With Death on My Shoulder

The Spirituality of Depression

Bonnie Joia

ReflectivePublications

Salt Lake City, Utah

http://www.spiritualdepression.com

ISBN 0-7414-2764-8

Published by:

INFINITY
PUBLISHING.COM

1094 New DeHaven Street, Suite 100
West Conshohocken, PA 19428-2713
Info@buybooksontheweb.com
www.buybooksontheweb.com
Toll-free (877) BUY BOOK
Local Phone (610) 941-9999
Fax (610) 941-9959

Printed in the United States of America

Printed on Recycled Paper

Published January 2006

With Death on My Shoulder
The Spirituality of Depression

Part 1: Growing Up Mormon

Prologue 3
Growing Up Mormon 11
My Perfect Mormon Parents 26
Love 36
For Time and All Eternity 52
Interlude 64
Mother in Zion 70
Moving On 90
Interlude 113

Part 2: With Death on My Shoulder

Prologue 119
Death on My Shoulder 129
Family Life and Sex Education 145
The Sound of Silence 162
Faith and Belief 178
Season of Content 195
Dr. Robert Kevorkian 211
Facing Conflict 237
Where Is Love? 257
Chrysalis 275
Betrayal 295
Moving On 302
What Is Truth? 321
Death 346
Epilogue 364

Glossary of Mormon Terms 373

Acknowledgments

Many thanks to friends who have offered encouragement: Anthony, Dick, Gary, Judi, Pat, Ruth, Vicki and Vivian.

To my children, Lowell, Ron and Wendy who have contributed memories, insights and support.

To Barbara Betz, whose feedback was invaluable.

And finally, to Dawn Marano, my editor, whose help and inspiration have made all the difference.

I dedicate this book
To my husband,
Jack Edward,
The love of my life,
The inspiration of my Soul,
And the support that makes my dreams come true.
Thank You!

With Death On My Shoulder

Part One

Growing Up Mormon

Prologue

Paradise Park, Hawaii, September 2002

When one lives in Puna, Hawaii—twenty miles south of Hilo where the yearly rainfall is 120 inches—blue sky does not go unnoticed. It's the day after Labor Day, and trade winds are back, bringing gentle breezes to cool the humid air. I lock my car, careful to slip the keys into my shirt pocket, and walk a hundred yards to our "veranda" two miles down the mountain from our home. Trudging through ironwood needles that blanket the well-trod earth, I step onto the black volcanic rock that holds back the ocean's crashing waves some fifty feet below. Chuckling, I recall cocktail parties we have hosted on this spot. The ritual begins about an hour before sunset. We place chairs in a semi-circle, around the ice chest, empty it of its *pupus,* usually fresh boiled shrimp and tangy seafood sauce for dipping. When Ka'u oranges are available, we serve fuzzy navel cocktails, which have become synonymous with sunset at the beach. Then, settling onto camp chairs, we witness the drama of day's surrender to night.

On this, the east side of the Island, we don't see the sunset, but the moonrise makes up for it. I especially remember one evening when Lowell, my eldest son, was visiting with a friend. Once seated, we became mesmerized by the crashing surf shooting at intermittent intervals some twenty feet higher than the rocks. Just as we were feeling the effects of the peach schnapps and the thinning ozone, just as we were relaxed enough to pay attention, the full moon slowly and silently inched its way into full view, revealing a whale, which breached in its mystical light. Perfect orchestration! Our guests were duly impressed, as were we.

But this morning, I am alone and aware that this enchanted time of our lives may be coming to an end. When we find a buyer for our house, we will leave our paradise and return to the Eden of my birth—the home from which I escaped so many years ago, Salt Lake City, Utah.

If ever anyone had a perfect childhood, I did. I grew up walking with God in the garden, hearing his voice through the mouth of my father, being enfolded by my mother's love. We were a perfect family, living in a perfect home in a perfect neighborhood, nurtured and protected by the "only true church" which had been established on this fallen planet to restore God's perfect gospel to a perfect people. We were Mormons, and the only people I knew until my late teens were also Mormons. Everyone thought alike, talked alike and lived according to the same code of behavior. I was aware of very little controversy. I never heard my parents fight or even have an argument.

I have two brothers, and I can remember only one fight with either of them. It was with Eric, who is three years my younger and seven years older than his brother, Dick. I must have been about ten and Eric seven. We were coloring Easter eggs, and our parents were not home. I don't know what upset us, but I do remember being so angry that Eric scampered down the stairs to his basement room to escape the hard-boiled eggs I was hurling at him. Even today, I experience a tinge of fear acknowledging the unsuspected demon within me who made its presence known, for the first time.

Dad taught me early about the imperative of forgiveness, but he also stressed that although we can be forgiven if we confess, even so, the result of our sins always marks us. He used the image of driving a nail into a board, and then pulling it out. The hole is always there to remind us of the sinful act. I can remember being haunted by the idea that my soul was like a board, so riddled with nail holes there was scarcely room for even one more. And God and everyone could forever see the bad things I had done.

Jimmy Myers, my father, was loved and respected by everyone. He was the perfect father, the perfect husband, and the perfect Mormon. He was my saint and my hero. The light of his goodness exposed my own darkness and drove me from Paradise. As I consider going back to Salt Lake City, I wonder if the cherubim with flaming sword will allow me entrance.

It's ironic that we're living in a place called "Paradise Park." I realize that my whole life has been spent searching for the Eden I left, so many years ago. A line by T.S. Eliot comes to mind: "…and the end of all our exploring will be to arrive where we started and know the place for the first time." I wonder if this means that the impending move is *meant to be*, smiling at the cliché we adopted during our New Age phase, more than twenty-five years ago.

I'm alone on the black cliffs this morning. I sit on my favorite rock, making certain my spine is straight, feet flat, head erect; focusing attention on my breath which has taken on the rhythmic ebb and flow of the ocean, watching the crashing waves explode as they reach the cliffs, shooting upward, as the Kundalini uncoils itself within my body to mimic the soaring geyser. Or is this the fountain of living water, gushing up to eternal life? I am convinced it is not either/or but both/and. In whatever language, the outer reflects the inner; the isolating barrier is shattered; the veil in the temple is torn asunder, and all creation becomes one—if only for a moment.

Why can it not last? Why are we created to taste such joy, yet unable to sustain it? Why do we search for Paradise when the kingdom and the garden are within? Hawaii? Salt Lake City? What difference does it make? Am I finally ready to find out?

The two-mile drive back to the house is a continuing meditation. I haven't seen another car on the road all morning. Mauna Kea is visible to my right, the day being clear enough we can probably see the telescopes from our lanai. The amazing albizia trees which were planted to reforest the area after a 1928 fire, still stand in separated groves throughout the area—forests of green lace umbrellas, offering shade from the hot sun and protection from the trade winds. Most residents see them as weed trees because they grow so fast and are almost indestructible. Too close to water tanks and houses, their invasive roots cause havoc with cement, but I rejoice in their beauty and feel grateful that so many still survive for our enjoyment. Another few years and they will probably be gone.

The area is covered with wild azaleas and tiny orchids, growing profusely wherever they find a bit of soil in the unbroken lava which flowed from the eruption of Mauna Loa in the late 1700s. That was the last time the volcano goddess, Pele, sent her molten fire into this region.

We live on Manako Street. *Mana* means spirit in Hawaiian, and one of the meanings of *ko* is *to be filled*. So the name of our street means *spirit-filled*—at least that's what I want it to mean. We decided to buy the house before knowing what the name meant, but discovering its meaning added much joy to our purchase. We are the second to the last building on the dead-end road. The one on the end is a large greenhouse owned by a prominent orchid grower. The acre lots in Paradise Park are zoned agricultural.

Jack is outside pruning the willy-willy hedge, which gives us wonderful privacy, but demands monthly care to keep it contained. We learned early precaution as to where cuttings are deposited because if there is any soil at all, the voracious hedge will root itself, and one is apt to awaken one day and find willy-willy happily taking over the property. Jack accidentally left a discarded stalk about five-feet long near the property line. When we finally noticed it, three new starts, about two-feet high, were growing out of its side.

I drive onto our property and, as always, gasp at the beauty we have created. We moved into the brand new two-story tan house two years ago. The only landscaping besides the willy-willy was a row of banana trees creating privacy from our only neighbors who live to the north. Our builder had also carelessly stuck the tops of his dinner into the ground so that a family of succulent pineapple now thrived in front of the bananas.

In order to develop property in this area, the lava has to be ripped with a monster machine to break up the lava, which is then covered with pebble-sized cinders like those sold in florist shops. Two-thirds of the acre had been prepared by the builder, but the rest of the property was untouched, preserving the natural albizia, azalea, orchids and wild guava.

Two years later, we have created a forty-foot circle of grass, crowned by an eight-foot mound in front of the house. A red bottle-brush tree gracefully dominates the top, while Queen Emma lilies, gardenias, poinsettias and other carefully chosen shrubs add interest and color in their season. Mondo grass now covers the mound, the deep green creating artistic contrast to the lighter green of the grass circle, which is ringed with pink hibiscus and white impatiens.

In front of the circle grow citrus trees, lychee, star fruit, apricot and figs. Ten coffee trees flourish along the south side; their limbs covered with red berries, ready for harvesting. Beyond the coffee stand six papayas, which have provided breakfast for us most of the summer. On the north side of the driveway, an unbroken mound of lava had escaped the ripper; it resembled a crater, some ten feet in diameter. The center is now filled with brilliant red ti plants, considered sacred to Pele. We allow them to grow to five feet before pruning them back. Deep red blood plants surround the upright tis around their base. In the morning light, our living volcano glows like fire; our tribute to Pele— or is it the Holy Spirit—or both. She blesses the property with the energy of creation!

After parking in the carport, I walk out front to check on Jack. He meets me halfway, carrying the biggest pineapple

I've ever seen. Lunch! He looks tired, as well he should after a whole morning's work. He celebrated his seventieth birthday this summer, and I look forward to mine next April. Everyone who knows us thinks we're crazy to be working so hard—until they see the property, and then they realize this is a work of love, the fulfillment of a lifelong dream of my "gentleman farmer."

I take the pineapple upstairs to the kitchen, stopping briefly on the lanai to admire Mauna Kea, in stark relief against the Wedgewood blue sky. This being the wet-side of the island, our mountain is usually hidden by clouds, but this morning, the telescopes are clearly visible as is the ocean below us.

Happily returning to the kitchen, I prepare the succulent white pineapple, keenly aware that if we move, we'll probably never taste another. And I ask myself, again, why do we want to leave? My eye catches Jack, on his knees weeding the grass, a never-ending chore, and I recall the exit from Eden when God warned our first parents: "...cursed is the ground because of you; in toil you shall eat of it all the days of your life...By the sweat of your face you shall eat bread until you return to the ground."

I find myself again struggling with disparate understandings of God, giving thanks for this Paradise, but wishing God could go easy on providing weeds. We're getting too old to work this hard. With resignation, I remember why we're contemplating leaving our paradise to go back to the place where I was originally planted.

☺

Lunch is over; dishes are done, and all my chores complete. Afternoons are my time for reflection and writing. If we do return to Salt Lake City, I want to understand more fully the long journey that has brought me to this moment. I have kept journals for many years, as did both my father and my first husband. Dad actually wrote two journals. The first, created to leave as legacy for family and friends, recorded his many accomplishments. The other, a personal, daily journal revealed his intimate thoughts.

When Dad died on January 1, 1998, my brother, Eric, quoted several entries from this writing to justify withholding my inheritance. Through my attorney, I asked for a copy. Eric, the Executer of the Family Trust, at first refused, until one and a half years after Dad's death, he finally relented in order to settle the estate. He had the journal photocopied, and I made plans to fly to Salt Lake City to receive my copy and sign the final papers.

I have been asked why I would want to read Dad's secret journal, knowing how critical it would be of me, but I have been on a search for Truth for many years, and understanding our relationship from his point of view seemed critical for my peace of mind. For many years, I have lived by the scriptural imperative: "Seek the truth and the truth shall make you free," even though I know that truth often brings pain—at least initially.

Before getting on the plane, I impulsively stuffed some of my own journals into the suitcase. When I received Dad's writing from my attorney, I hid myself away in solitude, and for three days poured over the journals. It was agonizing to face the truth of how deeply I'd hurt my parents, and after marking passages I knew were important for understanding our relationship, I cried myself to sleep.

The next day, after several hours of rereading and meditating on the marked passages, I remembered my own journals, which were still tucked away in my suitcase. I discovered I had written about many of the same incidents— from my own point of view. The two manuscripts pulled me back into the most critical time of my life, giving me access to thoughts and feelings as we each had experienced them. After attempting to take a neutral *witness* perspective, a skill learned in my Zen practice, I returned home with a more honest understanding of my father, and with an unexpected sense of appreciation for myself—for the courage it had taken to stand up to him for my perception of truth.

After those three days, knowing I needed more significant time with the journals, I put them away—waiting for my approaching retirement to read them again. During our time in Hawaii, I have written sporadically, with long periods of "writer's block"—a kind of paralysis, as I struggled to relive the decisions that brought me out of Mormonism and resulted in such animosity from my family.

Perhaps the real reason to return to Salt Lake City is that I have much unfinished business there. It has been wonderful to spend the first three years of retirement in this peaceful island paradise, but I sense there is more to the final years of my life than sitting on the lanai and watching the pineapples grow.

☺

I begin with my parents' story, before I was born. These scenes dominated my mother's life until she died, and became my own pre-history. I've attempted to capture the events, as they live in my soul, with the purpose of sharing, as honestly as possible, what I experienced growing up Mormon. I've recorded my memories with full awareness that others may have different perspectives. Some names of people and institutions have been changed to protect the privacy of those still living. My recollections are offered as creative non-fiction rather than autobiography.

☺

A Glossary of Terms used by the Church of Jesus Christ of Latter Day Saints (the Mormons) is found on the last page of the book.

CHAPTER ONE

Growing Up Mormon

Salt Lake City, August 1930

Margaret dashed through piles of fallen leaves carpeting the sidewalk outside the telephone company where she worked. Wrapping her knee-length coat tightly around her, she acknowledged the biting air as winter's harbinger. Mid-October, and Indian summer was now relenting to the inevitable change of season. *It seems only yesterday that mother went to the hospital,* she thought, *and then we complained about the heat wave.*

A cloudless sky sharpened the majestic beauty of the mountains protecting the Salt Lake Valley. Multi-colored asters and chrysanthemums smiled in the sunshine, almost summoning a smile in return. Newly planted pansies promised to survive the coming snow and brighten her walk in springtime. Dead leaves and spring flowers—the juxtaposition of life and death. Was it because her mother lay dying that Margie's senses were so keen? Her eyes blurred with tears, remembering the reason for haste. LDS Hospital had called five minutes before—the end was near.

Her bus arrived at the corner just as she did. Grateful to escape the biting cold, she climbed the steps automatically, and yet she'd remember every movement she made and everything she saw for the rest of her life. Why is awareness so sharp when we cannot think?

Etta lay in her hospital bed, sleeping peacefully, now free from pain that had convulsed her body for two months since her gall bladder attack. Jack Jarman, her second husband, sat with head bowed, shoulders stooped.

Standing, when Margie came into the room, he allowed her to hug him, his listless arms belying the deep affection between them. His face was haggard, and his eyes dull.

"Have you been here all night?"

He nodded without expression.

"You look exhausted," she said softly. "Let me sit with her awhile. A cigarette and coffee may revive you."

"Thanks, love," he muttered.

"And Dad, find a bench outside in the sun and breathe the brisk air!"

Nodding mechanically, he shuffled from the room.

Margaret hung her coat on a hook near the door, finally bringing her eyes to her beloved mother. It had been difficult to look at Etta's bloated face, but the swelling was now gone. *How will I ever live without you?* Taking the fragile hand in hers, gently stroking her mother's unresponsive cheek, she whispered, "Mother, you'll always be with me, always!"—allowing her pent-up tears to flow freely.

Etta's life had been difficult. She divorced her first husband, an alcoholic, when Margie was in junior high school. Two years later, she married Jack who took the young girl as his own daughter, ending the humiliation of begging child support from her birth father. Her heart ached even now thinking about it.

Margie glanced toward the door, wondering if Jimmy Myers, her fiancé, would get to the hospital on time. She'd called the *Deseret News* where he worked as a sportswriter, leaving word that Etta's death was near. He was covering a high school football game and probably wouldn't get the message until it was over. She longed for him to be with her at this crucial time.

"Oh Mother!" she cried softly. "Please get better so you can see us married. It's not fair for you to miss your grandchildren! How can God be so cruel?" Bending over to kiss her, she grimaced at the erratic breathing. "Jimmy's on his way. Please wait for him to come."

Etta's face seemed peaceful, although there was no response. *I wonder if she even knows I'm here.* Tears spilled over her cheeks, and Margie reached for Kleenex just as Jimmy pushed through the door, breathless and pale. The newspaper had sent someone to cover the story. As he squeezed Margie's shoulders, Etta opened her eyes, as though expecting him. Moving to the side of the bed opposite Margie's chair, he took her mother's hand.

"Mom, can you talk?" *If only she'd say something,* Margie thought. *Anything!*

Her lips moved. "Jimmy," Etta said weakly. "Sit with me for a few minutes. I want to talk to you alone."

Surprised and a bit hurt, Margie left the room and stood outside the door, trying to hear what was going on. She knew her mother and Jimmy were close, but why was she left out? She shuffled from one foot to the other trying to keep her tears in check. Inside the room, Jimmy sat down, leaning his head close to Etta's lips. She'd been an important part of his life ever since he and Margie got engaged, six years before. He acknowledged a surge of gratitude for her life, as well as the aching loss her death would bring. Neither Jimmy nor Margaret had experienced death before, and he self-consciously wondered if he were doing it right.

She had closed her eyes as he sat down; now she opened them again. Jimmy's personal journal recalls:

> (Etta) took my hand and said, "Jimmy, I love you, and I know you love Margie. I hope you will marry her and take good care of her." Then she pulled my head down and gave me a kiss.

With tears in my eyes, I promised her I would.

She managed a little smile. "I know you will."

He opened the door, finding Margaret standing uncomfortably in the hallway and ushered her back into the room. They stood, one on each side of the bed, silently watching the beloved mother relinquish her earthly life.

☺

Jimmy's plan to work long enough to have a nest egg before getting married was scrapped as his promise to Etta made waiting impossible. After all, he and Margie had been engaged for six years. It was time. One month later, on November 12, 1930, Jimmy kept his promise.

He'd graduated from the University of Utah in June, having paid his way through school working at the *Deseret News,* a plumb job for a college student, especially during the Depression. He now worked fulltime, and with Margie's job at the telephone company, he hoped finances would work out.

They were married in the Myers family home, 1125 East 27th South. The address indicates they were eleven blocks east and 27 blocks south of the Salt Lake Mormon Temple. Bishop Carl Burton officiated at the small wedding, which included immediate family and close friends, who were disturbed that the wedding wasn't held in the Salt Lake temple.

"Can't you wait a few months to get a temple recommend so you can do it right?" their friend asked incredulously when he heard the plans.

"No," Jimmy responded with determination. "Margie's stepfather's despondent and is selling the house. I promised Etta I'd take care of Margie, and I will."

"But what if you have an accident and aren't married for time and all eternity? Think what a catastrophe that would be!"

"I know, and we'll get married in the temple as soon as we can, but we're not waiting." Jimmy shrugged and swallowed words he wished he didn't have to say. "Actually, I can't get a recommend right now because I haven't been paying my tithing. And, I admit we've been doing a bit of drinking. That's just part of fraternity life."

"It's time to grow up, Jim. You need to protect your marriage. I'm not letting you rest until we go to the temple with you!"

The same friends who'd attended the wedding when the couple was united "until death do us part" were also with them six months later when they were married in the temple "for time and all eternity." It was April 1, 1931. The newlyweds had repented of their sins and done what was needed to assure their marriage would continue in the Celestial Kingdom of Heaven when they died. By this time, Margie was pregnant. In May, she had a miscarriage, a little girl whom she called Jean.

"Why?" she cried to her husband. "Why would God give us the promise of a baby and then take her from us before she was born?"

"I don't know, Margie. I don't know." Jimmy tried to console his disconsolate wife. They put the little cradle they'd bought away in a closet, hoping to use it some day soon.

Jimmy made $107 per month, and Margie continued her $50 a month job at the telephone company across the street from their apartment. In addition, he refereed basketball, giving them money to save for a future home. Entertainment was taking walks together and indulging themselves with nickel popsicles.

There wasn't much time to be together since both had irregular hours. Taking care of their small apartment took little time, and Margie had many hours alone to think and remember. Etta filled her thoughts. She remembered the beatings her mother had endured when her father came home drunk, and their terrible arguments and shouting. Sometimes the noise filled her head, vibrating through her whole body until she'd collapse on the bed, plugging her ears, trying to shut out the noise. She made a vow never to argue with Jimmy about anything. Never! She knew Jimmy would never abuse her—and she would be a perfect wife to him. She must find a way to avoid complaining when he was away so much.

Sometimes she thought about her lost baby, Jean, and imagined what life would be like had she lived. She'd go to the closet and look at the small wicker cradle, pretending a baby was there. Then she'd sit in her rocking chair and sing softly to the phantom child—weeping again.

In the fall of 1932, two years after Etta's death, Margaret crossed the street from the Myers house to the Jensen mansion, a place she'd grown to love. The owners didn't mind neighbors walking on the property as long as they didn't come near the house. The trees were losing their leaves, reminding her of walking to the hospital the day her mother died. Sitting on a bench near a blue spruce, she wept softly for the mother she missed so much and for the stillborn child who'd been taken from her before its birth.

As groundskeepers planted bulbs, which would bring color to the world in spring, new life was growing inside her. The child would arrive in April along with the tulips. Again, the juxtaposition of life and death awakened her awareness. The miracle of the seasons resonated in her heart: there is a time to plant and a time to harvest, a time to die and a time to be born. Intimately connected with the great mystery of life, she wept, this time shedding tears of gratitude, tears beyond understanding.

"Please, God," she prayed fervently, "please let my child be born healthy and alive. I'll be a good wife and mother. I promise you that with all my heart! And, please, let me have a little girl!"

☺

I was born on April 24, 1933. Was ever a child born more eagerly expected? My parents lavished love upon me. I was cuddled and held and sung to. Two songs still come back to me from those early days. Dad would hold me in his arms and walk around the apartment singing "Lazy bones, sleeping in the sun…," and my mother would awaken me with a catchy tune: "Good morning merry sunshine, it's such a lovely day. And the little birds are calling Bonnie! Bonnie! Come on out and play!" The songs were a ritual throughout my childhood.

My earliest memory is being three years old, sitting on the front steps of our house, waiting for Mom to come home from the hospital with my new brother, Eric James Myers. I remember being aware of how this baby, who was going to live in our house, was extra special because it was a boy. I didn't need anyone to tell me that boys were more wonderful than girls. At last, Jimmy and Margie had a son. God's blessings were truly on them!

I made two resolutions at that time. First, that I would always be good and do whatever I was told and never do anything to hurt Mommy or Daddy. And second, I'd prove to them I was just as good as any boy. In that act of choosing what I thought was *good*, I ate the apple in the midst of the garden, believing I could know the difference between *good* and *bad*. The first of these resolutions would dominate my life for forty years; the second would drive me for the next thirty. At this writing, I'm seventy years of age, and it is only now that I have the perspective to understand this truth.

My early years were like a dream. It's not easy to remember the good when there is no bad. We don't appreciate health until we get sick; only then are we aware and capable of gratitude. My only worry was my mother. She seemed sad most of the time, and I didn't know why. Everything in our life was perfect—except for me. I knew, at a young age, that I didn't have the pure thoughts I should have had. I was selfish and pudgy and lacked my mother's beauty.

By the time Eric was born, Jimmy had left his job at the *Deseret News* and gone to the *Salt Lake Tribune*, the more prestigious of the two local newspapers. He had a daily sports column, "From the Press Box by Jimmy Myers," and soon became the sports editor. Before Eric was a year old, Jimmy and Margie had purchased land and built their dream house on Fifteenth East, less than a mile from his parents' home. A number of their friends purchased property in the same neighborhood, and all went to Stratford Ward, our neighborhood Mormon church. The families were about the same age, and at one time, while we were growing up, there were twenty-eight children the same age as Eric and me, living on our block. We were all Mormons. That was our primary identity.

My father was born in Batley, England, a suburb of Leeds, in 1907. The family was Methodist, but after the Mormon missionaries told them about the "restored" Gospel and the opportunities in America, my grandparents joined the Mormon Church and made plans to leave for America. Grandpa took the long journey across the ocean alone, borrowing money for his passage. He worked for a year before he could send for the family. I'm not certain what he did to make a living in Utah, but he probably worked at the copper pit like so many other immigrants.

He sailed on the SS Corsican close to the time the Titanic set out on her maiden voyage. The story he told was that he was on the water not too far from where the Titanic went down, and he saw some of the huge icebergs that reportedly caused the disaster. Grandma was terrified until she learned he was safe.

Jimmy writes in his journal:

> Everything I have, or have done, I owe to the
> Church of Jesus Christ of Latter Day Saints.

> We came to America because of the church. The (Mormon) Church brought us to this "Promised Land" and has given opportunities, advantages and blessings we never, never could have had if we had stayed in England.
>
> I have thought many times about what our lives probably would have been…had Dad and Mother not had the courage, and conviction, to leave their family and friends behind forever and come to this great and wonderful land of freedom and opportunity.

Grampa loved his beer, pickled pig's feet and Limburger cheese. I can't remember him ever going to church with us. I don't know if something happened to take away his testimony, but I do know religion didn't seem important to him—which seems odd since it was the church that brought him to this country. I wondered if the motivation for crossing the ocean was more for the opportunities of the new land than the promises of the Mormon Church.

Dad's religious commitment is just as questionable, at least while I was growing up. His journal explains:

> When I went to the *Tribune,* I had to give up all of my church responsibilities. That was about 1935.
>
> I worked just about every night, sometimes seven days a week, and the only social life we had was having a few social drinks and food after midnight usually with friends who lived across the street—on Fifteenth East.

Mom lived through me, and as I grew older and my life became more interesting, I became the center of her life. If I came home feeling sad about something, she acted as though she had failed at being the perfect mother. She'd say, "Smile and be happy, Bonnie." I learned to do just that, in fact, I remember standing outside the screen door, preparing to go into the house after school, forcing myself to smile, to make her happy.

The other part of our ritual was just before bedtime. Mom would get in the bathtub and place a washcloth over her breasts, and I would sit on the toilet seat, placing my feet on the tub so we could talk. She seemed fragile to me, and I felt I was taking care of her. In fact, once when I was in High School and played Mama in the school play, *I Remember Mama*, I had a scene in which Uncle Lars was dying and I had to cry. I could bring tears every time if I just thought about my mother dying. That fear was at the top of my consciousness—but how could it be otherwise when her mother had died so young and she retold the story so often?

My brother, Dick, was born October 17, 1943, when I was in the fifth grade. I loved him; he was like a doll to me.

I had an early fantasy of being abducted by an Arabian king who was very rich and kept me in his harem— protecting my virginity, until I was eighteen when he returned me to my parents. It was a triumphant reunion for I had become the beautiful woman my mother wanted me to be. She was very proud, and the story always lifted my spirits and gave me hope.

Eden was a wonderful place, and my family was my world. It wasn't until fifth grade that I had significant playmates. A group of popular girls invited me to be their friend. We were all leaders in our elementary school. We formed a private *club*, which was limited to the nine of us. Using our middle initials, we coined the name, *Adeialaja*. Since I didn't have a middle name, I used *Etta* after my grandmother. I remember how special I felt to be the only girl on my street chosen to be an elite Adeialajan; all the rest of the girls in the school were left out. It was a Mormon equivalent to a sorority or gang, and provided us with an exclusive identity beyond our nuclear families.

All was well until I offended them. One of the girls got a Ouija board for her birthday; the group decided the occult device would work best at the Myers' house because my parents weren't as active in the church as theirs were. At the time, I didn't question their assessment of our unworthiness, I was just glad they'd come to our home; I knew it would make my mother happy.

The other event occurred at our promotion party. Mom insisted I wear a frilly blue dress to the dance. I didn't want to—it was too fancy—but I wore it to please her. I even told the kids how embarrassed I was, and we all laughed about it. After the dance, a gang of boys walked me home. I thought it was *neat*, but the Adeialajans didn't.

A few days later, Mom got a call from an adult leader in the Mutual Improvement Association (the MIA is the young people's organization in the Mormon Church).

"Margaret," she said. "I don't know how to tell you this but—well, Bonnie cannot be in the Dance Festival." This was a churchwide extravaganza being held at the University stadium. I had been to several practices.

"What do you mean?" Mom asked. I was sitting at the kitchen table talking to her before the phone rang and could tell by her expression that something was wrong.

"I'm sorry, Sister Myers," the voice took on a formal tone. "I don't know what Bonnie did to make the other girls in the Ward so upset, but they all say that if she dances, they won't."

"But that's ridiculous!" Mom scowled into the phone. "I can't imagine what Bonnie did to make them say that. Did they tell you what it was?"

"No," she answered coldly, "and I don't want to know. It must have been very bad, or they wouldn't have reported it to me."

"I'll talk to her and try to get to the bottom of it."

"That's fine, but you must understand that she is not dancing in the festival. It's settled!"

When she hung up, Mom looked at me with suspicion. "What did you do to the girls? They're so mad at you they won't dance in the Festival if you do. That was Sister Jones. She said it's all settled. You can't dance with the rest of them."

"But why?" I couldn't believe my ears. "I didn't do anything to anyone!" Tears filled my eyes. "Why won't they let me dance? It's not fair!"

"Bonnie, think." Mom's lips pinched into a thin pink line. "When was the last time you were with them?"

"I saw Sally at the store yesterday, but she turned and walked away. I thought maybe she hadn't seen me, but now I wonder."

"When were you together last?" Mom was insistent.

"At the promotion party; at the dance," I stammered. "But I didn't do anything to any of them. Honest!"

Mom was quiet for a long time, and then finally said, "That's it! They're jealous of you. They're jealous of your beautiful dress and all your boyfriends."

I was shocked at her words, but even more surprised at the glee I recognized behind her words. My friends' jealousy had made her happy! I went to my bedroom and sobbed my eyes out.

I didn't see any of the Adeialajans all summer. When I went to the ward, they turned their backs on me, and I had to sit alone, so I stayed away.

Now that I was out of the club I made some new friends. Dot and Carolyn also lived in the neighborhood, and we spent lots of time together. There was also another girl in the neighborhood, Rula, who lived two houses away from us. I liked her a lot, but Mom didn't want me going to her house because her father smoked, and she thought Rula was a *strange* girl. Whenever I had a chance to talk with her, I was fascinated. She had so many interests. Sometimes we'd play outside together with a group, but I didn't call her my friend because I knew Mom wouldn't approve.

In September, we started school at Irving Junior High. On Friday nights a movie was held for all the young people of our *stake*, which is like a diocese in other churches. A number of wards in the same locality meet together as a *stake* for special occasions.

One night, I went to the show with Carolyn and Dot. One of the *girls*, an Adeialajan, was there with two boys from my Latin class. Steve liked her, and Hugh had a crush on me. They asked if I'd go to her house after the movie to make popcorn. At first I refused, not wanting to leave my other friends, but Hugh insisted. He told Dot to let Mom know where I was and that I'd be home a bit later. Everyone agreed, and I felt very happy because I thought it might heal the rift with my former girlfriend.

We had such fun—making popcorn, laughing and joking. I thought the nightmare of the summer was over. The three of them walked home with me, about half a mile away, talking about how great it was to be in junior high and holding hands.

When we neared our house, Mom came out in a rage. Carolyn and Dot had stopped at the house on their way home and told her I'd been forced to go with the other kids.

She stood on the front porch and yelled, "How dare you make Bonnie leave her real friends! Go away and never come back here again!" I'd never ever heard my mother yell. I'd never seen her so angry. And as I watched the three of them scurry away, my heart sank. The enmity with the *girls* was sealed and never healed.

Although I was brokenhearted, I couldn't fault Mom. How could I? She thought she was protecting me. I remember crying softly into my pillow that night, praying I would never say anything to hurt her—even though I knew she was wrong in sending my friends away. We never mentioned it again. But the *girls* became the subject of much discussion and ridicule as we constantly looked for faults in anything they accomplished over the years. The incident was something to talk about during our long walks and the intimate time we spent together. It was as though she were teaching me to hate. I was so confused. I knew in my heart the *girls* had not meant to hurt me. A teenage scuffle had been taken over by adults and become a war. I wonder to this day why someone didn't step in to help us make up.

Until that point in my life, I hadn't allowed myself to have an opinion about anything. Even though I pretended to share Mom's outrage because the shared feeling made us seem close, there was a little part of me that did not buy in. I acknowledged that *little* part with shame. My conscious mind told me I must have done something very wrong to make the girls hate me, and now I was blaming my wonderful mother for my isolation.

I made other friends easily. The first day of school at Irving Junior High I met Donna, and because of the gossip she'd heard, she sought me out. Since I was not welcome in my own ward, I attended Mutual at hers. In addition, I often walked home from school with Carolyn and Dot and sometimes I'd sneak over to Rula's to sit on her bed listening to music and reading *National Geographic*. I soon found I didn't need the *girls* and, except for occasionally running into them at school, I simply wiped them out of my life—as my father had taught me.

At that time, everyone who was anyone wore Jantzen sweaters and Joyce shoes. I felt it was a badge of elitism. My new friend, Donna, could not afford to wear them and I remember standing up to my mother for the first time in my life when I told her I wouldn't wear them either. When we went shopping for school clothes, I purposely picked out cheaper sweaters and ordinary, less expensive shoes. Mom was upset but couldn't argue with my frugality.

She was proud of me in everything I did, except she feared I was getting too fat. Weight was a big problem for

Mom; she was always dieting. The highest priority in her life was being beautiful, and she worried that I'd have a weight problem also.

Finally, in ninth grade, her concern over my weight became obsessive. When I look at my pictures from that time, I don't see a fat girl at all, but she was convinced that I was on the verge of ruining my life—and hers—by getting fat.

One night during our bath-time talk, she told me about a pill she was taking. "It's called Amplus, but I call it my 'happy pill.' It not only takes away my hunger but makes me have more pep. It would be good for you. If you take it now, you might avoid getting fat for the rest of your life."

Her doctor prescribed for me an unlimited supply of Amplus, which was an amphetamine with vitamins added. I took the pills for the next twelve years without even realizing I was taking a drug!

☺

CHAPTER TWO

My Perfect Mormon Parents

Where was my father in all of this? Working! I assume he and Mom had some kind of relationship during the day, but he went to work before school was out and returned home at one or two in the morning, after he'd "put the paper to bed." I tried my best to stay awake and listen for his car to come up the driveway, which was next to my bedroom window. If I were lucky enough to be awake, I could sneak into the kitchen and get a hug and he'd share his Rocky Road ice cream. It was a special, secret time for me, almost like having an affair, although there was nothing sexual about it. Just a treasured time to be alone with the father I idolized.

Once, when we were sitting at the kitchen table enjoying ice cream, I asked him about my sister. "Mom said you had a baby girl who died before I was born."

"Sometimes things happen to people that are disappointing and we can't understand why," he explained. "Someday when we're in heaven and can talk to God, face to face, we'll understand, but for now, it's best to just forget about it and go on with our lives. Some things are best left unspoken." His voice was emphatic, so we never talked about her again.

That's the way Dad lived his life. When there was a problem, he did what he could to solve it, and then he put it behind him and went on. This was so different from my mother who was still hanging on to the problem of the *girls*. She couldn't talk about it enough. Maybe that's why she told me so much about her mother and my stillborn sister. Maybe Dad refused to talk about these things, even with her.

I wasn't certain which of them was right, but I realized that even though they were both good people, they were very different.

Dad must have been a very young man when he discovered the power of controlling his mind by seeing only the good. He seems to have adopted this method of handling the *unacceptable* on his own, and he lived his life accordingly. "Whatever happens," he told me, "you can always find something good in it. Whether it's an event or a person—you only talk about what is good." The three monkeys were his lifelong mascot: "Hear no evil; see no evil; speak no evil."

We had many conversations about how he lived out this philosophy of life. Having a daily column on the sports page gave him opportunities to criticize others. It was sometimes a challenge for him to be positive, but when someone did something wrong or made a mistake, Dad would remind his readers about the person's achievements at the same time he reported the error. He counted it as success when he could write the article so that they would avoid embarrassment.

He'd excitedly show me his column and say, "See, by reporting the news in this way, I've made a friend rather than causing further harm and creating an enemy." It was an unforgettable lesson and explained why my father, Jimmy Myers, was so successful and universally loved.

He had three favorite movies: *It's a Wonderful Life* with Jimmy Stewart; *The Christmas Carol,* which he watched on television every year from the time we got our first TV set until his death. The other was *The Magnificent Obsession,* which he probably saw on TV because I never remember seeing the book in our home. Later in life, I happened to read the book and it reminded me of him. When I told him I'd read it, his eyes got soft and watery and he said, "I know the story well." It is about a man who takes seriously the Gospel imperative to do your alms in secret.

I was always proud of my name, Bonnie Myers. Being Jimmy's daughter gave me immediate status with my peers who read the sports page as well as with adults everywhere in the Salt Lake Valley.

While I was still at Irving Junior High, Dad was secretary of the Utah Golf Association. He promoted two charity golf exhibitions featuring Bing Crosby and Bob Hope. One night, while I was studying, the phone rang and Dad said there was someone who wanted to talk to me.

A familiar voice came on the line, "Hello, Bonnie. This is Bing Crosby."

I couldn't believe my ears, even though Dad had talked about him coming to Salt Lake. "Are you really Bing Crosby?" I stammered.

"Yes, and I'll prove it," he laughed, and began singing "I've Got Spurs That Jingle, Jangle, Jingle."

Of course, I told all my friends about the phone call and later when Bing Crosby sent my father an autographed picture which read: "To my old and valued friend, Jimmy," and when Bob Hope kept sending Christmas cards for ten years after that, I proudly displayed the proof to anyone who visited us. I felt like a celebrity myself.

The summer before going to South High, I was invited to represent my high school at a Red Cross Leadership Camp in Missoula, Montana. Seven high schools from Salt Lake sent representatives; our chaperone was Evelyn Wood, who later became famous for her speed-reading course. She rented a large van, and the ten of us drove through the Teton to Flathead Lake, where we spent a week in classes and activities. On the way home, we visited Yellowstone Park. I had my "happy pills" with me; Mom made certain of that.

Mrs. Wood lived only three houses away from us and was not an active Mormon. She always took a special interest in me. She was aware of how I was shunned by the *girls* at the ward, and I believe she arranged to have me represent South High on the trip. Because of the training, I was one of the faculty appointees on the student council when I began my first year. Two of the *girls* were also on the council.

I could hardly wait for high school to start. I looked forward to more challenging classes and was especially excited about studying the Gospel of Jesus Christ at the Mormon seminary. This would give me an opportunity for serious classes about the church that I hoped would answer some of the questions I had. All of my friends would be in the seminary classes, as well as the *girls*. It was an eventful year through extracurricular activities. I was involved in the school newspaper, *The South High Scribe,* and played the lead in the school play.

In November, I invited my seminary class to a party at our home. Mom was eager to welcome my new friends, and went all out with an elaborate offering of snacks and soft drinks. It was wonderful fun, but some time during the party, one of the boys from the class looked in a cupboard and saw Dad's stash of alcohol. The student called everyone's attention to his discovery, and after the party, word spread that we were *Jack Mormons*, which meant I was not acceptable to the *good* kids.

About this time, I fell in love with Johnny, a boy from Pocatello, Idaho. He came over to my house a few times, and we talked on the phone for what seemed like hours. He never asked me to any of the dances, but in my mind, we were "going together." His parents were divorced, and he spent the school year in Salt Lake with his mother and the summers with his father on the farm where they raised potatoes. All I could think about was Johnny.

My conversations with Mom shifted from *girls* to Johnny and love and my dreams of getting married and having children and living happily ever after.

In June, Johnny went back to Pocatello and although I wrote to him, he didn't answer. In August, when I heard he'd come back early for football practice, I waited and waited for him to call, but the phone never rang. Finally, in desperation, I called him. He was kind, but made it clear he was not interested in "going with me" anymore.

I was too stunned to hang up the phone. Mom, who had been listening in the next room, was immediately at my side. When she took the phone receiver from me, the tears poured down my cheeks. I couldn't even form words to tell her what happened.

"I know," she said brightly. "Let's walk down to Sugar House and get some popcorn. The exercise will make you feel better."

Sugar House is a shopping area about two miles from our house, and the walk was one we often took together in the evening. We held hands, and she let me talk about it, saying very little, only listening. On the way home, I asked, "What's wrong with me, Mom? Why do I always lose my friends?"

"But Bonnie, you have lots of friends; everyone likes you except for the *girls,* and they're not worth worrying about."

"But why doesn't Johnny want to see me anymore? I don't know what I did to make him not like me."

"These things happen. There's nothing to do about it. You're a lovely girl, and there will be many more boyfriends."

"I don't want another boyfriend! I just want Johnny!" Tears spilled down my cheeks again, and my poor mother looked so miserable and helpless, I tried to shift the mood. *Smile and be happy, Bonnie*, I heard in my head. I managed a half-smile and told Mom, "Please don't worry about me. I'll be OK."

She talked about her first boyfriend, the one from Los Angeles, whom she had known when she was exactly my age—in tenth grade. "I really liked him and didn't want to come back to Salt Lake, but it must have been Heavenly

Father's will because I was supposed to marry Jimmy. I'm certain of that. But I wasn't sure at the time."

"How does one know Heavenly Father's will?" I asked seriously.

"It's a great mystery, Bonnie, but it's a kind of feeling you have, and you just know. You can't explain it, you just know."

During my junior year at South High, my whole life changed. My parents' partying had escalated, partly because of all the social obligations that came with Dad's high profile position at the *Tribune*. Without warning, he made up his mind to leave the *Tribune* and resigned. It was a huge decision, and I didn't learn the real reason until many years later when Mom told me the story.

One night, they came home from a party, and Dad was sick from all the alcohol he'd consumed. With his head in the toilet bowl, throwing up, he felt disgusted with himself. He made a decision right then and there that he would never drink again. And he didn't. In order to keep his promise, he decided to leave his job at the paper and get more active in the Church. He writes in his journal:

> (As Sports Editor) you become something of a celebrity. Everybody knows you and caters to you and wants their name in the paper. There were privileges at all the clubs and invitations to many major functions, tickets to entertainments, banquets, and award parties, etc., not to mention every sports event.
>
> It all wore thin after a while. What the heck difference does it really make if Utah does beat BYU or vice versa? It's not catastrophic if the Jazz loses ten games in a row or if the Utah gymnasts don't win the national title every year.
>
> Sure it's fun, and you meet a lot of wonderful people and get into a lot of excitement, but it

seemed like I should be accomplishing something of more import, something of lasting value. My views and ideas were changing and you can't stay in sports without being enthusiastic…So it was time to get out and move on.

I finally and definitely came to this decision while I was at my desk at the *Tribune*. I put on my coat and got on the elevator, and the first person I saw was a good friend and a writer himself.

He asked me what was new, as most newsmen do, and I told him I had just made up my mind to leave the *Tribune*. He was shocked and asked me what I planned to do. I told him I hadn't gotten that far yet; I just that minute decided to leave.

He said, "Well, if you are really serious, I think you might do well to talk to Dave Olson at the Evans Advertising Agency. I understand that he is looking for a writer. Do you know Dave?"

No, I didn't know Dave Olson, but he knew me when I went to see him the next day. You can't have your name and picture in the news every day for nearly twenty years without a lot of people knowing you. Dave not only knew me but also was glad to see me. He said he had read a lot of my stuff for a long time and liked my writing style. What's more, he was aware of the fact that I was well known and had a lot of contacts that might be helpful to the agency.

What this meant for me was that I simultaneously lost Johnny, the love of my life, and my greatest confidante—Mom. Now that Dad was home nights and all day Sundays, he had first priority on her time. It also ended my precious late-night conversations with Dad. In addition, I lost my bedroom because Grandpa came to live with us. I moved downstairs into what had been the family room. The walls were knotty pine, and I talked my parents into letting me paint the cement floor black. I was trying to create a Chinese effect, an attempt to be more like Rula. My memory calls up images of a dark opium den. It was such a different environment from my upstairs bedroom, which was full of light—where the sheer white curtains billowed softly into the room when there was a breeze. I wonder if the room itself may have had something to do with the depression that overtook me.

School was difficult. Now, I not only had the *girls* as enemies to avoid, but I couldn't bear seeing Johnny with someone else. Mom became upset that I wasn't happy all the time. For a high-schooler, I certainly had my share of dates. I went to all the dances; I still made straight A's; I was on the Student Council and actually wrote and directed several assemblies for the school. Most of my time was spent on the newspaper, and because I was editor, I had unlimited hall passes and could hide out in the *Scribe* office. I found my voice as editor of the *Scribe* when I won a national award for an editorial speaking out against cliques in school. My conviction came from personal experience!

My geometry class was a joke. The teacher was the football coach who knew very little about math. He depended on me and one of the boys in the class to do the teaching. I wanted to take a physics class, but my parents made me drop it because it wasn't suitable for a girl. They believed the only reason I wanted to take physics was to "chase the boys."

My literature class struggled to read *Romeo and Juliet.* It was so boring that later, when I had a chance to study Shakespeare, I was amazed to discover a passionate love of literature. How sad that it was stifled in school. My class schedule was so boring I actually wondered if I had anything more to learn.

Seminary was no better. Again, I found myself an outsider, judged as a *Jack Mormon* because of the alcohol found in our cupboard the year before. Also, I had real questions about what they were teaching: questions about the *Book of Mormon* and why Negroes could not hold the priesthood. These were innocent questions that troubled me, but I was strictly put in my place and warned not to question what I was being taught. Satan was always trying to make us lose our testimonies; we must be ever on guard.

Dad's conversion back to the church, plus the fact that he was home on Sundays, made it bearable to go back to the ward. I was so happy to be with him, I didn't even notice the *girls*. Mom often stayed home in bed with a headache, so that I had Dad all to myself because Eric and Dick were busy with their own friends.

I don't think Mom was really interested in the church at this time. For one thing, she was dependent upon her morning coffee. She was always worried about a neighbor coming in and catching her break the *Word of Wisdom,* the commandment from God to not drink coffee, tea or alcohol. It was confusing to me because in the *Doctrine and Covenants* it clearly states that the food proscriptions are not meant to be a *commandment* or *constraint*, but rather a wise teaching that the *Saints* should choose to follow for their own health. It was made a commandment by a later revelation. Now, drinking coffee is considered such a serious sin it will keep you out of the temple. Mom loved her coffee and lived with perpetual guilt over it, right up until her death. She went to great lengths to cover up her indiscretion. She was thrilled when instant coffee became available because it left no aroma in the house, and it looked like Sanka, which was OK with the authorities. She'd buy a big jar of instant coffee and pour the contents into a special, unmarked container so no one would know what she was drinking. It also meant that she would have to lie to her bishop in order to get a temple recommend.

Dad and I went to Sacrament Meeting together. This is the main Sunday service where we had the sacrament of bread and water that recalled Christ's death and resurrection. I asked my seminary teacher why we didn't have wine for the sacrament since the *Word of Wisdom* recommends it, but he wouldn't answer my question. When I asked about Jesus drinking wine, I was firmly taught that what Jesus drank was not alcoholic; it was only grape juice.

We also went together to Fast Meeting on the first Sunday of every month. I thought it a strange name for the longest meeting day of the month, but *fast* referred not to time but to the commandment to *fast* from food and drink until after the service. The money saved by not eating the meal was given as an offering to the poor, but since we did not *fast* in our home, it was difficult to make the connection. At Fast Meeting anyone who wanted could stand up and "bare their testimonies." That is, they would tell about religious experiences and affirm that they believed Jesus Christ was the Son of God, that Joseph Smith was a true prophet and that the Mormon Church was the only true church on the earth.

I remember Dad standing up one Fast Meeting telling everyone about how the Lord had heard his repentance and told him to leave the newspaper and how he had learned about the job with Olson from someone on the elevator *after* he had resigned. He believed with all his heart that God had intervened in his life and had called him to change his job as well as his lifestyle. I believed him with my whole heart also.

☺

CHAPTER THREE

Love

In January 1949, Mom took me for my *Patriarchal Blessing,* which is a once in a lifetime experience. The Mormon Church understands the need for guidance in the late teenage years, and the *Patriarchal Blessing* charts a clear course for living a faithful life, one which will lead to exaltation.

The patriarch told me that I was one of God's choice daughters who had been blessed far above most of His children here upon the earth. He explained,

> The reason you have been so blessed is because you kept your first estate in your pre-mortal life. You were valiant for the truth, and you were loyal and devoted to our Divine Master, the Lord, Jesus Christ, and therefore, of your own free will and choice, you have come into this world through goodly parents as a daughter of Zion, born in the dispensation of the fullness of times under the new and everlasting covenant…

He assured me that I came "into this life through the house of Joseph and the lineage of Ephraim and therefore (am) entitled to all the blessings which the Lord promised to our Patriarchal Fathers including Abraham, Isaac, Jacob, Joseph and Ephraim." He explained that this lineage carried with it the greatest promises made to both Joseph and Ephraim.

He continued:

In accordance with your faithfulness, you will also be entitled to the blessings of Sarah, which means that if you are faithful and have the desire in your heart, you will, in the Lord's own due time, have the opportunity of uniting your life with that of a son of God who bears the Holy Melchizedek Priesthood. You will have the opportunity of being sealed to him in the house of the Lord for time and for all eternity, and the Lord will bless your union further that you will have great joy and happiness therein. And from the choice spirits that are still in reserve to come forth in this dispensation, some will be sent to bless your home and to gladden your heart and you will have the power given you of the Lord to be a mother to them, a noble mother to guide their footsteps in the path of truth and right and your name will be held in honorable remembrance among the Mothers of Israel.

Further:

I bless you with the power to discern truth from error and right from wrong, even in the few tender years that lie immediately ahead of you. I bless you that in your everyday work and conversation and in your school life when you come in contact with the false ideas and philosophies of men, that you will have, even these days of your youth, the courage of your convictions under all conditions and circumstances to stand firmly for the truth and right.

This blessing became the promise, the goal and purpose of my life.

In early spring, I came down with a high fever. I was in bed for several days with nothing to do. Dad was now teaching the deacon quorum in the ward and had purchased a book by church historian, Hugh B. Nibley, a biography of Joseph Smith. Since it was the only thing I could find, I read the book clear through.

After finishing it, I awakened in the middle of the night, my bed soaked with sweat, my mind and body very still. A light shone in the corner of the room near the ceiling, and I perceived a loving *presence* who was blessing me. Was it Joseph Smith? I tried to bring him into focus, out of the shadows, so I could see a face, but to no avail. The *presence* said nothing, but I felt it was indeed Joseph Smith and that he was blessing me to do something important for the church.

After my recovery, the mystery of the experience stayed with me. I don't think I ever talked about this vision to anyone at the time, but it transformed my heart. I began reading the *Book of Mormon*, underlining and memorizing pertinent verses. The only fault I could find in Johnny was that he was not a Mormon. This was not an issue when we were going together, but now I wondered if breaking up with him had been God's will for me because he did not belong to the one true church.

One night, after my parents left for the evening, I went over to Rula's house to talk to her.

"Remember when you asked me what I wanted to do with my life?" I asked, lying on her bed, my head propped up by my elbows.

"Don't tell me—you've finally figured it out." She sat cross-legged next to me; her voice showing interest but also skepticism. I'd never been able to voice a dream of my own.

"I want to get married. In the temple!"

"I thought Johnny wasn't a Mormon," she responded flatly.

"He dumped me last fall; now I know why. I'm certain it was God's will."

Rula grimaced in disgust. It must have seemed a betrayal of all we had shared about the Mormon Church, but I forced myself to go on in spite of her frown. "I know now that I was born to be married in the temple and be a righteous mother in Zion," the words of my blessing had become part of my vocabulary, so often had I read it.

She took a minute to digest this news and then asked, "And this guy you're going to marry, is it anyone I know?"

"I don't know who he is, but I do know there is someone out there who needs me. I'm going to help him be very successful. That's all I know. But, Rula, I do *know* it—I feel it in my heart." I didn't tell her about my vision; I couldn't risk her making fun of me. "This is the purpose of my life!"

Rula scoffed, "Well, *I'm* not getting married—at least not for a long, long time." She always knew where she was going; I envied her dreams. She'd told me many times, "One day I'll walk the wall of China, and I'll climb the Swiss Alps. And I'll find a way to get out of this place so I can have the life I want! No temple for me!" This time she added, "It's a bunch of bunk! If there is a God, he loves everybody, not just self-righteous Mormons."

I stared at the wall. We had often wondered together how we could believe in a God who played guessing games with people. If they guessed right and became Mormon, they were saved; if they chose anything else, they were lost. This time, I didn't want to get caught on the wrong side of the argument. After all, I'd had a vision, and I knew I was supposed to do something important for the Mormon Church. I didn't know what that was, but it was obvious to me that it would be through a husband.

"Look at Alan Nathaniel," she continued. Alan was black and very popular at the school. In fact, he was the president of our class. "Just because he's a Negro, he's rejected by the church whether he's a Mormon or not. What kind of God would create a person with dark skin and bar him from the temple because of the way he was made? I can't buy it! And think about the Jeffs!" Rulon and Zola Jeffs lived next door to us. He became convinced the Mormon Church had apostatized from the true church when it condemned polygamy. He joined a fundamentalist sect and divorced his wife, Zola, because she wouldn't go along with him. I didn't understand the issues, but I knew it was a scandal in our ward.

I couldn't think of anything to say, but put my head down on my arms and closed my eyes for a moment trying to gather my thoughts.

Rula startled me by asking, "Are you really serious about wanting to marry a returned missionary?"

"Yes," I said softly, without opening my eyes.

"You know, I'm dating Doug. He's a bit older than me but a really nice guy. He has a friend named George who is preparing to go on a mission. What if I arrange a blind date?"

I lifted my head, startled at her suggestion. "I don't think Mom and Dad would let me go on a date with someone who is out of high school," I answered tentatively.

"You can always ask. You never know what parents will say. Why don't I ask Doug to bring George over one night and you can meet him? It wouldn't be a real date."

The idea of meeting a boy who was studying the Gospel was very exciting. I had no one to talk to about what I was reading. "OK," I agreed, "I could use some excitement in my life!"

Several nights later, Rula invited me to come over to her house. I told Mom and Dad I was going. When they looked questioningly at each other, I hurried out the door before they could object. "I won't be long," I yelled, amazed at my determination.

George was a dream man. Over six feet tall, he had dark hair and deep brown eyes—soft like a doe's. His look alone awakened sexual longing in me for the first time in my life. Rula and Doug left us alone in her bedroom, and we were immediately in each other's arms. We'd said only a few words, but his gentle kisses made words obsolete. My body suddenly seemed alive, a great river of warmth spreading from between my legs upward, flooding my whole body with the sweetest sensations I had ever known. When he withdrew his lips from mine, I felt shy and lowered my eyes. My arms and legs trembled, causing me to sit down on the bed. He sat next to me, put his arm around my shoulder and reached for my hand. We didn't speak—what was there to say?

Rula knocked at the door. "What are you two doing in there?" she asked.

"We'll be out in a minute," George managed to reply. He stood up and pulled me to my feet. Our eyes met, and I wanted him to kiss me again. Oh how I wanted him to kiss me—but he simply asked, "Can we go to a movie Friday night?"

I nodded, unable to form any words at all. We joined Rula and Doug, as though nothing special had happened. I went home in a kind of daze, hoping my parents wouldn't be there. I didn't want to talk to anyone! This was my first kiss!

My parents reluctantly agreed I could go with him, but he won them over the minute they met. He was poised and self-confident. I felt like an onlooker as he sat in the living room answering my father's questions, explaining that he'd just moved from Washington, DC, to Salt Lake to live with his two aunts who were sponsoring his mission. I don't remember what he said about his parents, but they were obviously out of the picture. He still didn't have a formal "call" but hoped to go into the Mission Home during the summer. He assured them that he would have me back before midnight.

When we left the house, I was relieved by my father's smiling face. I knew they trusted me, and it was obvious they trusted George.

He'd borrowed a car from his aunts. We drove straight up to "Passion Flats"—a parking area on the hills north of Salt Lake, behind the capitol. It was gorgeous up there. One could see the whole valley, cradled by the surrounding mountains.

We said nothing while we were driving, but I felt the mounting tension as we headed up the steep slope. He turned off the key and pulled me to him. "Now where did we leave off?" he asked softly. How long we were there, hungrily kissing each other, I don't know. I do remember the officer knocking at our window and how we pulled away from each other.

"You've been here a long time, young man," the officer scowled.

"Yes sir, but it's still light, and we're not doing anything wrong," George had amazing composure and no hint of guilt.

"Just be careful," was all that the officer said.

"Yes, sir," George responded, winding up the window.

We looked at each other shyly, and broke into laughter.

"Where did you learn to kiss like that?" he asked playfully.

"It could only have been from you."

He held me again, but this time we sat in silence, enjoying the powerful chemistry between us; playing with each other's hands; holding each other as darkness stole across the valley. The twinkling lights gradually illuminated the valley floor creating a lively display outside our window that mirrored the dynamic passion in our bodies and minds.

"Well," he finally broke the silence. "I don't know if meeting you is a great blessing or a terrible temptation. It's not what I bargained for. I've got to keep myself pure for my mission, and I wonder if we can handle this."

"Of course, we can," I assured him. "We're both committed to the same thing. And you are the answer to my prayers. I asked God to send me someone who could teach me the Gospel. Will you do that, George? There's so much I need to know and understand."

"You mean you think we could keep our minds on studying?"

"I'm certain of it. My Patriarchal Blessing promised me that I would have the power to rise above temptation. Let's pray about it right now." And we did. Right there in the car at Passion Flats.

The officer knocked on the window once again. "We're just praying, officer," George reassured him.

"Sure!" was the dubious reply, as the officer sauntered away to the next parked car.

And so began a most amazing courtship. We saw each other almost every day for four months. I met his aunts, and we loved each other! We went to church at his ward and joined a Fireside Group for young adults, which met every Sunday night in private homes. Elder Oscar Hunter was the leader, and sometimes there would be a hundred young people in attendance. He made the Gospel alive and powerfully relevant.

He read a passage from The Letter of James (1:5):

> If any of you is lacking in wisdom, ask God, who gives to all generously and ungrudgingly, and it will be given you.

He asked if we knew how God answered us. Then he opened the Bible and read from the Gospel of Luke where Jesus, after his death, appeared to his disciples on the Road to Emmaus. They didn't recognize him as he was teaching them, but later when he broke bread at their home, their eyes were opened and they recognized him, and he vanished from their sight.

They said to each other, "Were not our hearts burning within us while he was talking to us on the road, while he was opening the scriptures to us?"(Luke 24:32)

Brother Hunter told about his own conversion when he asked God if the Mormon Gospel was true—asking "with a sincere heart, having real intent and faith in the Lord Jesus Christ" that an answer would come.   With undeniable conviction, he shared with us how his own heart had burned within him.

I was riveted, because my own heart was burning within me at that very moment. I knew this was a verification of my vision and the experience of warmth I'd felt in my heart. Tears filled my eyes as I realized the importance of the teaching, and George squeezed my hand in recognition of my new understanding.

It was not easy to keep our hands off each other. We loved to kiss and desperately wanted more. First, we set a rule that there would be no touching below the neck. Later this was extended to the waist, and I admit that before he left for the mission field there were times when we hungrily felt each other, although we never removed our clothes. The urgency of our passion seemed sweeter somehow by the restraint. We grew in longing as well as respect. Our love of the Gospel united our minds. Our shared, deeply personal prayer became almost as intimate as our sexual exploration.

By the end of the summer, George proposed and asked me to wait for him until he came home from his mission. I said *yes* with all my heart. He could not afford a diamond, but bought me a beautiful zircon—very large and impressive. It looked just like a diamond and I never told anyone it was not real. Perhaps they knew, but I didn't care. I was engaged to a missionary, whom I loved, and I could join one of the groups of girls who were waiting for missions to end. This would give me a circle of friends who were interested in something besides clothes and parties and dating. It was perfect!

I didn't want to return to high school. My best friend, Donna, eloped with her longtime boyfriend, Bob, when her parents refused to let them get married, and Dot had a scholarship to the University of Chicago where she could simultaneously finish her high school requirements and earn college credit. I could see no reason to go back to South High School. It would be a waste of time.

Mom went with me to make arrangements to attend night school and finish the few classes I needed for graduation. Miss Dwyer, the dean of women, was heartsick. She'd planned to help me go to Stanford. I explained that I already knew everything I needed to know to be happy in this life. Now, I would be studying the Gospel. Her eyes were clouded and sad.

After working at a bank during the day, I went to night school. George went off to Germany, and we corresponded once a week, which was what the church allowed. I replaced my passion for him with passion for God and the Gospel. My spare time was spent in my basement room, reading the scriptures: *The King James Bible, The Book of Mormon, The Doctrine and Covenants* and *The Pearl of Great Price.* I also began hooking a rug to go in front of the fireplace in the home George would buy for us when he returned.

Once a week, I met with other girls who were waiting for missionaries. We prayed together and talked about our sweethearts. I loved being with them, realizing they could be themselves now that the pressure of finding a man was no longer ruling their lives. The other weekly event was attending the Sunday night firesides, which had been so significant in my relationship with George. Oscar Hunter is one of the most remarkable men I have ever met. He was there for us nearly every week, and the meetings were attended by young people from all over the Valley. If he was out of town, he would arrange for someone else to take the group. One of the most important of these meetings was held at Elder Mark E. Peterson's home. I remember clearly the message he preached.

He was talking about the passage in Matthew's Sermon on the Mount where Jesus commands: "Be ye therefore perfect even as your Father in Heaven is perfect." (Matt 5:48) He emphasized that we can never be completely perfect until we enter the Celestial Kingdom. "But," he said with all the authority of his high position, "we can be perfect in how we act and what we do. We can be perfect in paying a full tithing. We can be perfect in keeping the Word of Wisdom. We can be perfect in attending Sacrament Meeting. We can be perfect in meeting our obligations to our families and to the church." And then he looked at us for a long moment of silence, scanning each of our faces. "I want you to promise right here and now that you will be perfect in obeying all of God's commandments."

Again, my heart burned within me in my intense desire to do Heavenly Father's will. I promised that I would put the commandments of God above all else. I would love God with my whole heart and mind and strength by keeping His commandments as taught by the Mormon Church—without any more questions.

During my intense studies, I convinced myself that I also wanted to go on a mission for the church and I contacted the stake president to tell him I felt called to be a stake missionary. This was a mission to people in my own neighborhood. He smiled at me kindly and told me I was too young, but if my interest held firm, in a few years, we could talk about it again.

One day at Fast Meeting, I bore my testimony, talking about the burning in my heart and how it was verified by Luke's description of the Walk to Emmaus. I was using Oscar Hunter's words, almost verbatim, but by now, they had become my own.

Recurring dreams about George invaded my sleep—sexual, erotic, but unfulfilled dreams. Twice I dreamed that he was killed while in Germany on his mission. Because of my sanctity, the authorities allowed me to go to the temple and spend the night there alone. While I was in the Celestial Room, George came and impregnated me. I was a virgin, expecting a child. I had been fulfilled without sacrificing my virginity! Could there be a greater blessing!

If my parents worried about me during this time, I was not aware of it. I was gone all day working, and they seemed to go somewhere every night. Perhaps they were making up for all the nights they'd been apart before Dad changed jobs. Grandpa was there though. He and I would linger at the table after my parents had gone. He would get out his beer and Limburger cheese and pickled pig's feet and relish the special treats. I loved sitting at the table talking to him even though it was only chitchat. I tried to share my excitement about the Gospel with him. He listened politely and nodded but said very little.

When spring came, I found myself bored with sitting around, and the letters from George came less frequently. With little emotion, I sent the ring back and told him it was not working for me, and that if it were God's will that we be together, it would work out when he got home; for now, I needed to have a life. When I did this, Grandpa had a lot to say. He was very relieved—and so was I.

The first of April, I went back to Miss Dwyer and told her the engagement was off. I asked if I could participate in the graduation ceremony with my class. Of course, I could. She enthusiastically told me about a drama scholarship for the summer term at Denver University, and said that if I hurried and filled out the application, she was certain I'd get it. I sent it off the next day and was accepted. Grandpa was so proud he gave me $50 to help with the expenses. I was aware this was a very large sum for him, but I knew he wanted to be part of my new plans and gratefully accepted his help.

Next, I applied at the University of Utah for fall semester. I was so excited about going back to school. I wanted to be a psychotherapist and poured over the catalog of classes, planning out the next four years. Evelyn Wood, who was a counselor at Jordan High School and lived a few houses away from us, again reached out to me as she had when I was invited to the Leadership Conference. Her daughter, Carol, a year older, invited me to their house to talk about the university. I remember our excitement as together we made plans. Sister Wood's eyes teared as she revealed how worried she'd been about me and how relieved when she heard I'd broken up with the missionary and was going to school after all.

In April, only weeks after I'd sent the ring back to George, I went to Mormon General Conference at Temple Square. I was with my friend, Carolyn, when a young man introduced himself as Paul Harris. His brother, Dwight, had been my bishop. Paul had just come back from a mission in Uruguay. He said he hoped to see me again—soon. We dated a couple of times before I went to Denver.

It was the first time I had been out of Salt Lake City for any length of time. And it was the first time I was in a group of people where I was the only Mormon. I loved the classes and the plays we put on that summer, but I felt like an outsider. I didn't know what to say to people. They asked me questions about polygamy that I didn't know how to answer. They asked if I really believed that God was a human being. I explained to them that "as man is now, God once was; as God is now, we may become." It was a statement I had memorized but never really thought much about. Totally mystified by their shocked response, I felt judged and fearful that I'd not defended my church, as I should have.

I'd practiced what to do when I felt judged: When the *girls* rejected me, I shut them out of my mind; when the seminary students rebuffed me, I shut them out of my mind. And so I did with this group of young people. I just stayed to myself and did the work I had come to do, but I made no friends and left feeling relieved to go back to Salt Lake City where I knew who I was.

☺

As I write this, I realize that although what I've written is what I've told myself, it is not the whole truth. I remember there was a part of me that wanted to go back to Denver. Forgotten memories are flooding my mind. As I allow the memories to come back, I realize how much I loved the people I met. Here is the other story about Denver. I think both are true, but as I'm writing, I realize they come from different parts of myself.

I felt a sense of freedom as soon as I flew into Denver. Somehow the air was fresher, the sky more vast. I could almost feel myself growing taller, my spine stretching to hold my head high and walk in the clouds. Our dorm was next to a military academy. There were always handsome men standing outside, watching for coeds. I loved the attention and remember feeling beautiful and graceful, as I walked past them, relishing their whistles.

The program was designed for high school graduates from all over the country and all walks of life who were interested in drama. There were even two black students, a boy and a girl, and I remember a lovely young lady from Alabama with a charming accent. We were all excited and eager to be there, and I looked forward to getting acquainted with the others.

When the director of the program interviewed me, he asked me what experience I had. "I've been in several plays at my church; I took the lead in the junior high school play and played Mama in *I Remember Mama*. Oh, and I was the student director at South High for *Life With Father*, my junior year."

He mulled over my answers and surprised me by saying, "It sounds like you've always been the lead. Have you ever had a bit part?"

"No," I stammered, aware that no one in my school would have considered me being anything less than the lead—whether it was in a play or working on the school paper.

"Pity," he said. "One cannot lead without first learning to follow."

I liked this man!

The students were stimulating and interesting. They asked me a lot of questions about being a Mormon and especially wanted to know if my family was polygamist. I remember telling them that being a Mormon wasn't much different from being a Methodist or anything else, and no, my family wasn't polygamist although we had a neighbor who was. I told them how Brother Jeffs had left his wife to join the Fundamentalist sect of Mormonism that wanted to keep the practice of polygamy alive.

They listened with wide eyes as I told them the gossip I really knew very little about, enjoying the stature it gave me in the group.

We were all challenged by the exercises, the pantomimes, and the readings, which stretched our abilities, and we laughed at each other's embarrassments. Mine especially.

At the last play, I was supposed to speak about a dead man who lay at my feet. My line was, "And there he lay, her ring on his finger." I messed up and spoke the solemn words with deep emotion—"And there he lay, his finger on her ring!"

The audience broke out in uproarious laughter, and it took me a few minutes to realize why they were laughing. When I did, I was so embarrassed I wet my pants. There was no hiding the stream that ran down my legs or the puddle on the floor. I thought my life was over I was so humiliated, but the director came onto the stage and gave me a big hug, while a stagehand mopped up the mess I'd made. Never had I experienced such compassion—and from a group of strangers who weren't even Mormons.

I remember the closing party. We all knew each other very well, and it was difficult to leave. All of us promised we would try to come back to Denver for school.

It wasn't until I was on the plane going home that uncertainty hit me. Had I been unfaithful to my testimony? Was it the right thing to talk about polygamy the way I did? I was appalled at the things I had said. I was shocked that I liked these people more than any group I'd ever been with.

☺

By the time I got back to Salt Lake, I was very happy to see Mom and Dad. They told me that Paul had called several times and that he was eager to see me.

Once in his presence, the memories of Denver and the exciting people I'd met began to fade from my memory. I viewed the event as a temptation from Satan who had enticed me to be part of the world outside the Mormon Church. It was like the temporary joy I had known when I was with Johnny, and I knew how much grief that had brought. I embraced Paul with all my heart. Here was a true man of God. He was already a returned missionary, someone who could take me to the temple and secure my eternal life— now. I had a clear choice, and the deck was stacked in favor of staying in Utah and being a faithful Mormon. I can't remember ever thinking about Denver after that—until now, as I write the *other* story of that wonderful summer, which offered promise for a frighteningly different future.

☺

CHAPTER FOUR

For Time and All Eternity

After Denver, I was eager to begin classes at the University. Mom loved shopping with me for clothes, and she spared no expense. I was so excited about beginning a new life that I actually enjoyed our shopping sprees and the intimate talks about the future resumed. By now, Dad was well into his new position at Olson Advertising. One of his first accounts was with the Utah Symphony. He was helping transform it into a viable organization, and the whole family benefited through the guest passes he received for the concerts. Mom loved the social life, which came from Dad's new contacts. She was a beautiful woman, and Dad was always very proud of her. I loved hearing stories about the dances they attended and the people they met.

Attending the university was full of expectation, but I went alone. Because I hadn't taken my senior year at South High School, I'd lost touch with most of the students. I was no longer recognized as the popular daughter of Jimmy Meyers, and I was anonymous on the huge campus.

In October, a girl from the Tri Delta Sorority called, inviting me to a pre-rush function. When I told Mom, she was so elated it took me off-guard. She went on and on about how wonderful it would be for me to be in a sorority. I knew Carol Wood was a *tridelt* and had probably given them my name, but my aversion to cliques arose as a bleak fog through my being. I knew I did not want to join a sorority, but how could I disappoint Mom? She had never gone to college, although she'd attended Dad's *Pi Kapp* functions, the only girl in the crowd who did not have her own affiliation. If I joined, it would be a chance for her to make up for her own deprivation.

In addition to the loneliness on the campus, school was difficult. For the first time in my life, I actually had to study. I took a chemistry class for five hours credit and ended up getting a "C," which was failure to me, and my self-confidence bottomed out. Paul kept calling, and I was glad to have someone to go out with.

One night in November, after a mid-week meeting at the ward, he took me downstairs to the Relief Society Room, an especially nice space where the women of the ward met for projects and classes. Without turning on any lights, he asked me to kneel down with him, and in prayer asked our Heavenly Father to bless us and make us husband and wife. When we opened our eyes, he kissed me tenderly and slipped a ring on my finger. Simultaneous confusion and excitement focused into clear realization that this was the way out. If I got married, I would not have to face the sorority issue, and I could move into my dream now. Paul had not only filled an honorable mission, he was going to the U. Even though he didn't have any money at the moment, I felt certain he could eventually take care of me. We would be married in the temple, and I could live happily ever after, free from the pressure of trying to live up to the Meyers' expectations.

When Paul slipped the ring on my finger, there in the House of God as we knelt in prayer, it seemed my prayers were being answered. We walked back up the stairs to where our friends were still lingering in the Foyer and showed them the ring. It was settled.

My parents were utterly shocked when we told them. How could I go from such enthusiasm about the University and the chance to be in a sorority, to marriage? How could I go from a broken heart over Johnny, through a broken engagement with George, to desire marriage with Paul in less than eighteen months? In addition, Mom had real reservations about Paul's family, although his brother,

Dwight, had been our bishop and was a trusted friend. Dwight was the same age as my parents; Paul was twenty years younger. Nevertheless, remembering how Donna had eloped the summer before when her parents opposed her marriage to Bob, they reluctantly gave us their blessing.

At first, we intended to finish the first year of school and get married in the summer, but I dreaded going back to the campus, and besides, once we had pledged ourselves to each other, it became more and more difficult to control our sexual urges. The thing I feared more than anything else was having premarital sex. It was the worst sin of all. I had known of girls being disowned by their families because they got pregnant before marriage. I remember the mother of one of my friends saying, "I'd rather see my daughter dead than pregnant before she is married." I was paranoid about doing something that would make my parents ashamed of me. God was saving me from my inordinate passion, as promised in my Blessing. I think both of those reasons played into our haste, so we set the date for February 7, 1952. I would still be eighteen.

☺

In the Mormon world in which I grew up, the goal and climax of every girl's life was her marriage in the Mormon temple. Faithful boys have an expected and structured movement into adulthood. All children, male and female, are baptized into the "one true church" after eight years of age. This is deemed the age of accountability; after this rite, everyone is responsible for personal sins. Before that time, children are considered to be innocent. The Mormon Church strongly denounces "original sin" in the *Articles of Faith* that say, "All men will be punished for their own sins and not for Adam's transgression." Girls are prepared for their eternal calling by attending MIA, Sunday School, and the seminary connected to their high school, and, of course, they must be regular in attendance at Sunday Sacrament Meetings. Their salvation will be in the hands of their husbands.

For boys, much more is expected. They are destined to hold the sacred priesthood, which Mormons teach was restored to the earth through the Prophet Joseph Smith. At age twelve, a worthy young man is ordained a *deacon* by the faithful men of the ward through the laying on of hands. He has the privilege of serving the bread and water at the sacrament meeting. When he is about fifteen, if he has lived a godly life and is found to be worthy, the men of the church lay their hands upon his head and ordain him a *priest.* Among his other duties, the most visible is to offer the prayer of consecration over the bread and water so that members of the ward can duly remember the sacrifice of Jesus in his death. The next step is to become an *elder* in the church. Not all priests become elders, only those who show by their lives and through their diligence to the ordinances of the Gospel so far entrusted to them that they are worthy of such an honor—only these have hands laid upon them to be ordained an elder in the Church of Jesus Christ of Latter Day Saints. It is a high honor. Two other levels of priesthood await the faithful. Some men are set apart and ordained as *seventies*, often in their twenties or beyond. And still others go on to become *high priests*, the highest ordination in the church. These are men who have been faithful all their lives and are worthy of such a blessing. At this time, my father was a seventy, and my grandfather was a high priest.

Deacon and priest are considered to be the Aaronic priesthood, passed directly from Moses' brother Aaron down through the centuries, through the laying on of hands. The higher levels: elder, seventy and high priest are empowered through the Melchizedek priesthood, which was in existence from the very beginning. Melchizedek is said to have conferred the priesthood upon Abraham, more than four thousand years ago.

When a young man becomes an elder, he is eligible to go to the temple and take out his *endowments*. These are the secret rituals, which give the person access to the Celestial Kingdom after their death. Usually a young man goes to the temple when he is called to go on a mission for the church or when he is married. Girls are expected to be married, and at that time are endowed through the sacred rites of the temple. Single women may receive their endowments, but it was not encouraged

Paul Harris, the man I planned to marry, was an elder in the church and had been on a mission. In the eyes of the church, I was highly blessed. It was a fulfillment of my Patriarchal Blessing.

It has been over fifty years since I first went to the temple. Most of the ceremony is forgotten by now, and much of it has changed over the years. Because it is totally secret and a participant takes vows to never discuss what goes on outside the walls of the temple, very little is comprehended and remembered by most people. A person goes through the ceremony only once in their lifetime for themselves; however, they are encouraged to go as often as possible to take out endowments for people who have died and are waiting in heaven for the ordinances to be performed for them.

Following our marriage, I went to the temple several times, as a proxy for a number of deceased women, whom I was told were waiting at the gates of Paradise, thankful that at last someone had found their name and done the necessary work for them to enter the gates. I felt very holy that I had participated in someone else's eternal salvation. In fact, my Patriarchal Blessing promised me that not only would I be married for time and all eternity, but that I would come forth in the morning of the first resurrection and "stand as a savior upon Mount Zion" along with my family and kinfolk. Very heady stuff!

I remember the preparations for my wedding to be the perfect climax to my life in Eden. I had been faithful and had not done any of the things that would keep me from life's greatest blessings. When I met with the bishop to get my temple recommend, I was still a virgin. I didn't smoke or drink, and had never tasted coffee or tea. I paid my tithing on the small salary that came from the jobs I'd held while going to school. And I had found a man to marry who was a returned missionary and who I was certain would support me because he was going to the University and therefore destined to be successful. Never mind that I hardly knew him. We would have plenty of time to get acquainted after the wedding.

It was a relief when I actually held the precious temple recommend in my hand—proof that I was worthy of such a high honor. There were many stories that floated around about people who had not told the truth when interviewed about their worthiness. Their deceit was often discovered through the power of the Holy Spirit.

The most vivid example I can still remember was of a man from central Utah who came to the temple only to be turned away at the last minute. The temple worker discerned that the man had "black blood" in his veins. Black people were not able to go through the temple because they were cursed by the seed of Cain. In the "Book of Moses," found in the *Pearl of Great Price*, it is written that "the seed of Cain were black, and had not place among them." (7:22) I had been taught in seminary that there had been a great war in heaven and preexistent spirits took sides with either Jehovah or Satan. Those who were "on the fence" were born into bodies that were contaminated with the seed of Cain—and there was no way to become worthy of the priesthood or the blessings of the temple.

The story went that when the man returned to his home and did the research, sure enough his genealogy proved he had a black slave in his ancestry. I was quite certain that my own ancestry was pure, since my Patriarchal Blessing affirmed my select status among the daughters of Zion. Even so, I was relieved that I wouldn't be embarrassed like this man had been.

Mom was in her glory shopping for my bridal dress and making plans for the reception, which was to be held at Stratford Ward. I insisted on having a dance band so people would stay and not just go through the formal line at the reception. Our wedding announcements departed from expectations. They read, "Come dance at our wedding…" Not unusual for the twenty-first century, but almost shocking fifty years ago.

I wanted my wedding dress to be mid-calf so that I could wear it again someday—although I never did. Not liking the formality of most weddings, and since we weren't having a public ceremony, I saw no need for bridesmaids and a long train. Besides, I had too many girlfriends to choose among them and thought it safer to go with no attendants except for my best friend, Donna, who was my matron of honor. In addition, I was uncomfortable about Mom and Dad putting out a lot of money. So it was a unique wedding, which turned out to be wonderful! My favorite local band played, and the hall was full of dancers until nearly midnight.

Besides the wedding dress, we shopped for temple clothes, which is where the real excitement lay. We chose a beautiful pleated white robe along with the prescribed veil, sash and green apron, which is standard for the endowment ceremony that would be held the night before the marriage. When one goes through the temple, one is clothed with the white garments of sanctity which are worn ever afterwards, under one's street clothes. Mine were wonderfully soft and light, made of nylon, and I loved them from the beginning. Many people did not buy temple clothes. They could be rented, but since I believed we would be frequent participants in the temple for many years afterward, and I might be buried in these very clothes, I wanted my own. Mom and Dad not only bought mine but also bought a set for Paul. He had not been able to afford such a luxury before, even though he had been to the temple preceding his mission, three or four years before the wedding.

My picture was in both the *Deseret News* and the *Tribune*—for the announcement as well as the wedding. There were weeks of parties and showers from family and friends. Gifts poured into the house for Jimmy Meyers's only daughter. It was very exciting.

A week or so before the wedding, Dad knocked on the door of my bedroom. I was lying on the bed, thinking about our plans, aware of the anxiety in the pit of my stomach.

"Can I talk to you, Bonnie?" his voice betrayed concern.

"Of course, Dad." I sat on the edge of the bed, surprised at his unexpected visit.

He shut the door, pulled up a chair and sat pensively without saying a word.

"What is it, Dad?" I was alarmed at the unaccustomed sadness in his eyes and his dour expression.

"Are you happy, Bonnie?" he finally spoke, his voice flat and expressionless.

"Of course, Dad. I'm getting married—getting married in the temple. This is every Mormon girl's dream, isn't it?"

"But do you really love him?"

It was a question I'd asked myself many times in the past few weeks. "I don't know," I said honestly. "I don't know if I even know what love is—but I do know God wants me to get married in the temple, and Paul is the man He has sent to me."

Dad pursed his lips, as though he were trying not to say anything he'd regret.

"You don't like him very much, do you?" I said softly.

"Maybe I'd feel this way about anyone who was taking you from us. Mom and I—we're going to miss you. And we're worried that he won't be able to give you the life you deserve."

"He's going to the University. It will be hard for a few years, but we can make it. When he graduates, it will all work out."

For the first time, I was aware of doubt about the words I was speaking. The same kind of awareness that had made me doubt my mother's reaction to the *girls*, that tempted me to go to school in Denver, and now, that made me worry about making a mistake. I firmly pushed down the *voice* and answered with what I hoped was the assurance of a woman who had been blessed in her Patriarchal Blessing with "the power to discern truth from error and right from wrong."

Dad gritted his teeth. "How can he make a living with a degree in music? Have you even thought about that? What if you get pregnant right away? How can he take care of a family on the G.I. Bill?"

"We'll manage. If we're faithful, God will show us the way. I'm certain of that," I replied calmly.

Dad looked down at his hands for a long minute. When he raised his head, he seemed to be struggling for words. "Mom says you're not going to use birth control."

"God will not send us a child we can't afford to take care of," I said firmly. "And the church says we should not prevent a child from coming to this earth."

"For heaven's sake, Bonnie, you're taking all this too seriously. A person shouldn't go over the 'deep end' when it comes to religion. You can't throw caution to the wind. Mom and I use birth control. We have three children, and we carefully planned for each of you."

"And you were away from the church for a long time. You didn't pay tithing or keep the Word of Wisdom either, and now you know better and have repented. I *know* that the Church is true, now at the beginning of my marriage. How can I break the commandments with full knowledge of the truth?"

The more we talked, the more certain I became that my blessing was being fulfilled. I remembered that I had been promised that I would have "even these days of my youth, the courage of my convictions under all conditions and circumstances to stand firmly for the truth and right…"

"Dad," I looked him straight in the eyes, "I must be true to God's guidance. He wants me to marry Paul and help him be successful. Please don't worry. I love you so much, and I want us always to be a happy family!"

"OK, have it your way. But once the wedding is over, you're on your own. I'm not going to support Paul Harris!"

The intensity of his dislike tore at my heart, but I knew I must be strong. "We'll make it work, Dad. Please try to like him!"

"I will, for your sake, but Bonnie, if you change your mind—even if it's an hour before the wedding, we'll call the whole thing off. Do you understand?"

"How can we do that, when the invitations are already out? What would people think?"

"Who cares? We're talking about the rest of your life!"

By now, I was crying and so was he. He gathered me into his arms and held me for a long time. "I'll do my best," he finally murmured. "I love you, Bonnie, and only want the best for you."

"I know, Dad. And I love you, too!"

That night, Mom and I attended a shower that one of my aunts held for the women in the family and some of my friends. Dad invited Paul to come over to talk to him. I was worried about what he might say, but needn't have. When I got home, I learned that Dad had given Paul a check for enough to pay the loan we'd taken out for furniture. Dad didn't believe in going into debt and was teaching us a lesson at the same time as being generous. Paul was elated and felt he finally had a father who cared about him.

Two nights before the wedding, as we were sitting around the kitchen table finishing our dinner, the phone rang. It was for me. An unknown voice asked if the wedding was still on.

"Of course," I answered, surprised that someone would think it wasn't.

"Well, I won't tell you my name, but I was a missionary companion of Paul's when we were both in Uruguay." I listened intently. "I just want to warn you that you're making a terrible mistake. You're going to be sorry if you marry him." The phone went dead.

I held the phone in my hand, unable to move.

"Who was that?" Mom asked.

"Someone who doesn't like Paul. A voice from Satan. How can people be so cruel?" I hurried to my room, shaking, and fell on my knees asking for strength to meet the adversary who was trying to keep me from going to the temple. "Please God, teach me to be a good wife to Paul. He's probably never had anyone believe in him. But I do. I know that you want me to be his wife. And I will be faithful to your guidance." My heart burned with fervor within me as I rededicated myself to God's will. I felt sorry for Paul that something like this would happen, and my pity felt very much like love.

The evening before the ceremony, we went to the temple to "take out my endowments." I don't remember Mom and Dad being with us in the temple, and I strongly suspect that they were not yet paying their tithing. But I could be wrong. What I remember is a bit about the washing ceremony where a woman blessed me, anointing me with oil that I would be fruitful and bring forth children. Then I put on my beautiful garments, and they clothed me in the sacred robes. I remember very little after that, except that I promised to always obey Paul, that he would be the one who would call me forth in the "morning of the first resurrection." But I didn't really know what that meant. I remember being taught a secret handshake that would get me into the Celestial Kingdom when I died, and I remember being given a secret name, one that only Paul would know. And I remember taking vows that I would always support the church financially and with my time, and I would never talk about what occurred in the temple outside its walls. And I remember feeling very holy and good and special, and it was a feeling I never wanted to lose.

The next day, a small group of us met for the actual ceremony. Only those who had a temple recommend, and thus deemed worthy, could attend. Elder Spencer W. Kimball, one of the general authorities of the church, married us. He would later become the president. Before the ceremony, he talked to us privately about the meaning of marriage. The main thing he stressed was that marriage was to have children and to bring them up in the light of the gospel. He told us that there were special spirits who were waiting to come to earth to be part of our family and that we were to do nothing to prevent their coming. I agreed wholeheartedly. I wanted to have children more than anything else in the world.

We were married in a room lined with mirrors, where we could see our reflection repeated over and over again, as though stretching to eternity. When we left that sacred room, I had a new identity. I was now Mrs. Paul Harris.

☺

Interlude

Bonnie: I want to cry for all the missed opportunities.

Soul: Such as?

Bonnie: The wonderful people whom I couldn't fully appreciate. My friend Rula for instance; I felt guilty for being drawn to her because she wasn't a *good* Mormon. And Mrs. Wood was an amazing woman. One day after she'd spent an hour or so with me, I actually went home and, not knowing how to respond to Mom's questions, told her that Evelyn's kitchen floor was not clean; there was a crust of bread under the table. Why did I need to find fault?

Soul: Wasn't that what your mother wanted you to say?

Bonnie: You're right. She was threatened by any woman who had been to college, and she needed my reassurance that being a good housekeeper was more important than writing books.

Soul: Who else was there to aid you?

Bonnie: Miss Dwyer, at South High. She was heartsick when I dropped out of school and thrilled when I came back for graduation with a desire to go to the U. She must have pulled strings to get me the scholarship to Denver that summer—it was very late to apply.

Soul: So tell me about Denver? Do you recognize me in the events?

Bonnie: I certainly didn't at the time, but as I was writing about it now, I realize you were the one living the second story. It was the first time I felt a split in my personality. It frightened me, and I consciously forgot about you—just as Dad had taught me.

Soul: So what was going on? Think of what you now know about human development.

Bonnie: Dr. James W. Fowler, in his book *Stages of Faith*,[1] describes three stages of growth that were possible at my chronological age. What he describes as Stage two is focused on family relationships. Stage three gives authority to belief traditions—in my case the Mormon Church. Stage Four is a move to self-chosen, individual faith. I tried to be a part of a group outside my family with the Adeialajans, but when they rejected me, I retreated back to my mother as the center of my life—back to Stage Two dependency. But my mind was developing, and Mom was no longer stimulating enough. Intellectually, I was drawn to Rula and Mrs. Woods—to Stage Four—but I was not grounded in a belief system of my own. I felt like an ugly duckling, not belonging anywhere. Emotionally, I needed a place to stand, an authority outside the family system to tell me what to do. That's Stage Three—the Mormon Church.

Soul: Then what happened?

Bonnie: I had the vision, which I interpreted as being Joseph Smith. My hungry mind devoured everything it could of Mormonism. Instead of my primary identity being Bonnie Myers, I was now a Mormon, still holding fast to my parents. Dad's conversion into the church coincided with mine. I came to love him— no, worship him. He was the God of my faith, and Mom represented the superficial life I was trying to leave.

Soul: Was it an Electra complex?

Bonnie: I think so. But I didn't recognize it then. I only knew that I was competing with her for Dad's love. I felt that if I could be a better Mormon than she, Dad would love me more.

Soul: What role did Evelyn Wood and Miss Dwyer play?

Bonnie: They both tried to give me an intellectual focus. The only goal I had was to become a good wife and mother like Mom. Miss Dwyer wanted me to go to Stanford; she knew I'd never been challenged intellectually at South High. And Mrs. Wood encouraged me to go to the University and pursue a career in psychology. I got excited about it for a while, but the desire was not strong enough to override my lifelong programming that a woman's fulfillment was marriage and family. Besides, I had a subliminal sense that it would be threatening to Mom. Even though I hated her at times, I wanted to be just like her so I could have Dad. She wanted me to go to the U, but only to be in a sorority. I'd hated exclusive clubs, ever since my rejection in elementary school.

Soul: So Miss Dwyer got you the scholarship to
                Denver, and you allowed me to surface for a
                short time.

Bonnie: On the way home, I firmly rejected all I'd
                experienced. It scared me to death. If I had
                gone back to Denver, there's no telling what
                would have happened.

Soul: What would have happened?

Bonnie: I certainly wouldn't have married Paul. I
                wouldn't have my children. I might have
                become a therapist. I doubt that I would have
                remained a Mormon.

Soul: So, was it all a mistake?

Bonnie: From the perspective of now, I wouldn't
                change my life one iota. I am who I am
                because of the choices I made. The Mormon
                Church was developing along with me; they
                didn't understand human development and
                believed that a person was fully mature at
                nineteen. They believed that if people were
                faithful to the beliefs they had when they took
                out their endowments, they would achieve the
                highest reward in heaven.

Soul: Do you think the church has changed?

Bonnie: Not yet, but it's moving in that direction. I
                pray that my writing may contribute to the
                ongoing conversation.

                It's now scientifically proven that the human
                brain isn't fully mature until after age twenty-
                one. Most Mormon men and women go into
                the temple about age nineteen—the time
                when they are in the thick of their identity
                crisis, trying to become adult. At this chaotic
                period of development, they take vows that

they will never question authority, be bound to the same partner for all eternity, and go on missions, witnessing to others about a faith they've hardly explored.

It might have been excusable when I took those vows, but for them to continue the practices now is akin to conscious brainwashing. And there are many voices within the Mormon Church that are calling for further revision.

Soul: Do you actually believe they will make such fundamental changes?

Bonnie: The social results of repression are becoming more and more apparent. In Utah, where seventy percent of the population is Mormon, antidepressant drugs are prescribed twice more often than any other state,[2] and the suicide rate among young men is higher than any other state.[3] In addition, it's been reported that "10.97 percent of Utahans age eighteen and older have a diagnosable mental, behavioral or emotional disorder that substantially interferes with one or more major life activities. Only Rhode Island had a higher rate of serious mental illness, 10.98 percent."[4] I don't see how these statistics can be ignored.

Soul: Repression and suppression almost always lead to depression.

Bonnie: The good news is that the church has already revised many parts of the temple service, and I believe further evolution is inevitable. The Mormon Church itself is trying to be more inclusive. If they can find a way to see themselves as one path to God among many—they will play an incredible role in the coming of God's kingdom on earth. Which is what we all want, isn't it?

Soul: Let's continue with your story and see the result of your decision to crystallize your life as an eighteen-year-old Mormon girl.

---

1.   Fowler, James W., *Stages of Faith,* Harper San Francisco, 1981
2.   *L.A. Times,* February 20, 2002
3.   *Salt Lake Tribune,* August 18, 2004
4.   *Salt Lake Tribune,* February 15, 2002

CHAPTER FIVE

Mother in Zion

One night when our children were little, we drove through downtown Salt Lake City. As we passed the Mormon temple, Annie, then two-and-a-half years old asked, "What's that?" Lowell, eighteen months older, answered, "That's Cinderella's castle." Lynne, who is three years older than Annie answered, knowledgeably, "That's where you go to get married!"

They had learned well. For me, the temple was the final realization of all my dreams. I hadn't considered what life would be like after marriage. You meet Prince Charming, he takes you to the Temple, and you get married and live happily ever after! That was the promise and the expectation. But reality was soon to set in.

Proof of one's virginity on the wedding night was, and is, a must in the Mormon Church. I remember being told that a man views getting married like buying an apple. Would he choose one from which someone had taken a bite? Of course not! Neither would a decent man marry a woman who had already *known* another man.

The pressure in my teenage years to be popular and have lots of dates for Mom's entertainment was exacerbated by the terror I felt of losing my virginity.

Memories of my passionate romance with George still excited me and offered promise of ecstasy not yet realized. I was relieved that I'd met the temptation; I had proven I was alive and responsive, but absolutely committed to saving myself for my Prince. I leaned heavily on the promise in my Patriarchal Blessing that I was especially blessed with discernment of right and wrong and with the courage to resist all temptation. The fear of "going all the way" played a big part in my engagement to George and hiding in the basement for six months before I met Paul. I viewed my isolation as God's protection.

Before the wedding, I endured the required examination by Dr. Skidmore, whose father had delivered me, and I adamantly refused any birth control as well as his offer to puncture the hymen. I was appalled such a procedure was considered ordinary and was too embarrassed to discuss it.

The wedding night, which was to be the glorious fulfillment of my life and the climax of sexual bliss, was torture. Both Paul and I were virgins, and we had little understanding about making love. What I remember is trying not to scream with pain while he was on top of me, banging away, trying to break through the sealed hymen. I begged him to stop, but he said fiercely, "We're supposed to do it on the first night."

When he finally stopped, both of us were exhausted. While I was still sobbing from pain, he turned on the light to be certain the bloodstained sheet would proclaim my innocence. We lay, back to back, both of us shocked and humiliated; I cried into my pillow for most of the night. In the morning, I could scarcely walk, I was so sore. The rest of the hymen wasn't completely severed until nine months later when Lynne was born.

The pregnancy went smoothly except for intense morning sickness, which made it necessary to quit my job at the GMAC finance office. I was unprepared for the loneliness of this new life, so different from anything I'd ever known.

How was I to spend my time? Since neither of my parents found pleasure in reading, I had not yet discovered the treasures to be found in books. The only reading material in our house had to do with the Mormon Church, plus a few nutrition magazines of Mom's. I don't recall either of my parents ever reading a novel. They frequently told me it was a waste of time, and literature classes in school had been dismally dull.

Paul was amazed I didn't read. His mother had been an English teacher, and their home was full of books. He brought many with him into our marriage and introduced me to his favorites. I'll never forget reading *Pride and Prejudice* for the first time. I loved it so much I didn't want it to end, and it began my love affair with books.

If my marriage seemed a disaster in terms of sexual fulfillment, it was a blessing in many ways I could never have foreseen. The long days and nights spent alone while Paul was working, going to school or doing his church work were wondrous with the new world I discovered in books. I made my way through all of Jane Austin's novels and much of Charles Dickens. The discovery of Will Durant's *Story of Philosophy* kindled a lifelong thirst for knowledge. Durant became my first mentor, and I even wrote to tell him how important his work was for me. He responded with a gracious letter, and when the Book of the Month Club offered his books on Western Civilization as a bonus for joining, we took the offer without question.

I wish I'd known Paul's mother. I knew a bit about her from Mom. His family lived three houses east of my grandparents' house on 27th South. Dad knew about the notorious Harris family all the time he was growing up, and Mom knew them for several years before her marriage. Ella had three children from her first husband, whom Paul describes as "a tall, rustic coal miner who drank beer and smoked *Bull Durham* cigarettes." Although they were divorced because of his sinful behavior, he kept in touch with the family and visited Paul often during his childhood.

The divorce was instigated by Paul's grandmother, a staunch Mormon, who was intolerant of moral evil; she set her son-in-law's beard on fire to get rid of him. The second wife of a polygamist, she was a primary influence on Paul's early life.

My mother doubted that Ella had actually married William Harris; she was certain that Paul was illegitimate. Ella worked as a teacher and since she did not have a car, she rode the bus everywhere. Mom thought it disgraceful the way she picked up men. They'd stay with her for a few nights and then disappear. She was certain that Harris was just another of Ella's *friends*, but in his journal, Paul says they were married. Whatever the truth was, the biological father vanished before his son was born. Paul loved his mother deeply.

During the Great Depression, without a man in the house, Ella taught school in the daytime and had another job at night to support her family. She must have been a compassionate woman because a favorite story of Paul's was how she'd spent several nights comforting a woman whose son lay dying of Scarlet Fever. No one else would help because she was a polygamist. When the boy died, Ella prepared meals for the family and helped with funeral arrangements. He explained that although she was not active in the Mormon Church, active members stood by and criticized her while she went about more Christian charity than they. He thought that some of the negativity directed at him was because he was the son of the notorious Ella Harris. If my mother's opinion was any indication, he was probably correct.

Despite Mom's criticism of Ella, I appreciated how she'd introduced her son to the world of good literature at an early age. She also recognized his musical ability and found a way to pay for piano lessons. He was an excellent pianist, much appreciated at parties and informal meetings at the ward. He could whistle like a bird, and I loved hearing him play the piano and whistling "To a Nightingale."

My parents, on the other hand, had no background in literature, art or music until Dad became public relations manager for the Utah Symphony. Free passes enabled us to attend concerts and have exposure to classical music. My parents took seriously the Mormon warning about being lured from the truth by the "philosophies of men," and Dad limited his reading to Church publications. Paul, on the other hand, devoured music and books. He always had a symphony or concerto playing. It became the background for our life together, along with reading. I thrived on the stimulating discussions that arose from shared ideas, as a new and exhilarating kind of relationship arose, for which I am forever grateful.

Mom disliked Paul so much she couldn't stand to be around us. She and Dad seldom visited, although they were always available to answer a call for help. We saw them casually, only when we called on them, and on those special occasions when they took us to the symphony or a play. They'd both told me they would not *interfere* in our lives, no matter what happened, and they were true to their word.

My pregnancy went smoothly, after the initial morning sickness, until the last six weeks when I had a kidney infection and was in the hospital for over a week. Mom was frantic when the doctor said he might have to bring the child early because she was counting the days. She wondered if my desire to marry so quickly was because I was already pregnant. Finally, the doctor let me go home for bed rest, and Lynne was born one day short of nine months of marriage, on November 6, 1952. Mom justified the early date by pointing out it was leap year, thus saving herself the worry of "what will people think!"

There are two graphic memories of my early days as a mother. The first is the enormous work of keeping the baby clean. Since we didn't have a car to go to a laundromat, we bought a small agitator washer, which had to be filled with boiling water, for each wash and two rinses. It took hours to boil the water and wash the diapers, which were dried on wooden racks placed around the living room.

The other difficulty was Lynne's severe colic. She slept all day while Paul was at school and work, and she cried all night. I did everything I could to keep her quiet, but had no experience with babies, and Mom was not available to help. I sang to her, danced with her, walked her up and down the living room, rubbed her back and feet—but the moments of quiet lasted only long enough for her to get her breath to begin crying again. Paul became furious about 2:00 AM; it was as though his personality changed. He held me responsible for her misbehavior and screamed at me to keep her quiet, or he wouldn't be able to function at school. I felt guilty for being such a terrible mother. After a week of frustration, utterly exhausted by the nightly ordeal, I called the pediatrician. He recommended giving her *paregoric* mixed with sweetened water. I felt that I was drugging her, but she eagerly gulped the "pink medicine" from the bottle, succumbing to sleep within minutes—saving our sanity and perhaps our marriage. What remained of the ordeal was fear of Paul—I had seen anger in him I had not suspected.

At my six-week checkup, Dr. Skidmore wanted to fit me with a diaphragm to prevent another pregnancy. But remembering the promise I had made in the temple and the words of Brother Peterson about being "perfect in all things," which meant being true to the commandments of the church, I told him firmly that God would take care of us and would certainly not send us another child until we were more settled.

In the spring of 1953, we moved into student housing at the University. Stadium Village was created from surplus Quonset huts that had been made into apartments. Our rent reduced to only $28 per month, including utilities, and we now had laundry facilities. God was answering our prayers.

Although our housing was simple, I loved the Village. All the men were going to school on the G.I. Bill. Most of us were Mormons who had several children by the time our husbands graduated. The ward became our family, and I enjoyed the services, even though they were chaotic because of all the children. I looked forward to attending for the social contacts, however, after Lynne was born, we found it increasingly difficult to pay the mandatory ten percent tithing to the church. Before we moved to the Village, I worked at an all night job typing chinchilla pedigree records while Paul slept and was home with Lynne. Even with this additional income, we could not make the full tithing payment. I kept track each time we cut the payment a bit, certain that when Paul graduated and had a good job, we would pay it all back.

We started anew when we moved to the Village, determined to be faithful in every way. We would not use birth control; we would keep the Word of Wisdom by not drinking coffee or tea or alcohol, and we would pay a full tithing.

☺

I was pregnant again that summer.

Paul took his role of financial provider seriously, sometimes holding down two jobs as well as going to school. One was a paper route, near our apartment. Since the most time-consuming part of the job was to collect money, for several months, I did it for him, finding it increasingly easy as I became more visibly pregnant. I remember going from door to door in February, when the snow was knee high. It was freezing cold, and I was only a month from delivering my second child. Every person I called on gave me the money, no questions asked.

Lowell Harris was born March 29, 1954, while his father was on his paper route. Mom and Dad answered my frantic phone call by coming to help immediately. Mom stayed with Lynne, and Dad took me to the hospital. By the time Paul got there, his son had already arrived. We took the *paregoric* home with us, just in case, but he was such a compliant baby we used it only a few times.

I got a job at night and on weekends, working as a cashier at the Rialto theatre. We still did not have a car so I took the bus to work. One night, President David O. McKay, President of the Mormon Church and the Living Prophet, brought his wife to the theatre. He was tall, had snow-white hair and an inner light that radiated from his being. I was overwhelmed to be so near him; my hand shook as I gave him the tickets. His eyes caught mine, and his deep compassion touched the depths of my soul. When they left the cashier's window, I wished I'd paid for the tickets myself. Taking the money out of my purse, I placed it in an envelope along with a note telling him I wanted them to be my guests for the movie. I gave the envelope to the usher, instructing him to hand it to President McKay when they left the theatre—by then my shift would have ended. Several days later, I received a thank-you note from him. He had gone out of his way to discover my name and address. I treasured that note for many years.

During the summer when school was out, I found a part-time job at the Salt Lake *Tribune* selling classified advertising, arranging my hours to work when Paul could be home with the kids. He graduated in 1955, but wanted to earn a master's degree in music, hoping to become a composer. I wasn't clear what he'd do with the advanced degree, and my father was increasingly agitated that he was wasting his time. Dad could see the merit of graduating from college, but to keep going to school, when we had two children, seemed frivolous to my practical father.

Since most of his classes were now offered in the afternoon and night, Paul took a job with Cloverleaf Dairy, delivering milk. This gave us a bit more money. He needed a car and finally bought one—a true luxury that freed us from riding buses everywhere we went. Not easy with two babies!

By then, I was pregnant again. I quit my job at the newspaper, and Paul bought an inexpensive sewing machine. I loved spending my days learning how to sew, taking care of the children and being a housewife, especially now that we could see an end in sight for the financial problems.

Annie was born on October 18, 1955, while Paul was delivering milk. Again, my parents came to our aid. She was the sweetest baby one could imagine; she hardly ever cried, and we never needed the *paregoric*. She was so quiet that one time when we were visiting my parents, we got in the car to leave with Lynne and Lowell when we realized with a shock that we had forgotten Annie. She had a way of being almost invisible; I knew I must make special effort to give her the attention she deserved. Lynne was one month short of her third birthday when Annie was born.

After a difficult winter delivering milk and struggling with his classes at the University, Paul finally decided there was little opportunity for him to support his family through composing music. He took a job selling insurance with Prudential Life, taking on a *debit route*, which was a designated area in which he sold and serviced an established clientele. His territory was in Magna, a small mining town west of Salt Lake, the main industry of which was the copper mill. The company insisted on us buying a home in the area to cut down on driving time. We found a small house for $9,999 with a low down payment—another benefit of the G.I. Bill. At last we were settled.

I was thrilled to have a home of our own with room for the children. We had three bedrooms with plenty of space for my sewing and the kids' toys. There was a spacious yard to landscape; it was such fun playing house! Paul did well with his clients. He was a hard worker and before long was making enough money to buy a new two-toned Buick. He worked long hours, but I was used to being alone. I had my children and my books. Paul quit going to church regularly when he was in school; I went whenever I could get a ride with someone, but it was difficult in Magna with three babies. We spent most Sundays at home.

Before we moved from Stadium Village, I talked to the bishop of our ward about our current standing. I was hoping we could go to the temple again, once Paul had a good job.

"How do you figure your tithing?" the bishop asked.

"We pay ten percent on the money we receive. We haven't always been able to pay it all, but I have kept track, and when we're on our feet, we will make up what we owe," I explained, lowering my eyes to hide my embarrassment.

"But that's not the way to figure your tithing," he scowled. "Do you expect God to pay your taxes?"

"What do you mean?" I tried to remain calm.

"Tithing is to be paid on your gross income—before taxes! That is the commandment and the standard of the Church." His voice was like steel.

I returned home desolate, realizing I had calculated what we owed on the wrong basis. How could I even figure the correct amount? How could we ever make it up? My desire to follow Christ's rule, "Be ye therefore perfect" in following the commandments of the church now seemed impossible. I kept the tally as best I could and was determined that when we moved to Magna, full tithing would come first.

We had no sooner moved into our home than I realized I was pregnant again. When Doctor Skidmore gave me the news, anger hardened his voice. He scowled, "You seem to be *Fertile Myrtle*. If you don't use some kind of birth control, you're going to have problems with your back and you may not live long enough to raise the children you already have."

"But I took a vow…"

"I know it will be a difficult decision for you, but you must give it your careful consideration."

I was distraught. The God I believed in was intimately involved in my whole life. His Spirit lived within me and told me what to do. He guided me through the day, and I talked to him all the time. Maybe it was just thinking out loud, but often I would actually receive an insight that I *knew* came from Him. If children were sent by God, and I was supposed to do God's will, how could I possibly prevent a child's conception if God wanted me to have that child? And I had no doubt that my beautiful, perfect babies had been sent to me directly from Him. I agonized over the dilemma throughout my pregnancy.

At about the same time we moved into our new home, the Mormon authorities gave its members a new commandment about being prepared for a predicted catastrophe. The Church believed that in the Last Days there would be general chaos in our country. One *revelation* quoted frequently said, "Blood would run like water in the streets of Salt Lake." The new commandment had an urgency about it that made us think the End was very near. We were to have two years supply of food, water and clothing stored up in our homes. If we did not do this, we were subject to condemnation.

I was terrified about the prediction, and desolate, because there was no way we could pay for our new house, the car, another child, daily living expenses and tithing, and be expected to store up two years supply of food, water and clothing. *Maybe if I had more faith things would work out. Is God testing our faith?* I tried to talk to Paul about my concerns, but he shrugged it off as though it didn't matter, just as using birth control didn't seem to bother him. He'd go along with anything I wanted; he was much too busy making a living to give it more thought.

Paul had always been more comfortable ignoring the commandments of the Church than I had. In my mind, the Church was either completely *true,* or it was not. To not obey was a sin against God. I sometimes worried because he seemed to have lost his testimony about Mormonism being true. His studies in philosophy at the University had brought up questions about theology that threatened his beliefs.

My testimony was not based on intellectual understanding. I kept my tally of unpaid tithing and even though I could not attend meetings as often as I wanted, I had faith that when the kids were a bit older, things would change, and we would be able to be active members once again. Isn't that what happened to my own parents?

The realization that we simply could not buy and store all that food and clothing along with the necessity to make a decision to use birth control led to deep anguish. I felt like an apostate, when I asked Dr. Skidmore to give me a contraceptive after my baby was born. He was relieved and so were my parents!

Ron was born on January 18, 1957. I was still twenty-three years old and had four children. Lynne had turned four in November.

During each birth, I had been given *ether.* When I went under during Ron's birth, I saw a large circle which spiraled into itself, becoming a funnel, gaining speed and power, until it was only a dot—and the dot began to pulse incessantly. I sensed that when the pulsing stopped I would die. I was terrified, but when I awakened, Ron had been born. After regaining consciousness, the nurse placed him in my arms, and I marveled that what I thought was death was actually life.

The same dream reoccurred when I went home. Once asleep, the circle returned, slowly spiraling downward through the funnel until it became the pulsing dot. Screaming out loud I'd awaken myself and Paul, deeply agitated and drenched with sweat. I had the dream off and on for several weeks. Afraid of going to sleep, I prayed that God would take the dream away. Eventually it stopped, and for many years afterwards, I couldn't remember dreaming at all, as though my dream life was completely shut off.

What died in the pulsating dot was my confidence in the Mormon Church, as I understood it. We no longer went to the ward in Magna, but sometimes we attended my parents' ward. I felt like an outsider. It was sheer torture forcing myself to go through the front door, and I would sit in the pew, my mouth dry, my body sweaty, feeling unworthy and condemned for something I had hidden from my conscious mind.

Paul was gone most nights selling insurance. I thought it strange that he was home so seldom, and did not understand how far from the teachings of the Church he'd actually strayed until years later when I read in his journal that often he would go to movies with his sales manager and frequent pornographic bookshops.

He sold enough insurance that year to be a top producer, and with his new success, he felt he could do even better with New York Life. The manager was a General Authority in the Mormon Church. Paul thought he could get back to church if he had such an influence—just as my father became a devout Mormon when he got away from the newspaper business and joined Olson Advertising.

Because his new customers were in Salt Lake City, we sold our Magna home and bought one more centrally located. We made enough on the sale to have a good down payment and moved again, this time into the home of my dreams. It was on Millstream Lane. A three-foot wide stream sang its way along the back property line, and I couldn't wait to plant trees and bulbs to make it beautiful. There were three bedrooms upstairs and a full basement, which could be made into another bedroom, laundry and family room where the kids could play and not have their toys all over. I loved that house, and I loved the neighbors. Paul worked long hours and was seldom home, but I got involved in the ward again, teaching Mutual, the young people's organization, and took the kids to Sunday School and Primary. I even wrote and directed a play for a stake road show.

The night my play was performed, when I was exhausted and let down from the pressure, Paul and I had a terrible fight. I have no idea now what it was about, but he stormed out of the house without eating supper. I waited and waited, finally putting the children to bed, wondering where he was. About 2:00 AM he called, saying he was at the bus station downtown. He said he was leaving me; he couldn't take any more of my demands; he would never be able to make me happy. He was taking a bus to an undisclosed destination and would leave the car in the parking lot. It seemed unreal, and I didn't believe him; he was only trying to frighten me.

Returning skeptically to the bedroom, I lay on my bed, stunned, but alert and without tears. I had wondered for a long time if this might happen, an intuition that had been growing since his late nights in Magna. I wrestled all night with what to do, realizing how vulnerable I was. I had four children, and with only one semester of college, my only way to make a living was doing office work, which bored me. The situation was a wake-up call; something needed to be done.

He came home early in the morning and apologized, saying he was under a lot of pressure with his job, but assuring me he would never leave his family. However, our relationship was never the same.

I'd been practicing a radio program with some women from the General Board of the Relief Society (the women's group of the church). A few days after Paul "left me," I was at KSL radio station ready to read my part when the floor beneath me started spinning. Losing consciousness, I fell onto the floor, awakening to find I had vomited and lost control of my bowels. Humiliated and scared, I could not lift my head from the floor.

I remember the kindness of Sister Spofford, the Relief Society President. Someone took me to the emergency room of the nearby hospital where I was tested for everything they could think of, including a brain tumor and epilepsy, but could not determine the cause of my fainting. I went to an ophthalmologist who discovered that my left pupil was larger than the right one, but assured me this could not be the cause of my fainting spell. An ear specialist finally diagnosed my problem as Meniere's disease, an inflammation in the inner ear. But what had caused it? Could it be stress? The infection was real!

My doctor prescribed medication for vertigo, which did not prevent reoccurrences, but lessened their severity. It was frightening because the attacks would come unexpectedly. I remember one day when I was walking down the hallway at home carrying a load of laundry. Without warning, the dizziness returned. I stumbled and fell, dropping the laundry basket, spilling clothes all over the floor. Lynne ran to help me. After several minutes, I regained consciousness and found my five-year-old daughter sitting next to me, scared to death and crying. "What's the matter, Mama?" I struggled to my feet and hurried to the bathroom where I gave in to the diarrhea and vomiting. I was scared and felt completely helpless!

My doctor sent me to see a psychiatrist, hoping he could shed some light on my situation. I remember the appointment well. I told him about the guilt feelings that dominated my mind, but I didn't know what I'd done. I answered his questions as best I could, but could not explain my guilt—and yet there was no denying the pervasive darkness in my soul that I carried with me always.

I remember him saying, "If you could do anything you wanted to do and money was not an object, what would that be?"

Without hesitation, I replied, "I'd go back to school and get a degree so I could teach school." Under my breath, I added, *and support my children.*

He laughed at me. "There's no way you could go back to school with all those kids. You wouldn't last two weeks."

He said he could probably help me, but doubted we could afford ongoing psychotherapy. I was dismissed, the record showing that he could find nothing that would cause my fainting. When I got home, I couldn't shake the feeling of guilt that had surfaced during the interview. I must have done something very bad, and I was obviously hiding it from myself. It was then that I took off the sacred garments I had worn since my marriage in the temple. With tears in my eyes, I tucked them away in the back of my dresser drawer, vowing I would wear them again some day when I was worthy.

Paul seemed distant and unconcerned as though he thought I was engendering my condition to get sympathy. I later learned that he was struggling with his job. I knew that part of our salary was a *draw* on future earnings, but I didn't know how much money he was *borrowing* from the company. I did not know until the night he came home and told me we could no longer afford to live in the house. We'd been there less than a year, and we knew we could not sell it for enough to pay the mortgage and real estate fees. We decided to rent the house for enough to make payments on the loan and find a cheaper place to live until we could get back on our feet. We found a dilapidated house on the Avenues, an area on the north side of Salt Lake. It had only one bedroom, large enough for the two sets of bunk beds to barely fit. The kids would have that room and we would sleep in the living room. We didn't know it was infested with cockroaches until after we moved in.

My friend Donna's husband was a contractor. He agreed to help move, coming to our house after his workday with a flatbed truck on which we piled all our belongings, allowing us to slip quietly out of the neighborhood while it was still dark. In the move, the diamond from my engagement ring was lost; I didn't discover it was gone until the next morning. I never saw the house or the diamond again.

I don't remember how much we owed New York Life, but I do know we had every intention of paying the money back as soon as we could. That wasn't good enough for the pious Mormon authority.   He insisted on being paid immediately. Even though our only bills were the house and the car, the only recourse was bankruptcy. Since we had moved out of our house and were renting it, the court took our equity and the finance company took our car. During the negotiations, the elder called twice at our rented home and threatened to throw us out onto the street if we didn't pay him. I don't know what went on between him and Paul, but I do know how cruel he was to me.

Paul got a job at an all-night grocery store in the neighborhood. We decided he should go back to school to finish his master's degree and get a teaching credential. The Avenues house was easily accessible to the University by bus. It would be difficult to go back to school, but it seemed to be the best solution.

When I try to recall my feelings during this time, I remember only a gray haze. Bankruptcy was unthinkable in my ethical system. I was frightened about how we would survive, bewildered that a Mormon Authority would be so lacking in mercy, frightened that my *seizures* might continue and get even worse, and yet, there was a sense of hope deep in my soul—a sense that everything would turn out all right and, in fact, would be the beginning of a new and better life. But I also knew that it was up to me to somehow create that better life. I could no longer depend on Paul.

Several weeks after we'd settled into our new place, I called my father and asked him to take me to lunch because I wanted to talk to him. He took me to the Athletic Club, which was a prestigious restaurant for members only.   I always felt special when Dad took me there.

He told me that Paul had discussed his resignation from New York Life with him.   "Under the circumstances, bankruptcy seemed to be his only choice," Dad affirmed. "I'm sorry it had to happen, Bonnie. It's not the worst thing in the world; people do recover from bankruptcy."   He nervously folded and unfolded his napkin. "My greater concern is that you'll use this situation to turn against the Mormon Church." He thought a minute, his eyes focusing on something across the room. "Remember, Bonnie," he continued, "the church is more than one man. There are merciless people everywhere, even in the church. I admit I'm extremely disappointed in the elder's behavior toward you, but he is not the Mormon Church."

"I know that, Dad," I assured him, trying to keep my voice calm. "I don't understand the whole situation, but I do know there is probably fault on both sides. My problem now is that I'm having difficulty trusting Paul, even though I know he's done his best."

It was the first time since my marriage I'd even hinted to Dad about how unhappy I was. "I need to tell you what happened a few weeks ago, before we moved." I gulped, trying to fight back the tears that were threatening my precarious composure. Knowing how my parents disliked Paul, I did not want to add fuel to the fire, but I needed my father's support.

Dad's eyes softened as he reached across the table and took my hands, his obvious compassion helping me break through the barrier of silence I had erected over the years.

"One night we had a terrible fight," I began, tentatively. "He left the house in a huff and did not come back. He called me about 2:00 AM and said he was at the bus station and that he was leaving us. He said it was because he could never satisfy me. I now know that he was in the midst of the problems with New York Life, but then I didn't know what was going on.

"He came home the next morning, but during that long night while I was unable to sleep—frantic about how I would support myself and the kids, I came to realize how vulnerable I really am. Paul doesn't love me. And I don't love him. We made a terrible mistake, but I can't do anything about that. I know I should have listened to you before we married, but it's in the past now, and I'm trying to focus on the present situation, as you've taught me. I have no choice but to stay with him. I took vows in the temple to be his wife for "time and all eternity" and I must be true to those vows. I believe God will help me if I am faithful—but I wonder if Paul will do his part. I have a premonition that he will leave again. And I must be ready to take over the support of the children."

I was surprised that the tears I had been fighting had vanished. I was surprised at the strength and confidence I now felt as I confided my truth.

"Remember when I went to the psychiatrist about the fainting spells?" I had been sitting with downcast eyes through my confession, but now I raised my eyes to his. They had turned to rock-gray granite. I had never seen them so cold.

"Do you think the dizziness is because of the pressure?" he asked.

"I don't know," I answered truthfully. "But it's certainly possible. I know Meniere's disease is a physical diagnosis. It's real, but something is causing the problem. If I knew what it was, I probably wouldn't be so scared, and I wonder if my fear is making the symptoms worse."

We sat in silence for a few minutes, both of us staring at our clasped hands.

"Is that what the psychiatrist said?" His question brought me back to my intention for the conversation.

"No, that's my own insight. The psychiatrist asked me what I would do if I were free to do anything in the world, without considering the cost. I told him I would go back to school and get a teaching degree."

"And what did he say?" He leaned forward, surprise evident in his eyes.

And then I lied to my father. I lied to him openly and without the slightest guilt. "He told me that if I really wanted to go back to school, I should do it. I could find a way."

His eyes returned to our hands.

"I know it will not be easy, but I also know it is my only chance to have a life." I waited a few seconds before asking the burning question. "Dad, will you give me the money for one semester at the U? I'll work very hard, and I believe I can get a scholarship to cover the rest of my tuition. I only need help with this first semester."

"What will you do with the children?" He looked up again, confused, but intrigued.

"I'll find a way. There's always a way. In fact, I've been thinking that I could ask Aunt Norma to take them for a few hours in the morning. We could actually walk to her house from ours, but money's the big issue. I can't even talk to Paul about it, unless I have the tuition. We are totally broke, and even if we had the money, he wouldn't give it to me for something he'd consider to be frivolous."

Dad's eyes watered as he squeezed my hands. "If you can work out a way to go to school, Bonnie, let me know and I'll do my part."

☺

CHAPTER SIX

Moving On

I remember the broken-down old rental we moved into with warmth. It was April 1958, and what could have been a time for bitterness, became a time of transition. Understanding the pressure Paul was under when he *left* me kindled my desire to trust him again. I had learned well from my father that it is needless to dwell on what is past, and I did my best to put bankruptcy behind me.

The kids were wonderful. I don't know how much they understood about what had happened, but with my illness and our abrupt move, they certainly picked up on the gravity of our situation. They seemed to sense we couldn't handle much more stress. Lynne was ready for kindergarten that fall; Lowell was four, and Annie was two and a half. They were all healthy and active and kept each other company, making it easy for me to take care of fifteen-month-old Ron.

I hardly ever saw Mom. She was upset about the bankruptcy and the loss of our house. Our present home was a disgrace, and she couldn't stand to be there. She'd revived a secret desire to be a nurse and enrolled at the community college in a Licensed Practical Nursing course. I was excited when I heard her plans, knowing she was an intelligent woman, who had no chance to develop intellectually. She thrived in the classes since she was not only bright, but her outgoing, vibrant personality endeared her to everyone she met. I witnessed a remarkable transformation as Mom learned she was a person in her own right. When she graduated, two years later, she was the top student in her class.

My mother wasn't available to help me through the stress, but Vivian Stevens, our next-door neighbor was like a mother to me. An active Methodist, she was kind and sensitive and always knew exactly how to help when I was upset.

The day the elder from New York Life called me, threatening to turn us out onto the street, I escaped to the front porch to pull myself together, trying not to upset the kids. Stifling sobs in the dishtowel I'd been holding through the phone call, I noticed Vivian watering her lawn. She turned off the water and walked tentatively over to our porch.

"What's wrong, Bonnie?" she asked. "Is there anything I can do?"

I dried my face with the kitchen towel. "I don't think anyone can help," I began. "It's such a mess!" The tears flowed again, as though I'd turned on a faucet.

She took my elbow and gently pulled me down to the top step of the porch. "Let's sit here a while, and when you're ready, you can tell me what's going on. I'm not going to gossip; it's just between you and me."

I don't know how long we sat there, me blowing my nose and Vivian waiting. My only confidante had been Mom, and I hadn't dared talk to her honestly since I married Paul.

"We moved here because we had to declare bankruptcy," I began tentatively. "We had to leave our beautiful home, and…" The tears began again. "But it's over and done with; there's nothing we can do. I'm so stupid to be crying. I'm sorry!"

"You're not stupid, and why are you sorry?"

"I should be able to handle this better, that's all."

"Anyone who's just moved out of their home into this place, with four kids, has a right to cry!" I could see she was angry for me.

I stared at the dishtowel and in the silence felt frustration diminish. It helped talking about it.

"The reason I'm upset is I just got a call from the man we owe all the money. He's a bigwig in the Mormon Church. We rented our house to cut expenses so we could pay him back and save our equity in the house. Now he's forcing us to declare bankruptcy, and because we're not living in it, we'll lose the house completely. He just said if we didn't pay him every cent he'd have us thrown out into the street. I never thought a person in his position could be so cruel."

"It's always worse when cruelty comes from someone in a trusted position. Unfortunately, it happens in all churches. It's often the holiest ones who are the worst. After all, it was the religious leaders who crucified Jesus."

"I hadn't thought about it like that, but you're right—of course, you're right."

"Mommy, where are you?" Lowell called from inside the house.

"I'm sitting on the porch with Mrs. Stevens. Come on out and sit with us if you want." I squeezed her hand. "Thanks for listening, Vivian. I hope we can talk some more."

"Anytime, Bonnie. I'm alone over there and would love your company!"

One day, when the kids were having their naps, I took some homemade cookies over to her. She poured herself a cup of coffee, and I accepted a glass of water as we sat at the table in her lemon-yellow kitchen, which was full of light. A giant Christmas cactus with bright pink blossoms joyfully welcomed me.

"I'm having so much trouble with anger," I confided after admiring her plants. "Dad says I should just forget what the elder did to us—just put it behind us and go on. But no matter how hard I try, I keep thinking about him all the time, and it makes me upset and cranky with the kids. I don't know what to do about it."

"You can't expect yourself to forget. It's impossible. After all, your whole life has been changed through his unwillingness to negotiate. How can you forget about that?"

"But it's driving me crazy thinking about it all the time."

"What did Jesus tell us to do?"

"You know, Vivian, one thing I've realized from talking to you is that Mormons don't talk about Jesus that way. We would say, what does the church tell us to do?"

"Well, what does the church tell you to do?"

"What Dad says—just forget about it and go on. What does your church say to do?"

"Well, what Jesus teaches is that we must forgive."

"Isn't it the same thing? Isn't forgetting about something the same as forgiving? Forgive and forget—they go together."

"As far as I know, Jesus never said to *forget*. It's impossible in your situation. God wouldn't ask you to do something that's impossible."

I felt a sensation in my chest—not quite a burning of the heart, but it seemed like a sign; I knew I should pay attention to what she was saying. *God wouldn't ask me to do something that's impossible. Can I really believe that?*

"What is forgiveness, then?"

"Well, I'm not a theologian, but what I think it means is trying to understand where the other person's coming from and then asking God to help us forgive that person. In the Lord's Prayer we pray: 'Forgive us our debts as we forgive our debtors.' If we expect God to forgive our mistakes, we *must* forgive others when they hurt us. It takes time to let go of the hurt, but the *desire* to forgive is the most important thing. Our willingness to understand another person teaches us how to love—the most important thing of all because God *is* love!"

I had never heard anything like that before.

"Try this. When the angry thoughts come into your head, instead of letting them take over, just say something like: 'Please, God, teach me to forgive the elder, and forgive me for thinking these angry thoughts.'"

I practiced what Vivian taught me, and was amazed how much more peaceful I felt. I also needed to forgive Paul. He probably couldn't help the bankruptcy, and he was working hard to support us; I just didn't understand his priorities. He gave me so little to spend on groceries and running the house; it seemed impossible. There was not a penny to spare, and we were eating potatoes, packaged macaroni and cheese, and stuffing ourselves with bread. We bought powdered milk in bulk, which the pediatrician assured me was just as nutritious as fresh milk, but we certainly couldn't afford meat, vegetables and fruit. And yet, he always had money to buy another record for his collection. I kept my resentment to myself since I had promised to always obey him; I had no right to question him. I was so desperate that once I actually stole some vitamins from the pharmacy and another time slipped some *silly putty* into my pocket because Lynne wanted it so much.

Sometimes, I couldn't hold the resentment in and then I'd explode like a volcano. One night he brought home a pizza, and I had a fit because I needed the money for what I considered *good* food. My outrage spoiled the party for everyone.

Another time, on our anniversary, he brought me a dozen roses. I'd been saving pennies to buy Lowell badly needed shoes. I burst into angry tears when I saw the roses. He didn't buy roses for me again until many years later. The romance in our marriage seemed gone for good; even the diamond from my engagement ring, which was lost the night we moved out of our house, was never recovered.

The problem was that we didn't know how to talk to each other. I'd never learned how to acknowledge anger, let alone how to deal with it. If something bothered me, I'd stew about it—as Mom did. Then when I couldn't hold it in any longer, I'd explode, and the emotion was all out of proportion to the situation. When it was over, I'd blame myself for losing control. Guilt piled on guilt, showing unmistakable proof I was basically a very *bad* person. I wondered if this defect might be the source of my discomfort when I tried to go to church.

Remembering my discussion with Dad, I called on Mom's Aunt Norma who lived in a big old house about a mile from ours. It was an easy walk down the hill, though not so easy coming back. She tended children in the daytime to help with the family budget. I don't think it was an official daycare, but she always had four or five children in her home. When I asked if she would tend Lowell, Annie and Ronnie in the mornings while I went to school, she readily agreed and told me there would be no charge; she just wanted to do it for me. I guessed Dad was paying her himself, so I simply expressed my gratitude for her generosity. It was set; I was going back to school.

Since I hadn't studied for years, I bought a book to help improve my vocabulary, as well as Napoleon Hill's *Think and Grow Rich,* which I read religiously. Having a goal for my own life greatly satisfied much of the aching loneliness. I made clothes for the kids and myself, studied vocabulary and read my book, trying to think of some way I, too, could "think and grow rich." The summer flew by.

I'll never forget my first day at the University. It was early September when I registered for a full schedule, fifteen units, and made straight A's. Halfway through the school quarter, I applied for a scholarship, which was granted for winter quarter. Nothing could stop me now.

Although we seldom saw my parents, I talked to Mom on the phone several times a week. It was exhilarating to hear about her classes, and I reveled in her newfound self-esteem. We were both students now; the bond between us strengthened into a relationship between equals. I let go of my childhood need to take care of her, and she replaced her obsession with my life with interests of her own. What a blessing.

In the meantime, Paul was working very hard, and his professors were encouraging, saddened at our financial debacle. He had enough credits to finish a teaching certificate in August 1959. In January, a recruiter came to the campus to interview potential teachers for the Anaheim School District. They needed a band director, and Paul applied.

We were excited, feeling certain this was the opportunity we needed. The question of how we'd get to Anaheim arose. On faith that he would get the contract, I agreed to find work instead of going to school spring quarter. When the teaching contract came through in May, we bought a used 1956 Plymouth using the money I'd saved as a down payment and his contract as collateral. I was disappointed to quit school again, but with the one quarter I'd finished before marriage, I now had a full year of credits. I'd proven I could make good grades, and I was certain there would be another chance.

☺

In August, we hitched a small trailer to the back of our Plymouth and the six of us piled into the car, beginning the long trek to Anaheim, California. The trip was a nightmare. Paul was worried about the Plymouth pulling the heavily loaded trailer through the mountains. He was tense and on edge before we left Salt Lake, and his irritation increased with every sound from the kids.

We spent the first night in a campground in Zion's Canyon, leaving us only 250 miles to Las Vegas, but the drive over Mormon Mesa, west of Mesquite, took all day. It was near 100 degrees. We had no air conditioning, and the radiator kept boiling over. Luckily, we had brought water for such an emergency; even so, Paul's temper was simmering. No one was allowed to make a sound until we got to Las Vegas.

Dad had arranged for us to stay at the Riviera Hotel, a free night and meals, compliments of a client. Exhausted from the long trip, we were refreshed by the swimming pool. To make it up to me for being so mean during the drive, Paul called room service for the kids, and we went to the dinner show. He ordered filet mignons, together with appetizers and dessert. I questioned his extravagance, but he assured me it was expected when you were honored guests.

The next morning, the kids were absolutely wild. At breakfast, they insisted on running around the dining room and even tried climbing the potted palm trees that were part of the décor. We were asked to leave; I was humiliated. Never had the children been so unmanageable, and Paul was so angry and sullen that the entire drive to Anaheim was again made in heavy silence. The hotel passed their complaints on to my father who never forgot our lack of restraint and his embarrassment, even though he tried to put the incident behind him.

We had rented a two-bedroom duplex, sight unseen, through the local Mormon ward, intending the move to be a new beginning with the church also. We'd, once again, promised ourselves to pay our tithing and go to church the first Sunday we were there. The house was small, but the two sets of bunk beds fit into the larger bedroom, and we squeezed into a room of our own, a step up from the rental on the Avenues, where we'd slept in the living room. We were too tired to unpack, so we slept on the floor that first night.

The children were settled in their room about 8:30 PM, and we were trying to relax a bit before bed when a loud explosion outside our window brought us to our feet. Boom!

Boom! Boom! It went on for several minutes. The kids ran into the living room, terrified until we saw from our window that the noise came from fireworks. Our new home was a mile east of Disneyland, and we could expect the excitement as a nightly ritual. What fun—once we realized we weren't being bombed.

About 1:00 AM, we were awakened from sleep by another roaring noise. The whole house shook, as the nightly produce train rumbled past our house on tracks just feet from our bedroom. Not an auspicious beginning for our new life.

We enrolled Lynne in first grade and Lowell in kindergarten. A neighbor agreed to tend the children in the daytime, making it possible for me to work at an engineering company close enough to walk from our house. Paul settled into his new career and financial security was within our grasp.

The first day at my new job, I went into the break room, and someone asked if I wanted a cup of coffee. I still remember replying with disdain, "I don't drink coffee. I'm a Mormon!" I shudder as I remember the arrogance in my remark, even though the other employees took it in stride and didn't hold it against me.

On Sunday, we went to the local ward. Paul hadn't been to church for more than five years, and I hadn't been since the bankruptcy. It was exhilarating to get everyone all dressed up and have someplace to go together. I felt very righteous and prayed that nothing would interfere with church again. Paul presented himself as a returned missionary, and the Bishop invited us to be guest speakers at Sacrament Meeting two weeks after our arrival. We both were excited to have such an opportunity, but wondered what we could talk about.

A copy of a new magazine, *Wisdom,* had been sent to us as a promotion, and we'd subscribed to it. The first issue was about the Sermon on the Mount from Mathew's Gospel.

Since Mormons believe in the Sermon on the Mount, we took our respective talks from that magazine. We were well prepared, and we're both good speakers, but our talks were not well received, at least not by the bishopric. What we'd presented was not the prescribed teaching of the Mormon Church. I didn't know enough Mormon theology to know what we'd said that was wrong, and Paul was mystified also. The next week, the bishop talked to Paul after the service. I don't know what was said, but we never went back, and no one called on us as long as we lived in that ward.

I worked as a clerk typist, a skill I'd learned in junior high school. There were ten in the typing pool, and all of our work came through a supervisor. Sometimes I'd go several hours with nothing to do, but without fail, on Friday afternoon, a crisis would emerge, demanding weekend work—for overtime pay.

One Friday, after working two weekends in a row, I made an appointment with Lillian, the supervisor. I explained, "I have four small children plus a husband, and I can't keep working all week and weekends too."

She smiled sweetly. "But you said you needed the money, and, you've got to admit, the pay for weekends isn't hard to take!"

"You're right about that, but it's not worth it to me. I need to do laundry and clean the house and make meals ahead for the following week. Besides that, I want some time with my family."

"Let your husband do the housework," she taunted.

"I could never do that."

"Why not? Doesn't he live there too?"

"But, you don't understand. Mormon men do not do housework. That's the wife's job."

"Even when you're both working?"

"You don't understand. The fact is that I simply cannot come in on weekends. I'll work very hard five days a week, but that's it!" I was surprised that I could be so decisive.

"OK." Lillian thought a minute and then said confidentially, "Look, the rest of us depend on the extra work. I'll make a deal with you; I'll give you what work I can during the week, but the rest of the time, just look busy. It's the way we do things around here, OK? I don't care what you're typing, just look busy!"

"You mean I could write letters or personal stuff and it would be OK?"

"Just look like you're busy. That's all."

I was baffled by the dishonesty, but decided not to press the issue. All they expected was for me to show up and look busy. If I could use the time any way I wanted, I'd find some way to fill the time.

During the summer, I'd read a sexy novel that had taken the nation by storm. As I remember, *Peyton Place* was written by a housewife with little education. It wasn't very good, and I thought at the time that I could do as well as she had—if I only had the time. Well, guess what, I had just been handed *time* to write. Not a bad idea. Napoleon Hill would approve!

In order to sell a book, I knew it had to be sexy. OK. I'd write about a beautiful girl who looked like Lynne's Barbie doll.

The novel seemed to write itself. The heroine, Barbara, has a date with a tall, dark, handsome man who looks like George. He has large brown eyes, like a doe's. After a lovely dinner, he gets her drunk and seduces her.

Three times he brings her to the point of orgasm and leaves her unfulfilled. She stays with him for three days, as he teaches her the secrets of sexual pleasure. She learns how to bring ultimate fulfillment to any man and to herself. He gives her a new name. She is now *Barba*.

He has hypnotized her so that whenever she meets a man with dark brown hair and brown eyes who looks at her in a certain way, she will say to him, "Call me Barba," and with those words, she will be totally available to him for three days. When the time is over, she will, once again, become Barbara, mentally still a virgin, completely forgetting what has happened—even her new name. The lover will not understand why she is no longer available, but nothing he says or does will restore her to the woman he desperately desires.

The rest of the book was to be about the adventures of Barbara, the beautiful, chaste woman whom everyone admires, and who occasionally loses three days as the nymphomaniac she was hypnotized to be.

However, it was never written; somehow, the inspiration evaporated. For one thing, my supervisor reorganized the typing pool and separated me from the rest of the administrative staff by moving my desk into the engineering section of the building. My job was to be available to the engineers for urgent typing assignments—letters, inquiries and miscellaneous work that didn't require her supervision. The writing time was reduced to a minimum, and the book took second place.

☺

Call Me Barba was an experience of writing from a place inside myself that seemed to bypass my ordinary thought process. I wonder if this is what people refer to as automatic writing. It was as though there was a whole different self who inhabited the same body as the Bonnie I knew myself to be. I had experienced her briefly in the incident with my mother and the girls. But her questioning of my mother's actions was not acceptable to me and was therefore denied. Which self did Amplus enhance, and who would I be if I didn't take my "happy pills"?

I recognize two selves clearly in the two versions of my summer in Denver. The hidden one rose up again when I lied to my father, telling him the psychiatrist had encouraged me to go back to school. Now, here she was again expressing the double standard of my desire to be both sexy and chaste. Was she showing me that in order to be a perfect wife and mother, I had to repress the responsive woman George had awakened?

I don't remember showing the manuscript to Paul, but I blushingly admit that I sent it to my father. What was I thinking? Clearly, I wasn't thinking. I had no expectations of his reaction; I just sent it because, I believe now, it was really about him. I think I was telling him that even though I was having sex with my husband, the innocent daughter he loved was still faithful to him. I also recognize that this action could have been an awkward attempt to differentiate myself from my father, but I certainly didn't consider these possibilities in the moment. I simply sent him the book and asked for his opinion.

☺

Jimmy Myers was now the Director of Olson Advertising and had gleaned national acclaim through his work on the Colorado River Project. The Utah symphony was thriving under his influence, and he was now on the General Board of the MIA. He had just returned from a churchwide conference with young people from all over the country, when he got my manuscript.

A couple of days later, I called him. "Hi, Dad," I said in my innocent voice.

After a brief lull, when I wondered if the phone had gone dead, he said, "I'm surprised you called after dropping your bomb on me."

His anger seemed to suck the moisture from my mouth; the telephone lines were sizzling.

102

"You sound angry," I managed to say.

"Not angry, Bonnie. But I'm very disappointed. I was at an MIA conference with the wholesome young people of the church all that day. When I got home and saw your manuscript, I expected the same goodness from my own daughter. What a shock that was!"

"But Dad…" I stammered.

"I have burned the trash you sent me, and I never want to talk about it again. Not now or ever! Do you understand?" After a pause, he continued, "Now I'm going to hang up the phone because I want to put this behind me. And I suggest you do the same. Good-bye."

I put the manuscript in the back of a filing cabinet, feeling sad that I had revealed my evil self to him. *This only proves what a terrible person I really am*, I thought. But I would try to follow his instructions and put the whole incident behind me. It wouldn't do any good to brood over it, like my mother would.

In February, I lost my job. I was probably laid off, but I used the word *fired* when telling Paul. Lynne and Lowell both remember the conversation, thinking I was going to be burned up. Losing my job proved to be a blessing because it freed me from the need to work so that I could devote myself to the family. I remember wonderful weekends exploring the beaches. We especially loved Laguna Beach and went there every Sunday we could. We wanted to see if there were swallows at Capistrano, and from that outing, we made a project of visiting every mission along the coast up to Santa Barbara.

I planned to quit my job in June anyway because the family was going to Salt Lake City in the summer for Paul to complete his master's degree. I had three months ahead of me and wondered what I'd do with myself. It's been a truth in my life that when I let go of plans, something unexpected is bound to rush in to fill the void.

I was reading an article in the newspaper about an archaeologist, Kathleen Kenyan. Through her work at the site of Jericho in the Holy Land, she had disproved previous work by John Garstang, which provided evidence that the walls of Jericho had been destroyed at the hands of the Israelites. These conclusions were popular because they seemed to prove the authenticity of the Hebrew Scriptures. Now Kenyan concluded that Jericho was in ruins since 2300 BC, nine hundred years before the Israelites arrived at the scene; it had already been destroyed.

The article caught my attention because I had never thought about archaeology and the fact that people were trying to prove and/or disprove the Bible. Questions arose in my mind that sent me to the public library where I followed my nascent interest in archaeology to the study of Egyptology. I read everything I could get my hands on about Egypt and the historical criticism of the Bible.

Fascinated to learn about the early monotheism of Amon Hotep IV, I noted the connections between his heretical theology and the sacred city of Heliopolis, which seemed to be in close proximity to the land Pharaoh gave to Joseph's family and where they lived for 400 years before the exodus. I remembered how the "Book of Moses" in the *Pearl of Great Price* connected the blood of Cain with Egyptus and wondered if Joseph's wife, the daughter of a Pharaoh, had been contaminated by the blood of Cain. What did that mean for my Patriarchal Blessing, which said I was a descendant of Ephraim, a son of Joseph? If true, didn't I also have the "blood of Cain" in my veins?

The same enthusiasm, which resulted in my now defunct sexy novel, propelled me to outline a new story, this time about Joseph and his relationship to Amon Hotep IV and the genesis of monotheism. Did the Israelite religion come from the pharaoh or was the pharaoh influenced by Joseph and his descendants?

Excitement about my research and a longing for someone with whom I could discuss my findings rekindled my desire to return to school. Discovering that the junior college in Fullerton, California, was free to residents who'd lived in the state for at least a year, I realized I qualified! With Paul's permission, I made arrangements to enter school in September with the purpose of working toward a teaching credential so I could help him support the family. I took the entrance exam, sent for my transcript from the University of Utah and planned to register when we returned. Also, I decided that when I was in Salt Lake, I would ask someone in the church about my new theories.

We put our furniture in storage and piled into our Plymouth for the dreaded drive back to Salt Lake City. Paul could see no reason to waste money on a motel. It was only a sixteen-hour drive, and he could make good time driving across the Nevada desert at night. I couldn't help drive because I did not have a license. Before we got married, I had no access to a car so I hadn't applied for one. Paul made it clear that since he was the head of the family, driving was his job. Besides, he could never trust me to touch his precious possessions. The car was his.

Ron sat on my lap, and the other three children were in the back. They had games to play but no undue noise and no fighting were allowed. We stopped along the way, but only when Paul needed to go to the bathroom, and he seemed to have an enormous bladder. The rest of us had to hold it. We were careful to limit our liquids so as not to make Daddy angry.

Over the next twelve years, we would make that trip yearly and the rules never changed. Travel was a nightmare to be avoided if at all possible!

The summer with Mom and Dad was idyllic in almost every respect. Mom was well into her training at the community college and the hospital, so I got to be the homemaker. I delighted in cleaning the house and fixing meals for the family, and she appreciated my efforts. It was fun to have a nice meal waiting for them when they came home from work.

Two events of the summer stand out in my mind. The first concerned my old friend, Rula, whom I hadn't talked to since high school; the other was an interview with one of the General Authorities of the church, which Dad arranged to discuss my questions.

Rula was in town for a few weeks because she was getting married, and her mother invited Mom and me to an engagement party at the Salt Lake Country Club. She'd had an exciting life since I last saw her.

Her high-school interest in music had led to a passion for the harp. She contacted the harpist of the Utah Symphony and offered to tend her children in return for lessons. When the harpist's husband transferred to New York City, Rula went along with the family as a nanny. While there, she won a scholarship to Curtis Institute of Music. After graduation, she made a living playing her harp on an ocean liner. One of her trips took her to Hawaii where she settled down as harpist for the Hawaiian symphony.

This was in the late '50s, when Alan Watts and Timothy Leary were in the Islands experimenting with drugs. She was involved in their experimentation and also became a follower of Ron Hubbard, founder of Scientology.

The man she was about to marry was a research biologist, and they planned to make Hawaii their home. By this time, Rula had already walked the wall of China and climbed the Swiss Alps. And I'd realized my dream also— I'd been married in the temple and had four beautiful children to prove my worth.

We spent a stimulating evening together, amazed that in spite of our different lives, we were somehow intimately connected. It was as though we had never been apart. She freely told me about her life, and I told her about my dreams of going back to school and my interest in Egyptology and my questions about the authenticity of the Bible. We never mentioned Paul, and I temporarily forgot about the kids, so exciting it was to talk with someone who understood and cared.

When we parted, we never talked about keeping in touch, but there was an inner knowing that our friendship was permanent and that we would meet again many times throughout our lives.

Dad and I never discussed *Barba*. There was no embarrassment on either side when we saw each other. It was as though the manuscript never existed. I did, however, try to explain my research. He knew nothing about Egypt and had no interest, but when I told him I wanted to talk to someone in the church about what I was reading, he agreed to take me to see a General Authority.

I don't know who it was, but we met him in the Church Office building. The apostle was gracious and greeted me with warmth. I sat comfortably opposite him at his desk with Dad at my side.

"I've been deeply concerned about the church's stand against Negroes, ever since high school. I understand what the teaching is, but I have a question. I've been studying Egyptology and the history of the Israelites in Egypt, I know that the 'Book of Abraham' teaches that the blood of Cain was preserved through Egyptus, son of Ham, who survived the flood."

The apostle listened politely and nodded in agreement.

"Well, if the Egyptian people carry the blood of Cain and Joseph married Pharaoh's daughter, who was obviously an Egyptian, then Joseph's sons, Ephraim and Manasseh, also carry the blood of Cain. And Mormons are of the same lineage, are we not?"

The elder scowled at my father and then turned to me. "I can see that you have many questions which are not befitting a mother in Zion. Your job is to raise your children in the truth of the Gospel." He smiled at me kindly, as one would smile at a child. "It is best to leave the mysteries of the gospel to the men who have the inspiration of the priesthood." And then, he added, "It is Satan who makes you ask such questions. They can lead you to apostasy."

He sat silently in his big chair, allowing his wisdom to sink in to my incompetent mind. Finally, Dad stood up, shook his hand and thanked him for his time.

I felt like a stupid, six year old leaving that office; too intimidated to acknowledge feelings of any kind, but the secret self within remembered every word of that interview. She would bring it up later, when it could be used for her devious purposes. My father smiled lovingly at me, secure in the knowledge I had been put in my place for good. I was grateful he had been there to support me in my humiliation.

Paul drove the car home alone when his classes were over. The family followed a week later, after he found a suitable house near the college in Fullerton. We took the train. It was great for the kids because they could move about; however, it was almost impossible to keep them from disturbing the rest of the passengers. Lynne, still only seven, was very responsible and helped with the younger kids, but they insisted on making regular trips to the water fountain at the end of the car. I feared there would be a small river running down the aisle before we got to California. Thank heavens for our understanding steward!

The most memorable moment of the trip occurred when I went into the women's bathroom. A Negro woman about my age stood by the vanity, combing her hair. Involuntarily, I stopped short, hardly able to breathe. I wanted so much to speak to her, but it was as though an invisible wall stood between us. *Why?* I lowered my head and slunk to the john, staying for a long time, hoping she would be gone when I came out. She was, and I was relieved, but cried inwardly, realizing how I was a victim of society's hatred. The memory of that encounter haunts me even as I write about it.

Paul found a wonderful old house near the college. The first day we were there, Lowell, who'd climbed a palm tree, fell and broke his arm. We didn't have a doctor, and the poor kid was in terrible pain by the time we found help. But that didn't stop the climbing. The living room was the center of the house and had four interior doors, which led to other rooms. The kids learned to shimmy up the doorframes so their heads were only inches from the top. We'd come into the house, unsuspecting, and find our four children, making animal sounds, hanging from the openings. They called it "monkey business."

When I reported to my counselor, he surprised me by asking why I hadn't registered for medical school. Evidently my tests supported such a curriculum, and I recalled my adolescent desire to be a psychotherapist. But that was a long time ago. What I wanted was to major in English so I could teach school and support my family

"Why did you choose English?" he asked

"Well," I explained, "I love to read, and I have an interest in writing."

"What kind of writing?" was his logical question.

"Probably fiction," I responded. "I wrote the beginning of a novel last year, but scrapped it. Now I have an idea for a historical novel about Joseph in Egypt. I'd like help with my writing and especially want someone to read what I write and give me feedback."

"Do you still have the novel?"

I hesitated. *What have I gotten into? Would I dare show Barba to a college professor?* Before I could stop myself, I blurted out, "Sure, I have it in a file."

"I'd like to see it. It will help me know your skill and your needs."

I hesitated. "You see, Professor Smith, I wrote it after I read *Peyton Place* and thought I could write a sexy book as good as that. I don't know if you'd want to read that kind of thing."

"I would," he said emphatically. "You can trust me. I don't think I'd be shocked at anything you could write." And then he added, "I'm the head of the English Department, you know."

How exciting! Now I could get some feedback on my writing—and from a professor of English! I found the manuscript, and without rereading it, put it in an envelope and left it at the school office. I wondered how long it would take for him to get back to me.

It didn't take long. A few days later, a girl from his office brought the envelope back. I couldn't wait to see what he said, so I sneaked a peak in class. There was not a single note on the first few pages, but right after Barba had been hypnotized he wrote: "This is as far as I read. Bonnie, you sound like a nun trying to swear. You need to write from your own experience!"

I could hardly concentrate the rest of the class. I was glad he hadn't given it to me in person!

Another requirement for entrance was to have a complete physical examination. The doctor noticed from the survey that I didn't drink coffee, tea or alcohol and had never smoked. He asked if there was some reason for my abstinence.

"I'm a Mormon," I told him, without the arrogance of my previous announcement.

"Why can't you drink or smoke if you're a Mormon?" he baited me.

"Because we think the body is the temple of the spirit and we must keep it pure and wholesome for eternity."

"You mean you think your body will survive after you die?" He laughed.

I couldn't think of a reply. I felt stupid and belittled, very much like I felt when I'd talked to the apostle a month before. *Why is it that men so often make me feel inferior?* I asked myself. And then remembered Professor Smith who had given me harsh feedback but without making me feel worthless.

Still, the doctor's questions lingered in my mind. What did I believe about life after death? It was a question no one I knew discussed. Mormons ask the authorities what to think; I could never remember being asked what I believed. I knew I'd have to give this question concentrated thought.

Fullerton Junior College was known at that time as "a hotbed of communism." I don't know what that referred to because I certainly did not encounter anything un-American during my year of study. It was an excellent school with a dedicated faculty who had small enough classes to give personal attention to interested students, unlike the University of Utah where I felt completely invisible. My teachers took my questions seriously and showed personal interest, perhaps because in 1960, it was still unusual for a married woman with four children to be in school. I had never been encouraged to think for myself, and now I was being praised for my questions.

I earned all A's at FJC. The second semester, Mr. Jones called me into his office and asked me what I planned to do after graduation.

"I want to go on," I explained, "but there isn't a state college in the area, and my family situation prohibits commuting. Do you know of any possibilities?"

"As a matter of fact, I do." He picked up some papers from his desk, holding them out to me as though he were offering me a delicious apple. "Have you ever heard of Chapman College?" His eyes twinkled.

"No," I answered truthfully. "Is it in this area?"

"Orange, California, just a couple of miles from here. It's a private school, and I realize the tuition would be out of the question, but they have offered a fully paid scholarship to one graduate from each junior college in the county. Our faculty wants you to apply. We think you have a good chance of getting it."

"But won't they want someone who can be active in extracurricular activities? I can't—with my family."

"It will make it a bit more difficult for you to get it, but it's not impossible. What do you say?"

"It won't hurt to apply, and I have no other option."

I did apply, and my teachers' recommendations must have been very good because I received the coveted scholarship. Not only would it pay all of my tuition, but also cover my books.

☺

Interlude

September 2005

Soul: So, what thoughts are going through your mind as you read what you've written?

Bonnie: Feelings are more prominent than thoughts right now. Maybe you can help me sort through the emotion to enable articulation.

Soul: OK. What are you *feeling* about what you've written?

Bonnie: There's a whole range of emotions I could tap into. Perhaps the overriding feeling is exhaustion from all the energy spent trying to live up to the Mormon expectations—against all odds.

God blessed us with four beautiful children that we were ill-equipped to raise. We struggled financially trying to pay our tithing, suffocating in guilt for not living according to our promises in the temple, not even finding compassion in the Elder who forced us into bankruptcy. And when the doctor at the junior college asked me what I believed about a physical resurrection, I realized I was defending beliefs I'd never examined. No wonder I was always so tired— in spite of the amphetamines I was still taking.

Soul: What feelings, other than exhaustion, are begging for recognition?

113

Bonnie: Anger—and you know how hard it is for me to own my anger. But I'm furious at what appears to be deception in the church.

Soul: Can you be specific?

Bonnie: I've just finished reading *David O. McKay and The Rise of Modern Mormonism.*[1]

I bought the book because I've always loved and admired President McKay. He was president of the church during the period I've just recalled. I had been taught that Jesus met with the Authorities in person in the temple to instruct them. This new book is based on notes and diaries preserved by McKay's private secretary for thirty-five years, Clare Middlemiss. It presents a picture very different from my understanding.

Here are ordinary men with different points of view meeting together to make decisions for the church—a polity very like Episcopalian and other mainline denominations. We all make decisions in the context of prayer while relying on the Spirit's guidance. The book reveals there is no physical Christ in their midst to give them eternal, irrefutable answers. There are divergent opinions about almost everything. They debate and argue just like the rest of humankind.

Soul: And why is that so important to discover?

Bonnie: Because at the very time the Apostle told me that my questions about Negroes were coming from Satan, the Authorities were debating the same questions on the highest level of the church. Harold B. Lee wanted immediate rescission of the doctrine of the "black seed," but the best President McKay could do was to change the word doctrine to policy, thus paving the way for a new revelation, which came in 1978.[2]

Soul: What else could they do?

Bonnie: If they'd let the members of the church know they were wrestling with the issue, we could have entered into the dilemma with them. As it was, innumerable people I know were cut off from families because they dared question the authorities on this issue. It was the first theological run-in I had with my father, and because of my neurotic personality, it became another source of self-hatred, an indication I was unworthy of understanding the doctrine.

Soul: Why didn't they tell the whole church of their quandary?

Bonnie: They have to defend the teachings as Joseph Smith gave them. They lack awareness that all of life is evolving: that it is not a sin to grow in understanding and compassion and to look back at childish beliefs and see flaws; that confession and forgiveness are basic principles of the Gospel. If they would only seek the truth, it would set us all free.

Soul: You're making it a pervasive problem rather than an isolated one.

Bonnie: The Mormon Church teaches that "families are forever." And yet, I hardly know a family in this valley that doesn't have someone who is considered lost. Cut off emotionally—lost for all eternity because they dare ask honest questions. So much pain! No wonder there are so many emotional problems here.

Soul: So where do you see God in this narrative?

Bonnie: In love. I love my children; that has never been an issue. Their presence in my life brings great joy. Paul is like one of them; I love him in the same way. And I experienced divine help in meeting the challenges.

The problem was that, although I believed in God's love and guidance, I felt I wasn't worthy. The Apostle told me that Satan's presence was evident in my life. Satan's voice was always condemning me for not keeping the vows I'd made in the temple, constantly filling my mind with doubts about the "only true church," ever convicting me for not being faithful to the heritage I'd received at my birth. I was filled with self-loathing, and yet, there was something that helped me keep going and gave me hope that some day I would find the answer I sought. I know now that this was the voice of God.

Soul: What other emotions are you feeling right now, Bonnie?

Bonnie: Sadness. All my life I have wanted the Mormon Church proven to be the one true church. I feel sad because I feel betrayed. The church has not fulfilled my hope. Perhaps it was my expectations that were on the wrong track. Sadness is coming from deep grief that the very basis of who I've thought I am was crumbling.

Preparing to go to Chapman College, I was like a caterpillar crawling into a chrysalis, preparing to die.

☺

---

1. Prince and Wright, *David O. McKay and The Rise of Modern Mormonism,* University of Utah Press, 2005
2. Ibid, p. 74-75

With Death On My Shoulder

Part Two

Prologue

Salt Lake City, 1989

Ambling down the hallway at the University of Utah Medical Center, I grimaced at the loud clunk of my high-heeled shoes, wishing I'd brought the soft-soled flats I usually wear for hospital visits. It was Maundy Thursday, and I was just leaving the Cathedral when the page summoned me. A heart transplant patient had requested a priest to celebrate Eucharist with him. I was dressed formally in a black suit and shirt with gleaming white Anglican collar, and I hoped I wouldn't *scare him. He's probably frightened enough thinking of the coming ordeal without me barging into the room looking like death.* I usually wear a pastel blouse to soften the austerity of my clerical dress, but there wasn't time to go home and change.

Slipping into a pew at the hospital chapel, I took several deep breaths, bringing my mind to stillness. I imagined what my patient must have been feeling. *He's probably waited for the transplant for many months and must be relieved to finally get the heart. At the same time, fear of surgery and anxiety about his body's reaction will be vying for awareness. I wonder which emotion he will choose to focus his attention.*

Carrying my wooden communion kit in one hand, with the other I knocked cautiously at the door, caught short by the robust voice bidding me to enter. Instead of the apprehensive patient I'd expected, Bill Davis was sitting up in bed, his tanned face radiant with excitement, and his eyes warm with welcome. My eyes widened as I took in the scene before me. Next to his bed sat a silver-haired woman wearing a light green ultra-suede dress, a silk scarf of lavender and blue draping her slim shoulders. An arrangement of pink and white carnations and fragrant lilies graced a table at the foot of the bed, along with a bottle of champagne and several glasses.

I must have looked like a dunce, standing there with my mouth open, not certain what to say. "Thank you for coming," his wife said apprehensively. "We've never had a woman priest before!" They were as surprised as I.

"And I've never walked into a patient's room who was preparing for surgery with such extravagant joy!"

"Oh my goodness, you must…"

Bill broke in, "You must think I'm here for a heart transplant. Actually, I had my operation one year ago. This is my first annual checkup, and it is a celebration."

Self-conscious laughter knit our souls together as we adjusted expectations.

"What do we call you?" his wife, Hazel, asked, her eyes soft as a puppy's. "We've always called our priest Father."

"The kids in my parish call me Father Bonnie. Actually, I love it; it speaks to me of God's androgyny." I slid a chair up to the bed across from Hazel. "It's obviously been a good year for you. I'd love to hear about it."

"I was a VP for Standard Oil. We lived in many places throughout the country, most recently in Alaska. It was there I had my heart attack—at age fifty-six. They flew me here, to the University of Utah Hospital where the Cardiology Division is one of the premier facilities in the country."

Hazel and Bill took turns describing the five months they waited for a heart—the agony of not knowing if he would survive, and the impatience of having nothing to do. He wondered if his time on earth was limited; yet, he found himself killing time that seemed interminable.

Last year on Good Friday, a fifteen-year-old boy skipped school with a couple of friends. Leaving his companions upstairs while he went to the basement, he shot himself in the head with his father's rifle. The horrified boys called 911, and their unconscious friend arrived at the emergency room the same time as his parents. A few hours later the boy was declared brain-dead. His heart was beating, strong and steady, but there was no hope of him ever regaining consciousness.

The staff kept him breathing on machines for a few days, giving the parents time to think beyond their shock, and then suggested donating his heart to give life to a stranger—a way to redeem their tragedy with hope. The Davis's were summoned to the hospital, and within hours, the fifteen-year-old heart was transplanted into the fifty-six-year-old chest of Bill Davis.

As Bill told his story, tears flowed freely down their cheeks. Hazel stroked her husband's arm as we sat in reverent silence for many minutes, all three of us spontaneously praying with thoughts too deep for words.

Bill finally muttered, "The miracle is still too much to hold." He wiped the tears from his eyes and gazed at his wife with such love my heart ached with their joy. "I've loved Hazel, since the day I met her, thirty-six years ago. But not like this. Facing the reality of death and the possibility of losing each other changed our relationship forever." He looked up at me. "Before the heart attack, we didn't have time for God and church. We were too busy working and socializing and living the 'good life' for ourselves. But how can anyone ignore God when the heart that beats within you once belonged to a teenager whose life was cut short? Someone had to die so I could live! It's *the* fact of my life."

"Of *our* lives!" Hazel corrected.

"With this knowledge, we've both been more alive in the past year than ever before. Each day is an undeserved gift—God-given. Each day is holy—meant to be lived wholly. We feel blessed to know this truth, and feel sorry for the unhappy people all around us. We often speak at different churches when we're invited, and the hospital calls us to sit with patients awaiting surgery. God is using us in unexpected ways. We are so blessed!" They looked into each other's eyes, touching lips briefly. My heart sang with joy sharing this privileged moment with them.

The ritual of Holy Eucharist, anticipated as petition to preserve life, became a celebration of healing—an outpouring of thanksgiving for lives transformed.

After sharing the bread and wine, symbolizing the body and blood of Jesus, who promised to be with us in our suffering, we sipped the champagne in celebration of new life resurrected from death.

☠

Good Friday was especially poignant that year because of my encounter with Bill and Hazel. Suffering is central to the Christian message. With the belief that God became a man to lead us to abundant life—after passing through the valley of suffering—one would expect the Good Friday service to be the most widely attended of the year. But in our society, we don't like a corpus on the crucifix; we have removed the body and worship an empty cross. The handful of people who attend on Friday swells to overflow crowds on Easter Sunday to celebrate the Resurrection. We are a people who deny the reality of death. Although many say they don't fear to "pass on" because they know what awaits them beyond the grave, speaking of death is an embarrassment; polite discourse requires euphemism. We want Easter without Good Friday, just as we want joy without suffering, and life without death.

Following is the story of my journey, which began after I met *Death*—when she sat on my shoulder to lead me into life.

Before I continue, I must distinguish between two words: *religious* and *spiritual*.

Religious, as I use the term, refers to the doctrines and creeds of institutions, which have handed down their beliefs from generation to generation. Religion actually means to "bind together." It binds up our experience and gives us words and meaning so that we can communicate with others and join in common worship. Religion at its best gives us a container in which we can understand and participate in that which is holy and makes life meaningful. At its worst, it excludes those who do not agree with its particular teachings, causing pain and suffering which have little to do with God.

Spirituality has been called the lab-work of religion. Spirituality is concerned with our experience of the divine. It is beyond and before words. It is personal and intimate and relies on relationship rather than reason.

A religious path to God focuses on keeping commandments. Authority for our lives is found in the historical institution: the creeds, the doctrines and ordained leaders.

A spiritual path recognizes the longing in every person's heart for knowledge of that which is totally other—the meaning of the word *holy*. Guidance comes from the still small voice, the burning heart, the whispering of angels. When we pay attention to the longing, we find guidance in dreams, coincidence and intuition, and Holy Scripture acquires new and personal meaning.

Progress on the religious path involves ever-deeper adherence to the tradition and ever-closer attention to the commandments. The path is straight and narrow. The goal is righteousness.

The spiritual path is best described as a spiral of evolving consciousness. Each turn expands our perspective; we sense unity with evermore of creation. The process involves suffering, death and rebirth, as the Eucharist depicts. Like a caterpillar, we must go into a chrysalis to be changed in our innermost self. The transformation is often painful and demands that we die to who we think we are. If we can accept death, we will emerge as new creatures, as different from our former selves as the creeping caterpillar is to the butterfly in flight.

Jesus' familiar words to his disciples teach the same truth. "If any want to become my followers, let them deny themselves and take up their cross daily and follow me. For those who want to save their life will lose it, and those who lose their life for my sake will save it."[1]

Calling on the image of the butterfly, a symbol of the human soul, Marion Woodman describes the plight of those who refuse to die to their present lives. Her description could be a synopsis of the book before you. It is not only my story but also that of untold women and men who have resisted the journey. She writes:

"Birth is the death of the life we have known; death is the birth of the life we have yet to live…People splayed in a perpetual chrysalis, those who find life … 'boring,' are in trouble. Stuck in a state of stasis, they clutch their childhood toys, divorce themselves from the reality of their present circumstances, and sit hoping for some magic that will release them from their pain into a world that is 'just and good,' a make-believe world of childhood innocence. Fearful of getting out of relationships that are stultifying their growth, fearful of confronting parents, partners or children who are maintaining infantile attitudes, they sink into chronic illness and/or psychic death. Life becomes a network of illusions and lies. Rather than take responsibility for what is happening, rather than accept the challenge of growth, they cling to the rigid framework that they have constructed or that has been assigned to them from birth. They attempt to stay 'fixed.' Such an attitude is against life, for change is a law of life. To remain fixed is to rot, particularly if it be in the Garden of Eden."[2]

The spiritual path offers traditional teaching, but it is a map rather than dogma. It is meant to be followed rather than understood. Landmarks on the map are readily identified at four times in human life when the death/birth drama can be expected.

The biblical perspective as described by Rabbi Zalman Schachter-Shalomi, recognizes four seasons of approximately twenty-one years each, with an overlapping decade not unusual.[3]

The winter of consciousness extends to age twenty-one, the time modern specialists declare full brain maturity is achieved. For a child to be transformed into an adult, he/she must leave father and mother and establish a new identity. We must die to our childish selves. Depression and withdrawal are to be expected if the new self is to emerge.

The spring of consciousness invites us to establish careers and families of our own. If we have successfully let go of our childhood attachments, we are now free to replace tacit beliefs with new understandings based on our own experience. If we take time for introspection, we may discover new answers to old questions, and new vistas may open to us, revealing unimaginable possibilities. This is often a time of individualism, when we learn to stand alone.

The exuberance of spring slips into summer at approximately age forty-two when our children leave the nest and new questions again arise. We ask of our self-made philosophies, "Is this all there is?" Community becomes important again, and we are often called back to church, to synthesize our new beliefs with tradition.

The so-called "mid-life crisis," offering both despair and opportunity, is an invitation to again enter the chrysalis and endure the suffering necessary for a wiser, more encompassing self to be born. When the moodiness, depression and despair remind us of the trauma we experienced in the previous season, our descent into darkness can be more readily embraced. We now realize the necessity of dying to the old, so that the maturity of summer may yield its fruit.

Autumn begins around sixty-three with the approach of retirement, when the process calls to us again. Our identity in the workplace must be surrendered, and some of us may consciously crawl into the chrysalis to discover a new and fulfilling life beyond family and work.

Of course, we can resist these changes. The child can refuse to leave the structures of family and church that have nurtured it. However, without letting go, our wings will not unfurl. If still crystallized in the cocoon, parents will hold on to children, making unlikely the embrace of new possibilities beyond family. We can cling to unsatisfying work in the name of security, but we may never experience the fullness of our gifts. When autumn comes, we may become obsessed with keeping our bodies looking young through diet, exercise and plastic surgery; we may refuse to retire and spend as much time volunteering as we did working, rather than risk going into the darkness and discovering the wisdom meant to crown our lives.

If we decide to resist, there is a price to pay. Repression and suppression lead to depression. The dark night of the life cycle is prolonged when we don't heed its call. Drugs are the modern solution because they mask the pain of deep longing, allowing us to pretend everything is all right while refusing the call to transformation. Since the goal of spirituality is expansion of consciousness, if we inhibit our own awareness, how can we evolve?

Depression is a spiritual concern. For Bill and Hazel, their encounter with death brought new and abundant life. My story is about how *Death* became my friend and led me on a similar journey. Her guidance is available to everyone who dares enter the chrysalis and die.

☠

As I recount my life as a crystallized Mormon mother, I will attempt to be as honest as possible, often drawing from the words of my father and ex-husband to consider their points of view. In so doing, I pray that my writing will provide insights into the lives of others who are called to trust the journey through darkness, which leads to light.

Please note: Names of some persons and institutions have been changed to protect anonymity.

1. Luke 9:23-24
2. Woodman, Marion, *The Pregnant Virgin, A Process of Psychological Transformation*, Inner City Books, pp 14-15
3. Schachter-Shalomi, Zalman, *From Age-ing to Sage-ing.* Warner Books, 1995, pp 22-25

CHAPTER ONE

Death on My Shoulder

Anaheim, California, 1967

I first recognized death sitting on my left shoulder the night Annie threw up.

I came home to a messy house, exhausted from a long day teaching school, without plans for dinner. A student council meeting had detained me two hours, and it was nearly 6:00 PM when I faced the Friday dinner ordeal. A good meal on Friday nights often started the weekend on a happy note, but there was no time to shop and nothing in the house. My old standby, Kraft macaroni and cheese, would have to suffice. I dumped macaroni into boiling water, threw frozen peas into a second pan and hurriedly set the table. When I called the family to dinner, they gagged before they sat down.

"Is this the best you can do?" Paul, my husband of sixteen years, scowled.

"Peas again!" twelve-year-old Annie wailed.

The other four children took their places around the circular table, eyes lowered, glum faces speaking words unsaid.

"I'm sorry. I'll make something special tomorrow." Weekends offered time to catch up on grocery shopping, house cleaning, ironing and meal preparation for the week ahead.

We ate in tense silence. Paul gulped down my pitiful offering, and muttered sarcastically, "Thanks, Bonnie. A meal fit for a king—as usual." He pushed his chair away from the table, for escape to the living room. The boys moved macaroni to their mouths, one noodle at a time, as though eating fat white grubs. Annie hadn't taken a bite.

"Do I have to eat the peas?" she begged her father. "I don't feel good."

He spun around, glaring at his forlorn family around the table. "You'll eat everything your mother's fixed, do you hear me? Every pea, even if it takes all night!" He sauntered into the living room, put a Berlioz symphony on the record player and settled into his lounge chair to smoke his pipe and study a Perkins rose catalog.

The boys giggled at each other. Finger to lips, I cautioned them to be quiet. My own food stuck in my dry throat, as I tasted shame. If only I were a better wife and mother, I'd have a nice meal for them. I must manage my time better.

Lynne heroically finished eating. Now fifteen, she was going to the library with her boyfriend so I excused her. Lowell, our fourteen-year-old son, saw Ron, age eleven, dump peas into the giant philodendron near the window and couldn't help giggling again.

Paul stormed back into the room. "We'll have no funny business. Do you hear me?" Grabbing a boy's head in each of his hands, he cracked their skulls together with a loud thud. "Now eat your dinner as you're told." Taking two steps toward the living room, he suddenly turned back, eyeing Annie, cowering in her chair. "And that goes for you too. Do you hear me?"

It's my fault. He doesn't mean it. He loves the children. He's angry with me—taking it out on them. It's got to stop, but what can I do? I sat with eyes closed, teeth clenched, unable to respond.

Annie forced a spoonful of peas to her mouth, squinting her eyes, her pale face recoiling in repulsion. That's when she threw up—all over her plate and lap.

Grabbing a kitchen towel, I bolted to her side, wiping her face, telling her over and over, "It's not your fault, sweetheart. It's OK. Go lie down for a minute, and you'll be all right."

She scurried down the hall, hoping Paul wouldn't notice. I cleaned up the mess while the ashen-faced boys took their plates to the kitchen. "Maybe we could make peanut butter sandwiches—quietly," I whispered. No one was hungry. I finished cleaning up the kitchen, without interference from Paul. *It's amazing how much happens under his nose when he's into Berlioz and his pipe!* He didn't even look up.

With the kitchen in order, I checked the kids. Annie was sleeping; the boys studied in their room, and four-year-old Wendy played with her new paper dolls—as if nothing had happened.

Picking up my keys, I tiptoed past the living room to the garage. "Where are you going?" Paul challenged, without looking up from his catalog.

"Back to school, for papers I forgot." Slipping out the back door to the garage, my breathing shallow, as though escaping a dangerous enemy, I sensed cold fingers of anger thrusting up from my bowels to ensnare my heart. *I'll escape the colitis this time!*

I slid into the car and backed into the foggy January night, which perfectly mirrored my inner landscape: silent, menacing, impenetrable—obscuring the way ahead. Inching my way to the Santa Ana Freeway, I turned onto the exit, intending to drive against traffic until someone mercifully hit my car. *I'm so tired—I can't go on—I have nothing more to give.*

The next morning, I awakened in my own bed.

How I got there, I don't know. Had an angel rescued me, magically bringing the car to the garage and me to bed? Had a hidden impulse to live taken over and driven the car? My memory was blank, but the outcome undeniable. Somewhere in the cold ashes of my soul, a flicker of hope revived—inexplicable, but real.

It was as though the fog had penetrated my body. I felt detached from my life—anesthetized. I watched myself fix breakfast and make beds; saw myself and Paul and the kids move and speak, observing us all from a neutral place on my left shoulder.

To make amends with the kids, Paul took them to Laguna Beach, our favorite spot for family outings. I stayed home, relishing the time to contemplate my intended suicide and get ready for the week ahead.

I needed help. Watching myself thumb through the Yellow Pages, I looked for a psychotherapist; the names blurred. In slow motion, I replaced the phone book in the drawer. *I've been depressed before, and it's always worked out. I need fresh air—a walk. I need to get organized. I can do it!*

I strolled mindlessly to the grocery store—observing myself move down the aisles, choosing items I could carry home, watching from my perch on the left shoulder, almost enjoying the free ride. The clerk at the checkout stand brought me back to myself.

"Mrs. Harris, are you all right?" Her eyes registered genuine concern.

"I'm fine, Vicki," I answered truthfully. "My mind was wandering, but I'm fine." The presence on my shoulder watched me write the check; I smiled, relieved it was still there.

I feared it might vanish, but discovered that all I had to do was remember, and it would come into consciousness. I played at switching places. Sometimes I rode on my shoulder with it watching events unfold around me without judgment, and other times I became keenly aware of my body—every sense distinctly awake; every movement consciously chosen.

☠

The 1967-68 school term marked my second year teaching English and reading at Fillmore Junior High School in Anaheim, California, my fourth year in a public school. I considered myself a poor teacher because I wasn't a good disciplinarian, and I believed that what junior high kids needed was discipline.

After my intended suicide, I noticed a difference in my classes. Taking the perspective of the friend on my shoulder, I was able to handle disruptions with more skill. The detachment increased my awareness of the whole group, and projects were more easily accomplished. Students seemed more open and receptive; the student council, which I sponsored, was more engaged; and without effort I breathed new excitement into the literary magazine, which I'd founded.

Life at home became bearable because when a crisis arose, I retreated to my left shoulder and watched. Paul seemed to mellow, perhaps because I was less reactive. The kids kept their distance from both of us. Shortly after Lowell's fourteenth birthday, in April 1968, the suppressed tension erupted in an incident no one in the family would ever forget.

One night, Lynne was talking to her boyfriend on the phone when a boy from school came to see her. He tried to yank the phone away, and struggling for control, began tickling her. Lowell, who was in the room laughing at the ruckus, yelled into the phone that Lynne was being raped. Paul heard the noise, slammed down the phone and marched Lowell out to the garage where he beat him eighteen times with a two-by-four. He was black and blue from his kneecaps to the small of his back. My reaction to this horror was to jump onto my shoulder and escape into the bedroom where I sobbed—quietly—into my pillow.

Lowell couldn't leave the house for a week; he was so sore. Paul, who was the band director at Sunkist Junior High where our children were students, reported the incident to the coaches, requesting that Lowell be excused from P.E. since showering would reveal the bruises. The two coaches made the humiliated boy drop his pants for their inspection. In front of the victim, they congratulated Paul on the good job he'd done.

One could blame Paul's harsh disciplinary techniques on beatings he'd received as a child, but they were reinforced by the policies of the first school in which he taught. It's difficult to believe now how children were treated in the sixties. At West Junior High School, Tom Henderson, the vice principal, was notorious for his effective discipline. West was a typical Southern California school building, a sprawling one-story complex with wide locker-lined hallways.

It was customary for Mr. Henderson to take a naughty student out to the launching pad, the space between the rows of lockers, where the child was forced to bend over and hold his ankles. He'd be swatted a specified number of times with a wooden paddle, bored with holes to augment the pain. Thanks to the effective acoustics of the hallway, each whack reverberated through the building so that terrified boys and girls in classrooms could silently count the number.

My husband learned how to discipline his own children from both his grandmother and Mr. Henderson. It was a sanctioned punishment for disobedient children, which for Paul became a way to vent the smoldering anger and resentment he'd nurtured since childhood.

☠

One day in May, my principal sent for me; I hadn't been in his office since I was hired. He was a slightly built man, about five-foot-five. A picture of his family sat on his desk and an engraving of the Salt Lake Mormon temple hung inconspicuously on the wall behind his chair surrounded by framed diplomas. A devout Mormon, most of his faculty were also Latter Day Saints, including me, although I was not devout. He smiled kindly when I entered the room, indicating a chair opposite his. "I'm impressed with your excellent rapport with students as well as your good work with the student council."

"Thank you, Mr. Jensen." I relaxed into the chair. "I love teaching at Fillmore. The students are great, and the administration is very supportive."

"It's been a good year. But we may be in for a shakeup next fall." He leaned back, tipping the chair slightly, scrutinizing my face.

I squirmed, noticing my thumb exploring my cuticles, a habit signaling anxiety.

"You've probably heard about the Family Life and Sex Education program in the Anaheim District."

"A little," I apologized. "I've been busy with my own projects and haven't paid much attention to it."

He leaned forward, his grey eyes screaming anxiety. "I've avoided the subject myself, and wish I didn't have to pay attention now. Fillmore's the last school to implement the program, and the superintendent mandates it will be on this campus in the fall." Again, he leaned back in his chair as he scrutinized my face. "I want you to teach the class."

I gasped as my newfound detachment disappeared.

"I knew you'd be surprised, but I need you to fill this position." He looked me straight in the eyes; I lowered my own in bewilderment.

"Why me?" I stammered. "I'm an English teacher. I'd expect P.E. to teach a class on sex." I scrambled for words to express my anxiety. "Or a counselor or a nurse or someone qualified." My stomach knotted itself.

"You're a mother with five children—a Mormon with a wholesome background. The students like you, and I need someone I can trust. It's that simple. The class has to be taught, and it must be taught by someone safe."

I stared in disbelief. The fog returned, and I leapt for safety onto my left shoulder, beyond the panic. I was surprised that from this vantage point I could sense tiny sparks of hope glimmer in my heart. *Perhaps I'll learn how to manage my own family life.*

From a distance, I heard Mr. Jensen explain the extensive research behind the program. The thoroughly-tested curriculum had been written by a team of professionals: psychologists, doctors and clergy, as well as teachers and parents from the Anaheim District.

"This will be the third year since the program was adopted by the board of education," he explained. "Forty-one handpicked teachers from each school serve as facilitators to groups of about twenty-five students who come from gym classes daily for four and one-half weeks. Parents attend a meeting in the fall, before classes begin, having an opportunity to meet the teachers and view films and materials. They can decline the program for their child without anyone knowing because of the random rotation, but few take that option. We have ninety-nine percent participation." His intensity made me wonder if he were trying to convince himself as well as me.

"I appreciate your confidence, but I don't feel qualified," I mumbled feebly.

"The District has hired a professional, Dr. Norm Stevenson, who is a colleague of William Glasser, the founder of Reality Therapy. Have you heard of him?" Again, Mr. Jensen leaned forward, his eyes pleading for my assent.

"I have. I know his work is avant-garde, but highly respected."

"For preparation, you'll attend classes with Dr. Stevenson which meet together monthly. You'll be paid extra for the time you spend during the summer. By fall, you'll be fully prepared to meet your students. I need you in this position; I hope you'll say yes."

"I'm too stunned to know what to say," I stammered. "Can I have time to think it over and talk to my husband?"

"I need your answer by Monday. The monthly teachers' meeting is next Saturday."

I left his office, allowing *Death* to lead me. By the time I picked up Wendy from her Montesorri school, I knew I'd accept the job.

☠

In the four years Paul had been at Sunkist Junior High, he'd built a prize-winning band. One of the parents, Terry Jones, had been a drillmaster for the U.S. Marine Corps Marching Band in Washington, DC. His stepdaughter, known as Sam, wanted to be a drum major and Terry offered to help Paul make her dream come true. I hurried home from my interview with Mr. Jensen to get ready for the band's most important event, the National City Band Review. Sunkist had won the Perpetual Sweepstakes the last two years. The winner's name was inscribed on the trophy, but it had to be returned each May for the next competition. If a school could win three years in a row, it was theirs to keep. Students and parents alike were highly motivated to retain possession.

The band was a family affair: Lynne played flute; Lowell, trombone; and Annie, oboe. Ron was already excelling on the clarinet but had to wait another year before he could march with his father. Our house was often alive with cacophonous music, especially when they practiced at the same time—on different selections. One Saturday, Ron practiced for ten hours, until the neighbors begged him to stop. To us, it was a joyful noise.

Early Saturday morning, the day after my interview, the whole family climbed on the school bus to drive the 193 miles to National City. With simple uniforms of white shirt and trousers and a red sash over one shoulder, they had been good enough to win over forty-eight high school bands the two previous years. Sunkist was the first junior high school ever to win the coveted sweepstakes trophy.

After so many competitions, I knew that although marching bands are judged by ranks and files, it's the diagonal rows that indicate precision. Wendy and I found a spot where we could check them out. Sunkist's diagonals were flawless; I had no doubts about the outcome.

After the parade, we bought Cokes and ice cream drumsticks, and moseyed to the awards arena. The top row of bleachers offered a perfect view of the ceremony as well as the bands, which sat together in blocks, creating a colorful patchwork quilt. I knew each was hoping to win a trophy to display in their band room and justify their school's music program.

Lynne, Lowell and Annie were discernible among the mass of white and red uniforms, and I noted Ron hanging out with the clarinet players. Wendy found a friend and was seated two rows in front of me with the Anaheim High School band; the two girls jabbering away. I sighed with satisfaction, remembering how I'd encouraged the kids to play instruments. I knew the only way they'd have a relationship with their father was through the band. When I started teaching and had discretionary funds of my own, I made certain they got their own instruments. The Sunkist Junior High School band was the center of our lives.

I noticed a slim blond woman making her way up the steps of the bleachers and recognized her as a Sunkist parent. She motioned, indicating she wanted to sit with me. I patted the empty space on the bench and prepared to have my solitude shattered, forcing a warm Mormon smile.

"What are you doing way up here?" she panted.

"I like to see all the bands. Besides, I'm also soaking in the sunshine; it's such a gorgeous day!"

She settled next to me. "Isn't it thrilling? They were great! Do you think they'll win?"

"We'll know soon. In fact, I'm wondering why it's taking so long for the awards. The kids are ready to explode with tension."

"Do you know how much everyone admires your family?" Mrs. Jordan touched my arm for emphasis. "With three children in the band and Ron waiting in the wings, you must be very proud of them!"

"I am indeed." Purposely changing the subject, I added, "There wasn't a band in the parade that could match Sunkist's diagonals."

Mrs. Jordan smiled happily. "Whether or not they win, I want you to know we're all aware of how much you do behind the scenes to make it work."

I didn't know anyone recognized me as a part of it. "Thank you," I said, genuinely grateful for the acknowledgement. "There are dozens of parents working behind the scenes to make this possible."

"I don't see how you do so much. Teaching full time and taking care of five kids. And they always look so nice. I've heard you make all their clothes. And everyone knows how band members are welcome at your house for dinner any time they want to come, and tomorrow you'll probably have a big pancake breakfast for whomever shows up. How can you do everything and always be so happy?"

"Well, we all do what we have to do." I became increasingly uncomfortable with the effusive praise. "Actually, the pancakes were a strategy to get some of the band members to help clean up the mess they make. Toilet papering the house is a big deal for them—a way to let off steam. The first time it happened, some of the parents sent their kids over the next morning to help clean up; I made pancakes out of sheer gratitude. Now it's a tradition—much better than spending all day Sunday cleaning up the mess ourselves."

"If they win today, the whole band will be there tonight. Do you know Safeway's having a special on toilet paper? A four-roll pack for twenty-five cents! The kids have stashed them for the big event." Her smile indicated how much she relished breaking the confidence.

We called ourselves back to the awards, realizing only one trophy remained, and Sunkist had not received one. They'd either been disqualified, for some reason, or they'd won the sweepstakes. An expectant hush fell over the stadium as the head judge displayed the perpetual trophy, which had held a place of honor in the Sunkist band room for the last two years.

Then the stadium erupted. We couldn't hear the announcement, but when Sam flew up to the bandstand, Mrs. Jordan and I hugged each other and cried. A standing ovation brought even high-schoolers sitting near us to tears. Grabbing Wendy's hand, the three of us made our way down the bleachers, through the chaotic crowd to join the celebration.

Sitting in the front seat of the bus with Wendy, I had the entire four-hour ride home to absorb the meaning of their victory. It was the culmination of my hopes for our difficult marriage. Paul was successful! I smiled as Mrs. Jordan's words caressed my mind.

What a surprise. They all think I'm a perfect wife and perfect mother, just as Mom wanted me to be. No one knows who I really am. No one would suspect my intended suicide. No one knows how I resent Paul, and at the same time I want him to succeed. Even Mr. Jensen thinks I'm the perfect Mormon matriarch as well as a good teacher. What a phony

I am. I'm so stupid! I closed my eyes, trying to stop the gathering tears, and squeezed Wendy's hand to get attention off myself.

"What's the matter, Mommy?" her eyes widened with concern.

"It's nothing, darling, except I'm happy the band won; aren't you?" She snuggled up closer, relaxed her head into my shoulder and fell asleep.

☠

We were so tired after the long day we didn't even hear the nocturnal assault on the house. In the morning, the whole family gathered on the street to admire the handiwork. Hundreds of rolls of pastel toilet paper streamers covered the roof, the trees and bushes. Discovering some damage to his shrubs, Paul muttered under his breath, but we all knew it was a celebration, not an attack. A dozen boys from the band showed up at 11:30 and after taking pictures of their handiwork, happily climbed onto the roof, enjoying the cleanup as much as they had their crime. Even Wendy joined the party, stuffing toilet paper into garbage bags as though this were the event of the year.

When appetites were satiated, I cleaned the kitchen from the pancakes just in time to think about dinner, realizing the day was over, as was the weekend. I hadn't done the grocery shopping or corrected my papers for the next day's classes, and I hadn't talked to Paul about the Sex Ed class. He'd want to relax after dinner and hear a symphony and smoke his pipe, but I had to discuss my decision.

"I need to talk to you," I smiled sweetly. He was carefully trimming broken branches off the gardenia near the front porch and didn't like being interrupted when he was busy.

"Go ahead," he snapped, inspecting a leaf with increased scrutiny.

141

"Can we talk after dinner? I need your attention." I'd hopped onto my shoulder, and my voice had become calm but firm.

"You think you need an appointment to talk to me?" His sarcasm, aimed at my heart, was deflected by new perspective.

"I know you're exhausted, but perhaps we can talk after the kids settle down, OK?" He turned his attention back to the gardenia; I turned back to the house. There would be nine for dinner since Amy, Annie's friend, was sleeping over, and Lynne's boyfriend, Scott, was eating with us before they went to his Lutheran youth meeting. Spaghetti, salad and garlic toast, plus a chocolate cake I'd made after dinner the night before. The kids talked excitedly about National City, but Paul hardly said a word. Is he pouting or just tired? He's probably feeling let down from the adrenaline high.

It was 8:00 PM before the kitchen was cleaned up. I checked on the boys who were doing homework and Wendy who was in Annie's room listening to teenage gossip. Freshening up my face, I combed my hair and, purposely withdrawing to my shoulder, watched myself enter the living room and kiss Paul on his forehead.

He put down his magazine without speaking; I watched him watch me as I sat on the couch. He looked like a child afraid of his mother. *Is it possible that what I've thought was scorn is really fear? But what is he afraid of?*

I took my time before saying, "You were wonderful yesterday, Paul. The band was perfect as far as I could see. You must be thrilled!"

He looked up tentatively, relief relaxing the frown lines in his forehead. "Is that what you want to talk about?"

"You seem surprised. What did you think I was going to say?"

"I was expecting bad news. Every time I succeed, something unexpected smashes me down. It's too good to last!"

I jumped right down into my heart. No distance here! I'd never imagined he was afraid of both success and failure. "But what could happen? You've worked for years for your success. Those kids have been thoroughly trained; the trophy is no story you've made up."

Easing my way up to my shoulder, I continued. "I'm excited about putting in the swimming pool. It's a good decision. Only $25 a month and we'll know where the kids are because their friends will hang out here, and the band will be even more a part of our family. You've got a whole summer to plan the deck and make it beautiful. I don't know what more you could want."

Paul was pensive for a few minutes. "Now that your job seems secure, maybe I can relax a bit about money." The tension on his face disappeared, and a rare smile nearly betrayed itself. He reached for the handle of his recliner, relaxing his tense shoulders into the lowered back of the chair as his feet rose.

Now he's comfortable; now's the time to discuss the job. "I do have something to tell you, Paul, but it's good news, I promise." I scrutinized his face making certain my words sounded no alarm bells. "Mr. Jensen called me to his office on Friday and asked me to teach the Family Life and Sex Education class at Fillmore."

"Why you?" His reaction mirrored my own incredulity.

"He doesn't want the program, but the superintendent mandates it. He asked me to teach it because I'm a safe Mormon mother with high principles whom he can trust to not create problems."

"What kind of problems?"

"There's some backlash in the community. A survey shows ninety percent of parents want the program, but a group called the John Birch Society is threatening to shut it down."

"Can you can handle it?"

"I don't know. I have no background, but Mr. Jensen assured me I would be thoroughly trained by a psychotherapist who's a colleague of William Glasser—you know, Reality Therapy?" I could see he had no idea who Glasser is, but then I didn't know much about him either—only what I'd heard in faculty meetings. "The training's been going on for some time; the next meeting is Saturday so I need to give him my answer on Monday. What do you think?"

"It's OK with me if that's what you want." He picked up his magazine, a sign our appointment was over.

CHAPTER TWO

Family Life and Sex Education

Entering the conference room for our Sex Ed training the Saturday after National City was intimidating. Twenty chairs arranged in a circle announced this was not a typical faculty meeting. Placing my notebook and purse on a chair, sixth to the right of the presenter, wanting to avoid eye contact, I shyly looked around the room noting the apprehensive excitement. Spying the coffee pot, I inched my way in its direction, grateful for something to do. A handsome, middle-aged man smiled at me as he filled his glass with orange juice. I nodded slightly, busying myself filling a Styrofoam cup, doctoring the coffee with saccharine and milk. When I looked up, he stood next to me.

"When you came in, I thought you were the Mormon, but if so, why is a nice Mormon girl like you drinking coffee?"

A beautiful redhead standing next to me seethed, "She's hardly a girl, and what business is it of yours what she's drinking?"

"OK. Let's get started," interrupted an authoritative voice from a Levi-clad, graying man. After moving books off his chair, he sat down, a signal we were to do the same.

I quickly turned back to my seat, happy to escape a difficult conversation. *How did he know I was a Mormon?* I jumped on my shoulder, noting the people I'd just encountered had taken seats next to me—the man on my left, the woman on my right. *What have I gotten into?*

"I'm Norm Henderson." The leader's voice modulated to an easy conversational tone, looking at me. "Everyone has been here before except Mrs. Harris. Welcome."

I nodded to acknowledge his words, feeling extremely self-conscious.

"I'm the facilitator of the group but not the teacher," he continued, still addressing me. "You're the teachers. You have—or will have—the curriculum. You don't need me to explain it. We're here to learn how to help kids talk about their lives in a safe and confidential setting. The course is called Family Life and Sex Education because we want to communicate up front that these issues can be discussed; no subject is forbidden. In actuality, students may want to talk about alcohol or drugs or why they can't have long hair— who knows what will come up. We want to give them space where they can discuss anything, and everything, with a responsible, non-judgmental adult. That's you! You'll have about the same number of kids in your groups as we have here. And we'll run this group the way we hope you'll run yours." He took a sip from the cup he was holding. Then, addressing the whole group he challenged, "So, what do you want to talk about?"

No one spoke for what seemed an hour though actually was more like five minutes. I sipped my coffee, studying the milky liquid as though it might reveal some deep truth. I noted how uncomfortable I was with silence.

Finally, a woman said to the group. "Should we begin by introducing ourselves? Maybe we can fill Bonnie in on who we are, what schools we're from and what she can expect." Everyone nodded. She glanced around the silent circle. "OK. I'll start."

One by one, they identified themselves and talked about their classes. I was impressed by their enthusiasm for the program. One high school teacher expressed frustration that parents would not visit classes and experience what was happening. Rumors that the program encouraged premarital sex were gaining momentum in the community. "My students routinely discuss the values and consequences of promiscuity and can't find values," she said. "They look down on those who 'sleep around.'"

A junior high teacher told the group, "I'm finding the question box being used more now than ever before. Some kids want their questions to be anonymous. The group is more involved in problem solving when they know we're discussing someone's real concern."

An hour later, when nearly half the teachers had spoken, the redhead suggested a break; we all agreed on ten minutes.

The description of this meeting probably doesn't sound unusual to a twenty-first century reader, but in 1968 in Anaheim, California, it was unprecedented. I frantically wondered if this was one of the notorious encounter groups I'd heard about. If so, anything could happen.

An hour into the second session, I realized I'd have to say something. During an especially long silence, my heart thumped so loud I was certain it could be heard across the room. The man to my left—I'd learned his name was Steve, and he was a counselor at Kennedy High School—said he hoped the lady next to him would speak before our time was up.

My mouth was dry as an emery board. The group sat patiently; I glanced at Dr. Henderson, but he was staring vacantly out the window. No one moved. Finally I croaked, "I'm Bonnie Harris...."

Steve jumped up and got me a glass of water, which I drank slowly, finally managing to say, "I'm Bonnie Harris, and I teach at Fillmore Junior High." Scrambling around my brain, I looked for something appropriate to add. "This has been a very interesting meeting, and I'm happy to hear about all of you...and...and...I look forward to getting better acquainted."

It felt like someone had sucked air out of the room. All eyes were on me; I had stopped breathing.

Steve prompted, "Why are you here?"

Finally I blurted out, "I haven't the slightest idea why I'm here. But I am." Tears filled my eyes, and I tried to keep them from spilling over. When Steve handed me Kleenex, I remembered the friend on my shoulder. Sure enough, she came to my rescue. As my attention moved from myself to focus on my peers, I heard my voice say more confidently, "I'm a mother with five children, ages four to sixteen; my principal at Fillmore Junior High asked me to teach the class only a week ago, and I don't know anything about it." After a pause, I added, "I've never been in a group like this, and I'm extremely nervous about the whole thing."

Sandra, the redhead next to me, exclaimed, "You're not the only one, Bonnie. I'm scared shitless about the year ahead. I've already heard from parents who think the class is demonic and will corrupt our kids."

A dozen voices articulated concerns in a lively discussion, raising the energy several decibels. With only a few minutes left, a woman from Anaheim High asked when we'd meet again. We planned meetings for the summer and ended the session with smiles and enthusiasm. As we gathered our things, I couldn't resist asking Steve, "Why do you think I'm a Mormon?"

"Well, you are, aren't you?"

"Yes, but...."

"I can spot a Mormon anywhere, besides, if Brother Jensen finally agreed to have the program, everyone knew the teacher would be Mormon. By the way, I'm one too, only I don't drink coffee," he teased.

"Thanks for the water and Kleenex. I can't believe I was so nervous. It was stupid!"

"You're pretty hard on yourself, aren't you?"

"Aren't all Mormons—hard on themselves?"

"We should go someplace where we can talk. Do you have to get right home?"

Whoa, is this a come-on? I don't get that impression. He's probably worried about my soul. What the heck— Paul's taking the kids on a picnic, so why should I hurry away? Housework. Papers to grade. Out loud I said, "Maybe we could get a Coke someplace."

"There's a Burger King on the corner."

"Fine." Retrieving my notebook and purse, I left the room almost wishing this was the beginning of an affair. *Bonnie, do you know what you're thinking? I know. I'd never do anything like that, but he is attractive. Besides, he has a wife and three kids. No problem in having a friend. And he's a Mormon; I can trust him.*

I needn't have worried that Steve was attracted to me; he was all business. As soon as we settled ourselves at a table with burgers and Cokes, he started asking questions.

"You don't look old enough to have a sixteen-year-old daughter, as well as a college degree and teaching experience. How did you cram all that into your young life?"

"I was married right after high school," I answered between bites, not realizing how hungry I was.

"In the temple?" he asked matter-of-factly.

"Actually, yes," my voice quivered a bit, and I jumped onto my shoulder.

"Hmmm. I don't see evidence of garments beneath your blouse." His audacious remark seemed perfectly ordinary as he referred to the holy undergarments Mormons put on when they go to the temple the first time. They're supposed to be worn the rest of their lives.

"You don't miss a thing, do you?" I felt like the woman at the well talking to Jesus who told her everything she'd ever done in their first conversation. My eyes lowered in embarrassment.

"I'm a counselor in the bishopric of my ward. It's my job to pay attention to such details," he explained, waiting for me to look at him again. My comfort level was bottoming out.

"That said, let me ask again, how come a nice Mormon girl like you drinks coffee—and doesn't wear her garments?"

"It's a long story," I whispered evasively.

"I'm not in a hurry; are you?" He pushed his chair back a bit, providing a safe space between us while taking on the air of a professional listener.

Panic crept up my spine, but seeing his genuine concern, I threw caution to the wind.

"When I got married in the temple, I had every intention of being the most perfect Mormon who'd ever lived," I began tentatively.

Steve folded his paper napkin into squares. Without looking up, he commented, "You don't do anything halfway, do you?"

"I hate hypocrisy," I countered, as threatening tears caused retreat to my shoulder. From this perspective, I could see a genuinely caring man who was perceptive enough to recognize my pain. For many years, I'd resisted thinking about church and avoided talking about it to anyone.

I watched him make triangles with the napkin and realized he wasn't going to lead the conversation. I could either endure the silence, or tell him my story. What the heck!

I told him about the vision I had of Joseph Smith when I was sixteen and how I believed he'd called me to do something special for the Mormon Church.

Once I started talking, memories poured into my mind. I described the fireside with Mark E. Petersen when I promised to be perfect in obeying the commandments by keeping the Word of Wisdom and paying tithing. I told him of my intense desire to live up to the vows I made in the temple to always obey Paul and the authorities of the church.

I seemed to be reliving those difficult years when Paul went to school and we struggled to make ends meet while having four children in as many years. I felt again the shame of not paying our full tithing, but keeping track of the money we owed only to find I was calculating it incorrectly. I could taste the bitterness of resignation after Ron's birth, when the church demanded that we store food and clothing for a coming disaster.

I explained to Steve, "With our new mortgage, a new job, and four children, we could barely afford to feed our family day to day, let alone buy supplies for two years ahead. We were honestly trying to pay a full ten percent tithing ahead of everything else; the new commandment tipped the scales to 'impossible.' I gave up."

"You mean you'd give up eternal salvation because of money!" I forced myself to look at him before answering. The pupils of his eyes had diminished to piercing dots of accusation.

Guilt would have obscured my awareness, if I hadn't taken refuge on my shoulder. "You don't mince words, do you?" I stated defiantly.

"There's always forgiveness, Bonnie -- and starting over again."

Neither of us moved as he wrapped silence around us like a shroud. The thumping of my heart summoned awareness from its external sanctuary to the desolate tomb within my chest. I panicked, noting gathering tears that threatened betrayal.

"It's more than that." I sought words to override the emotion. "I've tried going back to church, but I feel barred from entering. It's as though there is a thick wall of glass through which I can see but cannot penetrate. I'm outside; I no longer belong, and..." my voice faltered, "I'd give anything if it could be different. But I feel cut off."

We both stared at the boat -- or was it a hat -- he'd created from his napkin. "When was the last time you were active in the Mormon Church?"

"In 1958, when I began having sporadic fainting spells. They were eventually diagnosed as Meniere's Disease, an inflammation of the inner ear, probably brought on by extreme stress.

"You had that much stress over tithing?"

"If I hadn't had the physical symptoms they may have called it a nervous breakdown -- or post-partum depression. But that wasn't recognized in those days. From what I've read, I deserved both, but there were also other circumstances that contributed to my problem."

"And these were...?"

"Are you sure you want to hear all this? It's so depressing."

"Now you've gone this far, I think you should continue, and yes, I do want to hear the rest." His pupils had opened again, emanating compassion.

"Paul was selling insurance under a man who was an authority in the church. He didn't realize his salary was a draw against future commissions until after he'd resigned his other job. Month after month we went deeper into debt. Paul kept the truth to himself, and I didn't know we were living on borrowed money." I took a deep breath, willing myself to stay above the turbulant darkness in my belly. I would not give in to self-pity.

Jumping back to my shoulder, I raised my eyes to Steve's, explaining dispassionately, "The Elder cruelly forced us into bankruptcy. We'd expected him to be our inspiration for going back to church." I looked down at my hands, put on a benign smile and assured him that even though it had been difficult at the time, it resulted in Paul finishing his master's degree and getting a teaching credential so we could move to Anaheim. "God works in mysterious ways, his wonders to perform," I quoted a well-known Mormon maxim.

Silence once again enfolded us, now like a warm blanket. I was back in control even though I hadn't thought about these events for years.

Continuing I explained, "I know there are merciless people like him in every church and organization. I have long since replaced anger with sympathy. I refuse to punish myself by not forgiving him; I won't live with resentment in my heart. I think the real reason for my antipathy against going to church is deeper than all that, but I can't figure it out. All I know is that this heartless man is one link in a chain of events that undermined my desire to be active. Perhaps some day I'll find my way back."

"I think you will, Bonnie, and I'm going to pray that it will happen soon."

I mentally added one more person to the long list of people who were praying for me -- even in the temple.

Before we parted I smiled at him, warmly appreciative. "Thanks, Steve, I can't remember ever talking so frankly to anyone. It was good of you to listen."

"My pleasure!" he smiled back. "I'll see you at the next session and perhaps we can continue -- if you want to. I'm curious about how you got to Anaheim and still don't know how you squeezed a college education into your life."

I floated back to the car. The whole day had been extraordinary. *So much to think about! I've never experienced a group coming together as ours did in those three hours. I want to know how to do that! If we can offer that kind of openness to kids, think how much can be accomplished! I want to know how to lead groups, and I want to learn how to listen like Steve does. He was wonderful! I'm amazed at how much I shared with him -- and he's a Mormon. Unbelievable!*

❦

"It's 2:30 PM. How long was the meeting anyway?" Paul mumbled from his recliner. "Do you realize you left us all day without a car?"

"Sorry," I tried to sound contrite. "We got through at noon. I went to lunch with someone and stopped at the store for groceries. I hope you had a good day!" I breezed into the bedroom to change clothes, determined to hold on to the lightness I felt, acutely aware of the oppressive atmosphere in our home.

When I returned to the kitchen to put away the groceries, Wendy came through the patio doors. She was wearing the floor-length blue nylon dress I'd made for her to play princess. A golden cord was tied at her waist, and she wore the jeweled crown Lynne had created for her. She loved to dress up; she loved being a girl. "Where did you go for lunch?" I asked, kissing her forehead.

"We went to Girlsen Park," she said defiantly.

"Girlsen? Oh, you mean Boysen Park."

"I've changed the name. It's *Girlsen*."

She'd changed the word *boysenberry* to *girlsenberry* a few weeks before. We happily went along with her new nomenclature.

"Guess what's happening on Monday?" I teased.

"We get our new swimming pool!" A huge smile brightened her face.

"Well, we won't get to use it; they'll just start digging the hole. It'll be a couple of weeks before we can swim."

"I know that!"

"Of course, you do. School will be out in two weeks and swimming lessons begin at the park. We need to go shopping and get you a swimming suit."

"Goody! When can we go? Tomorrow?"

"That sounds like a good time," I laughed. "We have a date!"

She ran back to her kingdom in the backyard, soon to be torn up by the bulldozer. For the first time in our marriage, we did not have major financial problems. The swimming pool was a luxury, but the payments were the same as our family membership at the Charter Motel near Disneyland. Swimming had been our recreation for several years, and all the kids were good swimmers, except Wendy. Swimming lessons were imperative for safety alone.

When we arrived at the park to begin lessons, I was surprised that she refused to get in the water. She sat on the edge of the pool and watched. The instructor tried every trick she knew to get the stubborn little girl to go in, but to no avail. I even put on a suit and went in first, hoping she'd come to me, but she sat immovable on the side of the pool. Every lesson for three weeks repeated the same routine, the teacher assuring me that eventually Wendy would join in. But that magical moment never came.

The end of June, when they filled our pool with water, I felt upset to have wasted lesson time without accomplishing anything. She didn't seem afraid of water, but she'd obstinately refused instruction. When the other four kids dove in, screaming with excitement, I tried not to pressure Wendy. In my peripheral vision, I noticed her carefully walk down the steps holding onto the railing, and hesitantly step into the water, unaware of being watched. Then, without fanfare, she immersed herself, even her head, as the teacher had instructed and swam to the other side of the pool. She'd taken in everything the class had learned, but was waiting to practice in her own pool. When she got to the other side, she finally looked up to see if we'd noticed. The whole family applauded, and she beamed with satisfaction.

Paul created a large patio between the pool and rose garden, which featured a brick fire ring about five feet in diameter connected to the gas line. Our family and guests sat around it nearly every night through summer and fall, roasting marshmallows, singing camp songs and talking endlessly. The house and pool were often filled with friends and kids from the band. It promised to be a good summer: Paul was successful, and I looked forward to the Sex Ed training and the challenges the class would bring. The summer of 1968 promised to be the happiest time of our marriage.

One night in early July, Paul and I found ourselves alone enjoying the evening. The fragrance from roses, jasmine and gardenias wafted intermittently on the soft breeze, delighting me with intoxicating pleasure. A full moon had sauntered above the rooftops, presiding over multitudinous stars that glistened like precious gems on the black velvet sky.

"Are you happy, Paul?" I barely whispered the question, not wanting to jar the stillness. The silence enfolded us for several minutes, suspending the question on the ether.

"Life can't get much better than this," he conceded.

"I've been thinking about all we've lived through, and this reminds me how happy we were in our cute house in Magna."

"The one you made us sell so you could move into that fancy house in Salt Lake?"

"What are you saying?" I was stunned. We'd purposely avoided discussion of the bankruptcy, but to suggest that I made him sell the house was preposterous. "I didn't ask you to sell; your job took you to Salt Lake; you complained you were spending too much time commuting. I was glad to be back with our friends and family, but it wasn't my idea to move."

"Well, have I finally made you happy?" His voice tinged with resentment; his question bordered accusation. I watched myself choose to hear words and ignore feelings.

"I'm proud of you, and all you've achieved with the band. I'm glad you feel more confident about yourself. I love our home, and I think the pool is a great idea. I enjoy having the band kids around. Life is good." I added, "And

I'm working hard, also, to make things work out for us." I waited, hoping to hear some small acknowledgement of my contribution, but he fell quiet and said nothing more.

What happened to the magical, moonlit night? Another missed opportunity for intimacy. If only we could get help learning to talk to each other. If only I could have a conversation with my husband, as I did with Steve—a perfect stranger.

Paul stood up from his patio rocker. He seemed to want to say more, but abruptly announced, "I'm going to bed. Are you coming?"

"I think I'll linger awhile and enjoy the moon. I'll be in shortly."

He turned and walked into the house. I relaxed into melancholy.

The beauty of the night was swallowed by the fog of emotions, which still threatened to overwhelm me ever since driving to the freeway to end my life. Anger, fear, helplessness—there was a lethal mix of undifferentiated feelings that I'd systematically buried over the years. I lived with the constant anxiety of uncontrollable eruption.

I consciously willed my awareness to my shoulder, where I could look more objectively at what had just happened. I recognized my longing for intimacy in the atmosphere of a sensuous night, and I tried to get inside Paul's skin and experience his reality, but insight was lost in the fog; the inscrutable Paul Harris was beyond my comprehension.

☠

It would be thirty years later before I found some clarity reading his journal. He writes about his lack of self-confidence and the ridicule he suffered from his peers. The same boys from school were also in his ward and ill feelings followed him to church. To compensate for his sense of inferiority, he often made up elaborate stories. Once he told a geography class he was born in Florida, but when asked for details, found he had to make up new lies to justify the first. He admits this became a familiar pattern so that he often had difficulty separating fact from fiction. Then he notes that since he excelled in reading, he learned from fictional heroes to make his own stories more authentic.

☠

That night, as we sat on the patio in the moonlight and he implicated blame on me for the bankruptcy, I had my first inkling of his penchant to rewrite history. Inside my head, I heard my father's voice: "See no evil; hear no evil; speak no evil." Mom's warning joined his: "Never question your husband." I remembered the vows I'd taken in the temple to be in submission to him or 'suffer my life to be taken.' I tried to minimize his lie, wondering how I could live with someone I didn't trust. *It's my fault he can't talk about painful events. I should be more trustworthy so that he can confide in me.*

Once the self-accusations began, the fog would have engulfed me again, except that from my shoulder, my new friend, *Death*, whispered into my left ear. "Seek the truth and the truth shall make you free," she coaxed. The new voice startled me, but I felt tension diminish as my clenched fists uncurled, and my arms relaxed. Time stopped as I stared into the burning fire.

Memories leading up to the bankruptcy begged my attention. I recalled how, after Paul graduated from the University, he gave in to my father's insistence that he get a real job to support his family; he'd never make a living composing music. Paul became a salesman for Prudential Life, a job that offered a salary as well as commission, because it serviced existing accounts in a particular neighborhood. He was assigned to a community about twenty miles west of Salt Lake, and since the company wanted him to live in close proximity to his clients, we purchased our first house on the G.I. Bill for $9999 in Magna, Utah. I loved it and was thrilled to have a home of our own.

Shortly after Ron's birth, Paul earned a trip to Vancouver, Canada, because he was a top salesman. It was the only trip we ever had alone, and I hoped it might renew our romance. However, once back home, he extended his working hours, leaving early in the morning and not returning until ten or eleven at night. I was busy with my babies and kept telling myself I should be grateful for all our blessings.

The success seemed to go to his head. He traded our old Plymouth for a big Oldsmobile. I questioned whether we could afford it, but he shrugged off my concerns saying he'd gotten a promotion that doubled his salary, and there was more to come. A few months later, we shopped for a home in Salt Lake because he was now working there, although he hadn't told me. We got more than our investment out of the Magna house and bought a much nicer home on Millstream Lane. It was my dream come true.

Before long, he quit his Prudential job to go with New York Life, thinking he could make more money, and because the manager was a General Authority in the Mormon Church. He didn't realize the check he received each month was a "draw" on future earnings. This led to the bankruptcy I'd told Steve about.

Why are these memories filling my head? Why did they intrude on our conversation on this lovely night? Why does it feel like we're living the same event over again? I remembered Paul telling me after National City that he was expecting bad news. He'd said, "Every time I succeed, something unexpected smashes me down. It's too good to last."

A sense of dread accompanied *Death* on my shoulder, and became a full-blown nightmare when, the middle of

July, Paul triumphantly announced that because of his success at Sunkist, the principal at Madison High School wanted him to be their band director. It was a complete surprise to everyone, including me. I tried to be excited, and don't think anyone noticed my shaking hands, or questioned my abrupt departure from the dining room.

What's going on with me? Surely, I don't think this is a repeat of the insurance debacle. How stupid! Is it because I talked about it with Steve? It's been on my mind ever since.

To my surprise, *Death* answered, "How is the promotion like the bankruptcy?"

He seems so arrogant. I'm happy he's successful, but...

"But what?"

The secrecy is similar. He'd been working in Salt Lake months before he told me. I must feel miffed that he accepted the new job without telling me. I feel left out. More of my stupidity.

Death continued her probing. "Look at the differences."

Paul is successful. Madison is in the same neighborhood. His Sunkist band members will be in his band. He'll have the same devoted parents behind him. How could anything go wrong?

I got a glass of water, put on a smiling face, and returned to the dining room where Lynne was gushing excitedly about how she'd still be in Paul's band. Lowell and Annie were wondering who would take their father's place at Sunkist, and Ron felt sad that he'd have to wait until high school to be in the best band in the world. They hadn't missed me. I joined the conversation with as much enthusiasm as I could muster.

"When will you tell your band boosters?" I asked.

"I've already called Sam and Terry, and by now, the grapevine will be working overtime."

"It sounds like we're the last to know." I tried to keep smiling.

"I wanted it to be a surprise for everyone. I've finally arrived, haven't I? Just look at the facts. In the spring, I was elected vice president of the Southern California Band and Orchestra Association, honors keep pouring in from all over the state, and now I'm going to be director of the best high school band in California—or maybe even in the whole U.S. Who knows, the sky's the limit."

He glowed with pride and kept talking about what it meant, over and over. When band parents came by to congratulate him, he recited his accomplishments with such relish it seemed he'd only at that moment understood how great he was. I winced and excused myself from the monologue. It was embarrassing, but I understood how much he needed this boost to his ego. I played the dutiful housewife, serving cookies and lemonade on the patio and smiling 'til it hurt.

CHAPTER THREE

The Sound of Silence

At my second session of Sex Ed training, Dr. Stevenson explained how a person's emotional reaction to words was an indication of mental health. He reminded us that verbs and nouns are symbols representing actions and things. A map is a symbol of place, but not the place itself; a dove is a symbol of peace, but not itself the quality of peace. Likewise, words are not what they denote, although we often relate to them as though they were the thing itself. For example, the word *communist* invokes fear in many people. We all know the emotion provoked by someone burning an American flag. Likewise, Christians pray in the name of Jesus; the word itself has power.

"One of the greatest challenges in discussing sex is the necessity of using words restricted in polite society. Forbidden words are packed with emotion beyond their meaning. In a restroom, scratched on the wall, you might find *shit* and *fuck* and *Jesus*—altogether." Nervous laughter rippled through the group. I nearly fainted; the emotional charge was so great.

He waited for us to settle down. I was relieved I wasn't the only one who reacted to the *dirty* words—well, Jesus isn't a dirty word, but—I had to admit, he was right about the emotional impact being equally shocking.

He explained the relationship between the limbic brain, which controls emotions, and the cortex, which in 1968 specialists assumed controlled intellectual functions. Semanticists had argued for decades they were interrelated, showing that strong emotion interfered with the intellect.

When we react emotionally to a word, like *communist*, we get stuck in our limbic brain and reason cannot be accessed. The good news is that we can be trained to pause before reacting. "The *cortico-thalamic pause* suspends the automatic response and allows rational functions to operate," Dr. Stevenson explained. "Counting to ten before one allows anger is an effective strategy."

I hadn't studied about the brain before, but the information brought a rush of excitement. *When I remember Death, I'm pausing to enable clarity of thought and greater objectivity!* The thrill of insight from this connection flashed from both mind and heart and was experienced physically— an experience of total unity! I had somehow been led to cutting-edge wisdom, authenticated by Stevenson's words.

I reluctantly called myself back to the group, setting my experience aside for later contemplation. Dr. Stevenson continued, "Our first task is to consider words we need in this class. We must be comfortable enough that our students can speak the words out loud without provoking emotional reaction from us. In other words, we must deal with our own limbic responses and discharge emotion from words necessary for discussing our bodies.

"I suggest you ask each other, and as many people as possible in the world outside, what words they use to talk about defecating, urinating and copulating." He paused; I realized my thumbs were nervously circling each other. "Notice," he continued, "you probably didn't have an emotional charge from any of these words. Ask yourselves, why?"

The list of words we came up with was revealing. Defecate: move bowels, gunk, grunt, crap, excrete, pass, eliminate, pass off, dump a load, number two. *Shit* brought the most titters and was the hardest for most of us to say out loud.

Urinate: go to the bathroom, take a leak, piss, go to the little boy's room, peepee, have to go, use the urinal/bedpan, make water, tinkle, wiz, see a man about a horse, number one. Interestingly, no one used the word *toilet*. Why?

Copulate: intercourse, mess with, make out, screw, cheat, go all the way. We learned that *fuck* was a Dutch word referring to breeding cattle. We noted that most of these words had nothing to do with *making love,* but instead expressed rage, contempt or disgust. *Making out* and *intercourse* were exceptions, but they were also neutral in emotional impact.

I was so uncomfortable during the session I considered excusing myself and getting out of there, but resisting my desire to flee was practicing the *pause* that allowed the intellect a chance to override the limbic brain. Although uncomfortable, the honesty of the conversation and the discovery of my emotional reaction to words were mind-boggling. I recalled the current hit song "The Sound of Silence" and Paul Simon's lyrics: "The words of the prophets are written on the subway walls and tenement halls, and whisper'd in the sounds of silence."

The second half of the class was spent on the vocabulary of the body. What are the common words for *penis* and *vagina*? The four-letter words again were said aloud: *cunt, dick, cock*, etc. Stevenson noted that each year a survey was taken to evaluate the program, and the most helpful topic students noted was terminology. A ninth-grade boy said, "I only knew four-letter words and slang for parts of the body, and I couldn't talk about sex with anyone except people who used this same language. My own parents didn't know the correct words."

There was a heated discussion about Freud, which I didn't understand. At one point, someone lamented, "Shit, we're so fucked up over these goddamn words, how can we teach this class?" Blood drained from my face, and someone asked if I was OK. I nodded my head, withdrawing to my shoulder in embarrassment. *Why is it the graffiti we see most commonly are fuck, shit and Jesus? Are the limbic reactions intensified because our polite culture forces them underground?*

Before we ended, someone asked how I was doing; it was a compassionate question. I struggled for words, finally offering, "Maybe I'm in this group to represent parents. If one of my children came home and told me they'd had this conversation at school, I'd be irate. And yet, I recognize my repulsion is a sign of unexamined reactions to words. It has been an uncomfortable session, but something I needed. Thanks for letting me just listen."

I found enough control to blink away surfacing tears; several teachers thanked me for my courage and honesty. I felt deliciously accepted for who I was. Steve couldn't meet with me after the session, but promised he'd help me debrief after the next meeting.

☠

Shortly after Paul accepted his new position at the high school, I attended my third meeting of the Sex Ed teachers. The semantics session was still vivid in my memory. The group's acceptance of my extreme reaction to the *dirty* words increased awareness of how uptight I really was. The atmosphere in the classroom was cordial, and as we greeted each other, I sensed closeness with colleagues arising from trust and respect.

The day's focus was two anatomy films we'd show to boys and girls separately: *From Girl to Woman* and *From Boy to Man.* All students would see both films, but they'd be separated by gender. Several of the teachers lamented that we could no longer use *How Boys Grow*, which was one of the pilot films in 1962. Parents had objected to the explanation that masturbation was to be expected. We brainstormed ways to discuss it without the film. How could we help alleviate the guilt propagated from disproved myths, such as that masturbation causes blindness—without provoking the ire of critics?

During the morning, we explored our personal reactions to the material as well as appropriate responses to student questions. As in the previous meetings, after his brief introduction of our task, Dr. Stevenson hardly said a word. The films were the authority in the room, and the dialogue came from participants. I began to realize that if I could allow students to own their discussion, I wouldn't have to say much. That was the point—to trust that boys and girls would help each other form wholesome attitudes about human sexuality. I marveled at the way Dr. Stevenson let us struggle with our own insights without interference or manipulation intended to enforce some agenda.

☠

With twenty-first century eyes, I realize we were experiencing brainstorming techniques, which would become commonplace, especially in corporate America where creative minds are valued and nurtured. Sadly, most institutional learning still follows the old academic model of feeding by lecture and digesting by tests that demand *correct* answers. When humans are given the opportunity to think together freely, the energy which arises is evolutionary. But evolution demands change. We began to realize that we were a small part of a far-reaching movement occurring throughout the country, spreading out from Berkeley and Esalen, from Kent State and Montgomery, Alabama, provoking change in attitudes about sex and war, women and minorities, religion and the environment.

☠

The need for sex education had been acknowledged for years. The Anaheim program began its research in 1961, shortly after birth control pills became widely available and fear of pregnancy was no longer reason for abstinence. It was only in 1965 that the Supreme Court struck down the

Comstock Law that had banned contraception since 1873. The times demanded open discussion with young people to help them make positive sexual choices.

An eleventh grade girl was quoted in the *L.A. Times,* "With the pill so easily available, I feel like we will all have to reevaluate our moral standings. Now that the fear of pregnancy is being removed as a deterrent to premarital sex we have to learn to make our moral decisions with some responsibility…This class helped me strengthen my own convictions—I will wait for marriage before experimenting with sex."[1]

With change comes fear and resistance, as I had experienced when faced with the dirty words. Vietnam War protestors, the flower children, the Watts riots, and a growing militancy in the Black community were similar responses to voices for change in our country. *Open Marriage* was a national bestseller. Fear had led to violence when Martin Luther King was assassinated on April 4, 1968, and Robert F. Kennedy was killed in California on June 6th— both murders occurring within a few months of our group's first meeting.

For the first time in my life, I experienced personal connection to events in the wider world. People felt helpless in confronting the national problems; there wasn't much an ordinary person could do. The Anaheim Sex Education Program, perceived by some local residents to be akin to the moral breakdown in the country, would become the target for repressed emotions far beyond its relevance. We were about to experience a community's *limbic response*, which made rational discourse impossible.

☠

Steve and I went to the Burger King in high spirits. After some initial chitchat about the group and the exhilaration we'd experienced in exploring the challenges of our upcoming classes, he got right to business.

"OK. I want to know how you got to Anaheim, how you managed to get a college degree with four children and what's behind your resistance to the Mormon Church." He looked at me with admiration. "You'd make a wonderful Relief Society President, you know. The church needs you."

I actually shuddered. It took a few moments before I could even begin talking; the idea was so repulsive to me. *Is this another example of limbic brain takeover?*

"It's that bad, huh?"

"Sorry. My reaction took me off guard. I can hardly remember where I left off."

"You told me about the bankruptcy and losing your home and car. I can understand how your fainting spells came about, especially since you could have been suffering from post-partum depression."

"There was something more I didn't mention. Paul kept his financial situation to himself. I knew nothing about it, but the tension between us was unmistakable. We had a terrible fight and he left the house. About 2:00 AM he phoned and said he was leaving me; he could never make me happy. I didn't really believe him, but spent the whole night wrestling with the fact of my utter dependence. If he did leave, how could I possibly earn a living and support my four kids? Lynne wasn't yet six years old. He came back in the morning, but I never felt secure in my marriage after that.

"Before diagnosing my vertigo, the doctor sent me to a psychiatrist to consider if there was a psychological problem. To his many questions, I kept saying how stupid I was; that I was guilty of something, but I didn't know what I'd done. He finally asked, 'If you could do anything you wanted, without consideration for kids, money or time, what would it be?' Without a moment's pause I told him I'd go back to school and get a degree to support my children."

"What was his response?" Steve asked.

"He laughed at me, and said there was no way I'd last even one quarter at the university."

"You evidently didn't believe him, so what happened next?"

"We moved out of our house into a rental near the University of Utah so that Paul could go back to school to get a teaching credential. He worked at an all-night grocery store.

"One day I asked Dad to take me to lunch. I told him about Paul's threat to leave, reassuring him that his action was due to pressure over his job; I understood it and held no anger, but I was concerned. I told him about my visit to the psychiatrist and that I'd realized I needed to go back to school and get a credential myself, so that I could support myself if he ever really left me. I asked him to pay my tuition for one semester, convinced I could earn scholarships to pay the rest. He agreed.

"I completed a year of school at the U. Paul was hired to teach in Anaheim, and I quit school to earn money for the move. Once we were settled in California and established a one-year residency I enrolled at Fullerton Junior College, which was free, and I graduated with an Associate's Degree. The faculty suggested I apply at Chapman College which offered a full scholarship to a graduate from each junior college in the area. To my delight I won it, even though I couldn't promise involvement in extra-curricular activities because of my family."

"That's an amazing story," Steve was genuinely impressed.

"I agree. I still don't know how I did it, but I graduated *magna cum laude* and was listed in *Who's Who in American Universities.* I proved to myself that I wasn't stupid, at least not academically!"

"Wait a minute," he looked puzzled. "I thought you said you had five children. When did the fifth come along?"

"I discovered I was pregnant one month before graduating from Chapman. At the time it seemed like the end of the world, but I love her dearly!"

Steve had finished eating and was now playing with his napkin again, as he had the first time we talked. *Oh boy*, I thought, *here come the church questions. Sure enough.* "So where was the Mormon Church in all this?"

I told him about the fiasco of speaking about the *Sermon on the Mount* at sacrament meeting when we first arrived in Anaheim, and how our talks offended the bishopric.

"When we moved to Orange, California so I could attend Chapman, two men from the local ward called on us. We hadn't been visited since our faux pas in Anaheim and were genuinely happy to see them, thinking they were ward teachers. I invited them into the house, and both of us wondered if this was the time we'd get reconnected. But these men were not teachers; they were members of the finance committee, soliciting funds to build a new ward-house. They wanted us to contribute several thousand dollars that we did not have. When we told them we were struggling financially to get through school but planned to be active when I graduated, they offered to arrange a loan at a finance company. That way, they'd get their money immediately, and we could take our time making the payments. Paul erupted in anger. He told them to get out and never come back. They never did."

"Money again," Steve lamented.

"Yes. Money shouldn't be so important, but from day one of our marriage it was a critical issue."

"Others have done it. When the law of tithing is followed, especially during hard times, the Lord rewards us with abundance we could never imagine. It seems you wrestled with your commitment throughout your marriage and always chose *other* gods."

"We always intended to be faithful." I could feel the cloud of fog pulling me down to oblivion.

"You know what they say about that: 'The road to hell is paved with good intentions.' But Bonnie, it's not too late. You've just built a swimming pool. You're both working. Now is the time to do what you've always intended. Come back to the church and pay your tithing."

I hopped onto my shoulder, aware of my friend, *Death*. Together we watched Steve and me sitting in the booth of the Burger King, me staring at the rabbit-shaped chip in the yellow Formica table top. Steve watched me intently, probably praying. I couldn't think of a thing to say; I didn't understand my resistance.

When I didn't respond, he leaned back into the booth. "You still believe in the Mormon Church, don't you? It sounds like you do."

My dispassionate voice answered him. "I know I'm a Mormon—born and bred. It's my identity. But I don't know if I believe in the teachings of the church. Perhaps I'm too stupid to understand them."

"Why do you keep saying you're *stupid*?" his voice was gentle and sincere.

"Every time I've asked questions I've been put down."

"Give me an example."

"Twice I went to a General Authority with troubling questions and both times was sent away with a pat on the head, being told to leave thinking to my husband who held the priesthood."

"So there *are* doctrinal issues. Have you been reading anti-Mormon literature?"

"Never. I don't consider myself to be anti-Mormon or anti-anything. In fact, I wouldn't know where to find such material."

"So what questions did you ask the Authorities?"

"I was—and am—deeply concerned about the Mormon position on Negroes. I've done some independent reading and frankly can't see how the brief passage in the *Pearl of Great Price* justifies the painful discrimination of the Church. In fact, if the Mormon Church has the only legitimate prophet on the earth, I wonder why they're not leading the movement against discrimination." I noted the intensity of my words.

Steve smiled, indulgently. "So you took your question to one of the General Authorities?"

"Yes, my father didn't know how to answer me so he made an appointment. I don't know who we talked to, but he was kind and listened politely. He asked if I had been reading anti-Mormon material, just as you did, and I told him no. Then he smiled at my father and turned back to me with words appropriate for a six-year old. He told me to go home and take care of my family and leave such questions to the priesthood. He said my questions came from Satan to lure me away from my birthright; I must be steadfast in turning away from conjecture. He warned me that I was in danger of apostasy, and I should encourage Paul to go back to church. Then he proclaimed his testimony that the Mormon Church was the only true church, that Joseph Smith was a true Prophet and that my eternal salvation was dependent upon following the commandments.

"I went away feeling stupid, but now worried that my resistance to attending church was due to Satan's influence. The Apostle's words added fear to the guilt I'd experienced in the psychiatrist's office when I had Meniere's disease. I worried that Satan had taken up residence within my soul."

Steve looked down at the table and ground his teeth. He stuttered, "And what was the second question you asked?"

"The question arose while studying at Chapman College, which is a Christian school where Bible classes are required. I learned that Christians understand that the Bible is not always accurate in its translation. I was encouraged that scholars agree with the Eighth Article of Faith I'd learned as a child: 'We believe the Bible to be the word of

God as far as it is translated correctly.' I became excited about the work of Christian theologians in discovering inaccuracies by examining early manuscripts, which were not available when the *King James Bible* was translated in 1611.

"I compared Matthew's Gospel with 'Third Nephi' in the *Book of Mormon* and wondered how the words of Jesus to the Nephites could be identical to the King James' translation of Matthew if Joseph Smith was using an independent source, written by someone in a different country and a different century. Everyone knows that two people translating the same document will come up with variations of wording. These were supposedly different manuscripts. Even more troubling was that scholars have discovered in the Lord's Prayer, that the phrase 'for thine is the kingdom and the power and the glory' is a gloss inserted by an ancient scribe. Someone had written words into the manuscript—words not found in earlier codices. I reasoned that if Joseph Smith's translation had not contained these words, the authenticity of the *Book of Mormon* would have been confirmed. Unfortunately, it seems he copied the flawed text." Steve made no visible response.

"When I asked my New Testament teacher about this, he told me he wouldn't comment, but suggested that I contact one of the Mormon Authorities about it. Dr. Jenkins was an excellent teacher, careful not to intrude on anyone's beliefs.

"While visiting my parents that summer in Salt Lake City, I tried talking to Dad about the translation, but he refused to listen. Instead, he took me to another General Authority. This man also told me Satan prompted my questions. He said that a woman should not be involved in such studies. He said I should not be going to a Christian school where my mind was being corrupted. I again left feeling like a six-year old who had been dismissed as too stupid to be taken seriously. My sense of guilt increased, and I felt helplessly lost.

"I never seriously considered going back to church after that. Even tithing was no longer an issue. We began drinking wine, and I even tried smoking, but since I'm allergic to nicotine, I soon quit, although Paul smokes a pipe. The Mormon Church is a dead issue to me—yet I grieve for my loss. I keep hoping that somehow I'll receive a testimony again and resistance will dissolve. I am a Mormon through and through, but a Mormon who stands outside and can't find her way back. In the meantime, I'm trying to raise my family and be as good a person as I can without a church. All of the kids were baptized when they were eight years old, but we let them make up their own minds about attending Primary and Sunday school. If they want to be Mormons, we'll support them. If not, we'll be there for them in any choice they make. At least they'll have the freedom to find their own way."

Steve quietly considered his response. After a lengthy pause, he looked me in the eyes and warned, "Your purpose on earth is to have children and bring them up in the Gospel. You realize, don't you, that you are abandoning your responsibility for five precious lives entrusted to you by God."

I was aware of the gravity of my response. "I don't want to break the commandments, but I can't avoid breaking them. My life may have been different if we'd waited to have our children until we could take care of them."

"Why didn't you wait?"

"Because we promised we would not use birth control. We promised in the temple."

"You take things too seriously. You've got to use your intelligence and do what's best for your individual situation. I use birth control. I have two children, and we planned carefully for each. Everyone I know uses birth control. Why were you so stubborn?"

"The God I knew was my intimate father in heaven. He walked with me. I talked to him many times a day. He sent those children to me; I know that for a fact. It was unthinkable to prevent him from sending a child if he wanted to. How could I dare? If I couldn't trust God in this matter, how could I trust Him in anything else?"

I was shaking with repressed emotion over the *catch 22* dilemma that had dominated my married life. When I looked up, Steve's eyes betrayed both sadness and confusion. Whenever I'd had this conversation with parents, friends or anyone using birth control, the same response revealed their own guilt.

"Look," I went on, hoping to change the subject—I knew he didn't have an answer to my dilemma, "I hate hypocrisy. I grew up with a mother who drank coffee. She drank it in secret and used air freshener to mask the aroma—always hiding her sin from neighbors who might stop by to chat. She even lied to the bishop to get her temple recommend. What's worse, drinking coffee or lying? I don't get it. If one can't be honest, there's something wrong." I again thought about the Mormon maxim that it's OK to tell a small lie to protect a greater truth—a rationalization that probably arose when early pioneers were expected to lie about polygamy.

Steve looked at his watch and said he had to go; we'd been talking for over an hour. We stood outside the Burger King, awkward about how to end the conversation. Finally, he took my hands in his and said, "I hope I haven't been too hard on you."

Funny, I was concerned about *his* feelings. "Actually, I appreciate what you said. If you hadn't told me to go back to church, you'd have neglected your responsibility." I smiled shakily.

As he hurried to his car, he assured me he'd keep me in his prayers.

My mind was jumbled; I knew I was too upset to drive. Besides, I didn't want to talk to anyone until I'd thought through what I'd just said. I'd never told anyone about the

General Authorities and certainly not about Egypt or the Lord's Prayer. I'd never said anything derogatory about the Mormon Church—not to anyone. I didn't even talk about it to Paul. We'd taken vows in the temple never to discuss the ceremonies with anyone or criticize the Authorities. We'd sinned in many ways but keeping secrecy was not one of them. The reason I'd opened up to Steve was that he was in the Mormon bishopric and was a respected counselor. I smiled to myself, realizing the mandated silence about the temple put the Church in the same category as the dirty words society condemned. *Fuck, shit* and *Mormon* together screamed from the sewer of repressed anger.

I found a picnic table under a tree behind the school building, not far from where I'd parked. The day was hot, but comfortable due to low humidity. I noted the graceful palm trees—long-legged ballerinas in tutus, back-dropped by the cloudless azure sky. Pink and white Oleander fenced the school grounds, and a garden of azaleas and Bird of Paradise challenged my agitated mood.

Maybe I should try going back to church. As soon as the idea came to mind, *Death* reminded me of the last time I'd been in a ward—last Christmas. I was in my deepest depression, only a few months before my intended suicide. I wanted so much to reconnect with the meaning of Christmas. We'd spent much time and money on presents for the kids, decorating the house and sending out cards—but I'd realized the holiday no longer held meaning beyond Santa Claus and gifts. My heart ached for spiritual meaning that had slipped away.

Christmas 1967 was on Monday. Mormons don't have services on Christmas Day, but they'd have a regular sacrament meeting on Sunday. Paul didn't want to go, but I did—not to our neighborhood ward where I'd be recognized, but another, where no one would know me. I hoped they'd sing Christmas carols, and I ached to hear the familiar story of Jesus' miraculous birth. Determined to enjoy the service, I pushed through the accustomed resistance, willing myself through the front door to find a seat in the center of the chapel. To my dismay, it might have been a PTA meeting: lots of announcements, two short talks by young people on unrelated subjects, and although we sang one carol, the main speaker talked about deer hunting in Colorado. The only mention of Jesus was the formulaic "I say these things in the name of Jesus Christ" at the end of each talk and during the perfunctory prayers. There was no word about Mary or the wise men or the angels or the fantastic star or how God loved us so much he sent his only begotten son. I was so dejected by the time I left that I wondered if I'd ever go to a ward again.

---

1.   *L.A. Times*, November 26, 1967

CHAPTER FOUR

Faith and Belief

Telling Steve about my college days loosed a flood of memories crying to be explored. Luckily, it was a lazy summer for me since the family's focus was on the swimming pool and Paul's preoccupation with his new position at Madison High. The school, only a year old, had sadly neglected the band. Although a part-time director tried to enthuse students, his discipline had been lackadaisical, and Paul inherited juniors and seniors unwilling to practice the long hours necessary to win trophies. In addition, since the fledgling music program required only two classes, he was assigned three American literature classes, which meant hours of preparation and papers to correct. Football half-time shows were also a new challenge, which meant he'd have little time for me before or after school started. Having ample free time, I retrieved my class notes from Chapman, which I'd stashed in the filing cabinet after graduation in 1962.

As I thumbed through the papers, I recalled how, when I applied for the scholarship, I had no idea the college was a Christian school. Most private schools in California had religious origins, but Disciples of Christ, which founded Chapman, was still involved in its policies. A student was expected to take a semester each of Hebrew Scriptures (Old Testament) and New Testament, and it was mandatory for all students to attend chapel on Thursday mornings. The services were conducted by ministers from local churches; evangelizing was prohibited.

I'd never been to a church other than Mormon and the requirement to attend chapel was unsettling. I was also leery of taking religion classes outside Mormon seminary. However, since there wasn't another college in the vicinity, I had no choice but to make the best of it. I reminded myself how fortunate I was to have a full scholarship, which even paid for books. Classes were so small there was no way to be a passive observer. I'd have to participate in discussions and feared revealing my stupidity. I prepared myself to be severely tested by the *enemy*.

Dr. Jenkins, the Old Testament teacher, caught my interest the first day when he challenged us to make the distinction between faith and belief. He used the definition of faith from Hebrews 11: "Faith is the assurance of things hoped for; the conviction of things not seen."

"Faith," he explained, "is an inner state of being that propels us toward our actions and desires. One can have faith in many things. Some people have faith in bank accounts or their investments. But the point is that faith refers to a movement—an action—more like a verb than a noun, although it can be used both ways, just as hope and love are both.

"On the other hand, *belief* is a noun. The verb would be *believe*. When we talk about our beliefs, we are talking about things or ideas to which we have given intellectual assent. We could say that we have faith in our beliefs."

He explained that this distinction was important because in the class we were going to examine our beliefs. "Some of you might change your beliefs because of what you learn. This will be uncomfortable, but it does not mean you will lose your faith."

"How many of you believed in Santa Claus when you were a kid?" he asked.

All twelve of us raised our hands.

"How many of you had faith in Santa Claus?"

Several students besides me raised our hands.

"When you found out there wasn't a Santa Claus—that your belief was wrong, what happened to your faith? Did you still celebrate Christmas in the same way? Or did you quit giving presents in your family?"

"We kept giving presents, but we knew it was our parents who were giving them to us," I replied.

"Was it the same faith that allowed you to depend on your parents giving you gifts at Christmas? Did your unbelief in Santa affect your faith in Christmas?"

"No, but it changed my faith," another girl joined in.

"Think about it," Dr. Jenkins challenged. "Did your faith change or did your belief change? I'm willing to bet most of you still have faith in what Santa stands for, even though you lost your belief in Santa Claus as a man who literally comes down your chimney on Christmas Eve. I'm going to ask a question about the distinction between *faith* and *belief* on our first exam; I'll be more interested in your reasoning than in the answer you give.

"There are two other words that I want to consider before we begin reading the scriptures." The professor wrote the words: *eisegesis* and *exegesis* on the blackboard.

"I want you to understand how you've been taught to read scripture. How many of you look up verses that prove what you already believe—and sometimes even memorize them?" I raised my hand without hesitation; that's the way I was taught in seminary classes. We were given a Mormon belief, and then we'd go to the Bible to prove it was from God. I especially remembered talking about "baptism for the dead" and then reading a passage in the Bible where it was mentioned. I couldn't grasp the relationship of the Biblical words to the temple practice, but maybe now I'd learn how to answer my questions about Mormonism. Perhaps it was possible to not believe all the teachings of Mormonism even though I knew I'd never lose my faith in the Mormon Church. I *am* a Mormon.

Dr. Jenkins brought me back from my thoughts. "This way of using the Bible is called *eisegesis*," he explained. "Another word is *proof texting*. You prove beliefs you already hold by finding something in the Bible to support them. We'll find examples of eisegesis in the Bible itself— especially in the New Testament.

"There is another way to read Scripture, which we'll practice in this class. It's called *exegesis*. It's the opposite of proof texting. We read the Bible to learn something new, or to explain something we don't know. We ask the question: 'What is the writer trying to communicate about God?' rather than 'How does the text prove what I believe?'

"*Eisegesis* leads us to take words literally to prove our point. *Exegesis* asks questions of the text itself, such as: How does the passage fit with the rest of the text? Are there words that meant something different centuries ago than they do today? *Exegesis* questions the text. Questions are good. Don't ever let anyone tell you otherwise. It's through asking questions that we learn and grow. In this class, we will ask lots of questions, and we may come up with different answers and that's OK. I know it will be uncomfortable for some of you, but I promise, you are free to draw your own conclusions."

I could hardly believe my ears. I was in a religion class where questions were welcome!

"Can you give us an example of exegesis?" I asked.

"Sure. When the Bible says you must obey God, what does that mean?"

"To do what you're told," a boy next to me answered.

Dr. Jenkins smiled, "That's the way we usually read it. But if we were to study the Greek word *hakuo*, which is translated *obey,* we'd find it actually means *to listen.* So the original meaning was that we were to *listen* to God. Do you see the difference? The first meaning makes God into an authority who tells you exactly what to do. If God is asking us to *listen* to him, he is asking us into relationship. He invites us into a conversation. Asking a question about what the word *hakuo* meant to the original writer, is what we call exegesis."

Wow! I thought. *This is going to be fun!*

"Your assignment for tomorrow is to read anything you want from the Bible and bring in at least one passage you wonder about. We'll exegete what you bring."

I knew exactly the passage I'd bring: "Be ye therefore perfect."

I wondered what the dictionary would say about the word *perfect,* so I looked it up. It listed synonyms: complete, sound, entire, absolute, comprehensive and whole. I found myself thinking about it all night, wondering what paying tithing had to do with perfection. I couldn't wait to take my passage to class the next day!

☠

Our family had moved into a wonderful old house in Orange, California, just four blocks from Chapman College. Ron's kindergarten class was four blocks in the opposite direction from the college. I arranged classes so I could leave him at school in the morning and be through in time to meet him when he finished.

The first day I left campus as soon as possible, hoping to get to Ron's school before he left. I made it just as he was coming out the door. He looked sad.

"Hi, baby!" I said softly, so no one else would hear my endearment. "Did you have a good time at school?"

"I don't know how to skip!" he mumbled. "So I sat down on the floor. The teacher's mad at me."

"Well," I assured him. "We'll take care of that; we'll practice!"

After lunch, the two of us practiced skipping. Once he got the hang of the little hops between steps, we skipped all the way to the town square—about a mile from the house. Laughing and breathless, we treated ourselves to an ice cream cone, and then skipped all the way home.

When Paul came home, I couldn't wait to tell him about my religion class, especially the difference between belief and faith, even though I didn't really understand it.

"It sounds picky to me," he scowled. "Scholars try to make things so complicated. The Bible means exactly what it says."

I remembered how much fun we had when we were first married, and he'd talk to me about the books I was reading. I'd hoped my studies would be something we could share again, but when he came home from school, he was so tired he just wanted to sit in his easy chair, put his feet up on a stool, listen to music and smoke his pipe. I prepared dinner, disappointed he wasn't interested in what I was learning, but reminded myself how important his career was. We all depended on that!

☠

The next day, I waited expectantly for the Old Testament class. I wondered what Dr. Jenkins would say about Mark E. Peterson's interpretation of being perfect. When it was my turn, I presented the passage for discussion and explained that I'd looked up the word *perfect* in the dictionary.

"Perfect!" He explained, "You got the idea of how to exegete a passage very well. So what did you learn from the dictionary?"

"The synonyms for perfect are: complete, sound, entire, absolute, comprehensive and whole. But when you said *perfect* just now, it sounded like you meant it was right. And that's my question. I remember an authority in my church telling me that although we can't be perfect as humans, we can perfectly keep God's commandments.

183

"You're on to something important, Bonnie. The way I used the word *perfect* just now was to play on the word. Going to the dictionary wasn't really perfect because it was only a first step to a complete exegesis. Thank you for calling that to my attention. As far as the text is concerned, it will help to ask whether the passage in question is referring to *being* or *doing*. What do you think?"

I repeated the verse thoughtfully. "Be ye therefore perfect as your Father in Heaven is perfect." Mr. Jenkins gave me plenty of time to think about what I'd read. Finally, I said, "Well, it says that God *is* perfect, and it seems to be telling us to be like God. It doesn't refer directly to anything we *do*."

"So what does perfection have to do with following God's commandments?"

"Could it mean that if we paid our tithing 100%, we would be perfect in paying our tithing?"

"Good. Now, what does perfection in an action have to do with your own perfection?"

"I don't know." I was working hard trying to understand the connection.

"What if you baked a perfect cake? Would that make you a perfect baker?"

"Of course not!"

"Bonnie has brought up a profound principle; one that's basic to understanding religion. I'm going to write this on the board, and we'll think about it throughout the year." He wrote: "What is the relationship between doing and being?"

I felt great about my contribution to the class! Maybe I wasn't as stupid as I thought.

☠

School and home could not be separated in my experience. Ron was very young to be walking alone, even for a few blocks, and I warned him that if anyone tried to talk to him, he was not to answer but to keep walking to where I'd meet him. One day, he turned the wrong corner and got lost. I frantically searched the neighborhood, finally calling the police to report him missing. As I hung up, I noticed a police car driving slowly down the street. Racing out the door, I caught sight of Ron sitting on the front seat.

"Ma'am," the officer said, "you taught your little boy very well not to talk to strangers. He wouldn't even talk to us!" He broke into a grin. "I found him two blocks away; when I asked his name, he wouldn't say a word. I even tried giving him candy, but he wouldn't take it. I've been going up and down the streets, hoping to find a frazzled mother to identify him."

Grabbing Ron into my arms, I hugged him so tight he struggled to get free. "I've been so worried! But you're safe," I cried joyfully. "He does know his name, address and phone number," I explained to the officer, "but I didn't think to tell him it was OK to talk to a policeman. Thanks for everything!"

The kids were wonderful. We didn't own a television set; we couldn't afford one. Evenings after dinner, we studied—all of us. Even Ron had books and art supplies to keep him busy. A couple of nights a week I had classes, and other times I'd sneak away to the bathroom, fill the tub and read. It was the only place in the house to have privacy.

☠

Classes at Chapman were more demanding than they'd been at the junior college. The expectation of the teachers was high, and I felt I must maintain an A average for fear of losing my scholarship. I probably put myself under a lot more stress than I needed to, but it paid off.

In addition, the religion class and chapel were turning me inside out. I devoured every word from Dr. Jenkins, and couldn't get enough of the profound sermons and beautiful music provided by local churches at our chapel service on Fridays—none of it Mormon. In the two years I attended, not once did a Mormon speak at chapel. There was constant tension trying to figure out what I believed. Guilt was often present, born of the fear I was betraying my father. I remembered the words of my Patriarchal Blessing that promised ability to discern right from wrong, but since we weren't going to church, perhaps the blessing no longer applied.

Of all my teachers, Dr. Jenkins was my favorite, although his classes provoked constant anxiety trying to balance what I was learning with Mormonism. The final exam for Hebrew Scriptures covered the books of Samuel and Kings. I was appalled when we read the story of King David—about how he killed Uriah, seduced Bathsheba and committed adultery. I hadn't studied that in my Bible classes in Salt Lake. The first part of the exam was made up of true/false, multiple-choice questions, the last being whether or not King David had been righteous. When we finished, we handed in that part of the exam after which we received the following instructions for an essay: "What was your answer to the question about the righteousness of King David? If you said he was righteous, write a two-page essay showing why he wasn't righteous. If you said he was not righteous, defend his righteousness."

I had said he was not righteous because I thought that's what Dr. Jenkins believed. I was surprised to have to take the other position, but it was easy; I just slipped into my Mormon mind. I don't know what I wrote, but I got an A+ on the paper and a comment that I certainly did well defending a position not my own.

The second semester was New Testament. We spent several days talking about how manuscripts could be traced to multiple writers and sorted out through the Documentary Hypothesis. This gave a very different meaning to Genesis 1 and 2 compared to what I'd been taught through Mormon doctrine. There wasn't time to do the subject justice or understand its full implications, but the concept was filed in my mind for further investigation. We also learned there were extant codices that helped researchers track how changes in the text had occurred as they were hand-copied by succeeding generations of scribes. I recall telling my teacher, "What we're studying corroborates the Mormon *Articles of Faith,* which say that we believe the Bible is the word of God only if it is translated correctly."

Dr. Jenkins explained, "The difference is that Mormons claim to have a completely new source for their translation, one which is no longer available. The rest of the church does its research from manuscripts that still exist."

I smiled as I read the notes from my first year at Chapman. The issues had long since been put on the back burner of my concerns—that is, until I talked about them with Steve.

☠

In preparation for doing my student teaching, we discussed how to deal with the growing drug problem infesting the schools. It was then I realized that *Amplus,* which I'd taken for many years, was a drug. My "happy pills" were what they called "uppers." I was taking them myself!

I recalled when I first started using them. I was in the ninth grade at Irving Junior High School in Salt Lake City. Mom was concerned about my weight because I was a pudgy child, but her concern became obsessive in my teenage years. Above all, she wanted me to be beautiful, popular and wear lovely clothes. When I look at pictures of me from that time, I don't see a fat girl, but she was convinced that I was on the verge of ruining my life—and hers—by getting fat.

One Saturday while Dad was refereeing a football game in Logan, Mom invited me to go with her to visit her mother's sister, Loni. We drove several blocks past my grandparents' home, then pulling into the driveway of a brick house, drove to the backyard past the garage and parked in front of a small, unkempt shack. The shingles were falling off and what used to be white siding was now a dirty gray, so weathered it exposed raw wood. Papers and cans littered the yard, and a torn blind hung precariously from the window near the door. A lazy white cat, sleeping on the top step of the rickety front porch, didn't move a whisker when we cautiously stepped over it.

Mom knocked at the door. No answer. She knocked again, calling out, "Loni, it's Margaret. I've brought Bonnie to meet you. Can we come in?"

"The door's open," came a guttural voice.

I stepped anxiously into the dark room. Repulsed by the heavy air, thick with cigarette smoke, I perceived the outline of a woman sitting in a rocker. Her bulk filled the chair like pillows; her arms scarcely had a lap on which to rest. Her straight hair was uncombed, and her face so swollen I could barely make out the features.

She ground her cigarette into an ash-filled saucer, and looked at me with small piercing eyes. "So this is Bonnie. You're as pretty as your mother said you were."

I was flattered. I didn't know my mother thought I was pretty. The surprise helped me relax a bit in the strange environment.

"Come and sit down so we can talk," she pointed to a footstool. "Just push the magazines off onto the floor, it's OK."

Mom disappeared into the shadows of the room, stacked with newspapers, magazines, dishes of half-eaten food and piles of clothes. She emerged dragging a chair. Using her lace handkerchief to wipe the dust and crumbs from the wooden seat, she sat down as gracefully as if visiting one of her wealthy friends.

"It's been a long time since you dropped by," Loni whined. "I do love to see you!"

"Well, you know how busy it is when you're raising a family," my mother said, confidently ignoring the implication of neglect. "I wanted you to meet my precious Bonnie."

Loni looked back at me. "What grade are you in?"

"I go to Irving. This is my last year. Next year, I'll go to South High."

"Irving. Just like your mother and father." She closed her eyes and for a second or two seemed lost in thought.

This ugly woman was trying to be kind, yet, I had no idea what else to say. I just sat there watching her immense body shift awkwardly in the creaking chair. The two women recalled memories of Mom's years at Irving, but I only half-listened. I stared at her swollen legs, wondering if she could even stand.

Finally, Mom said we had to get the car back, which was a lie, but I was glad to get out of there. It's OK to tell a small lie for a greater purpose. Loni groped for another cigarette. I wanted to get out of there. My eyes itched and were watering from exposure to the leftover smoke in Loni's disgusting house. The contrast of walking from the stale, choking gloom into sunlight and clean air was like moving from death into life.

I looked back at the shabby house, as I slid into the car beside my mother. "How can anyone live like that?"

"She does the best she can," was all Mom would say.

We drove home in silence. I went to my bedroom and lay on my bed, allowing the soft breeze to blow the white gauze curtains into my room. *How blessed I am*, I thought. *What if Loni were my mother? YUK!*

After dinner, I listened for Mom to draw the water for her bath. When I thought she was settled and relaxed, I knocked on the door.

"The door's open. Come in and we'll talk."

I took my usual place on the toilet seat, placing my feet on the edge of the tub. Mom lay comfortably with her back against the tub, her ample breasts modestly covered with a washcloth.

"What did you think of Aunt Loni?"

"She's so ugly I could hardly look at her. Why did you take me there?"

"I want you to know what it's like to be fat. Bonnie, you have the same build as Loni. You must realize that if you don't take care of yourself while you're young, you'll look like her in a few years. I don't want that to happen to you."

She might as well have slapped my face. I could hardly breathe. It was the first time I experienced the gray, cold fog of fear fill my body. I knew Mom worried about me being fat, and now I knew why. Gradually, awareness of her love warmed the cold space in my being, and the tension built up in those minutes…seconds…of shock released itself in tears.

"I don't want to be like her. Please Mom, help me to not be like her," I sobbed.

She reached a soapy hand out to me. I clasped it like a drowning swimmer grasping a lifeline. "You know I have the same problem. I have to be very careful about what I eat, or I'll gain weight."

"But you're beautiful, Mom—the most beautiful mother in the whole school and ward."

"Well, I wouldn't be if I hadn't found a solution." She withdrew her hand, which disappeared into the water.

"A solution?" I leaned forward, eager to receive every saving word.

"The pill I take in the morning."

I knew she took a pill but hadn't paid much attention to it.

"It's called 'Amplus,' but I call it my 'happy pill.' It not only takes away my hunger but also gives me more pep. It would be good for you. If you start taking it now, perhaps you too can avoid getting fat for the rest of your life."

Mom took me to the doctor who gave her an unlimited prescription for me. Amplus was an amphetamine with vitamins added.

Everything Mom ever did for me was done because of her love. But taking the pills made me feel inauthentic. *What would happen to me if I couldn't get them?* It was unrealistic, of course, but I imagined myself not having the pills and suddenly ballooning up into Aunt Loni. Mom knew what was good for me far better than I did. I knew I must always do what she wanted me to do and never, ever hurt her.

Fourteen years later, in 1962, as a senior in college, I realized I was addicted to the very drugs I was supposed to teach my students never to use. Bewildered by the realization, I threw the remaining pills from my prescription down the toilet.

The result was several weeks of withdrawal, headaches and depression. I finally talked to a doctor who suggested I drink coffee instead. And thus began my downward spiral into breaking the *Word of Wisdom*. I started drinking wine once in a while and even tried cigarettes, but I was so allergic to them I didn't use them long. On the wall in our small bedroom was a vertical rectangular mirror. In one corner, I placed a picture of my father and in the other a clipping from *Reader's Digest*, which said that cigarettes caused cancer. I'd sit in front of the mirror, looking at my father's picture, drinking my coffee and wine, and, at least for a week or so, smoking a cigarette.

☠

The past is alive in the present, as well as the future. As I read my college notes and experienced these memories, I realized that Death had been a recurring presence in my life. She'd appeared briefly in the cold, gray fog, warning me about my mother's advice, but I was unable to perceive her. She was present when I threw away the pills and when I courted her in my mirror, watching myself enter into sin. And she has been with me on my shoulder ever since she saved me from suicide.

☠

Before graduation, my mind returned to the need to distinguish between faith and belief. I went to the dictionary to see if I could better understand the words. *Faith* was listed as a noun. I was certain Dr. Jenkins told me it was a verb. The synonyms were confidence, trust, assurance, expectation, hope, etc. Remembering *Corinthians I,* where Paul lists the three greatest virtues as faith, hope and love, I looked up the other two words. They are listed as nouns also, but in addition are listed as verbs. I realized I could hope or love something, but I could not faith something. Then I noticed that a secondary definition for *faith* is "a formal system of beliefs, religion, doctrine, creed, dogma, etc." I needed to talk to Dr. Jenkins again. I was certain he'd meet with me, even though I wasn't his student that semester.

"Come in, Bonnie," he beamed. "It's good to see you. How are you doing?"

"I'm struggling with my church and all we learned in your class," I began. "There's so much I question, and yet, I *am* a Mormon. My whole family's Mormon. I don't want to lose my faith!"

"I don't envy your struggle!" He looked sad.

"I often think about the difference between faith and belief. I think it could be a way to reconcile the conflict in my mind. In the dictionary, *faith* is not listed as a verb as I think you said. Can you explain that?"

"In the original Greek, *faith* was a verb, but in the Age of Reason, the seventeenth century, humanity defined itself by thinking. You recall Descarte's famous statement: 'I think therefore I am.' The meaning of *faith* became synonymous with the word *belief.* That's where our difficulty lies. But it was not the original meaning. Faith is more dynamic than beliefs which are objects of faith."

"So that explains my second question. I noticed that the secondary dictionary definition for *faith* is a formal system of beliefs. Does that come from the same historical shift?"

"That's it, but even the word *belief* has it own history. The word *credo*, from which belief comes, is a Latin word which means 'to put one's heart on.' The historical creeds of the church or the Mormon *Articles of Faith* state the beliefs of the community. Instead of saying 'I believe in God the Eternal Father...,' it sometimes helps to say, 'I put my heart on the concept of God the Eternal Father...,' or you could say 'I choose to believe in....' This implies that you have made a choice to believe this way, knowing there are other ways to believe. Faith encompasses words and concepts but is bigger than the ideas it holds. Our beliefs can change and grow; in fact, if we're alive and our minds are developing into their full potential, our beliefs *will* grow. If they don't, the intellect will stagnate."

"Is that why I don't know what to believe about God?"

"Tell me more about that," he asked gently.

"I can't really believe that God is a man in heaven. I believe there is a God who created the universe and is somehow connected to human beings, but I don't know who or what God is."

"So you're saying the beliefs you learned as a child, are no longer adequate?"

"Something like that," I acknowledged.

"Just be patient, Bonnie, and live with the question of who God is. Some day, your faith will help you grow into the answers."

When I left his office, I understood only a fraction of what he said. My mind was spinning trying to hold it all. But I liked the way he talked about our beliefs growing and changing as we progressed. I remembered Jesus saying: "Seek ye the truth and the truth shall make you free." Could that be what he meant? So much to think about!

☠

As I reviewed my notes from 1962 at Chapman College, on a warm August day in 1968, after talking about the church to a respected Mormon elder, the longing to know Dr. Jenkin's God flooded my soul. Imagine a god who wanted to be in relationship with me—a god who wouldn't condemn me for questioning. Why didn't I go to one of the other churches when I felt so alienated at the Mormon ward? I loved the chapel services. It would break my parents' hearts if I did such a thing. "Seek ye the truth and the truth shall make you free." But I'm not free enough to seek! What is the answer?

☠

194

CHAPTER FIVE

Season of Content

From the perspective of 1968, I recalled my senior year at Chapman College, five years earlier and wondered how I'd made it through. The year was a blur of stress. Not only did I have my classes at school and the family at home, but also I was student teaching at West Junior High where Paul taught band.

In March 1963, I sent out my resume, including one to the Utah Teacher's Association, halfway considering leaving Paul and taking the children back to Salt Lake. *Was that Death's prompting?* But I also applied in Anaheim, Fullerton and Orange. Bill Cullen, the principal at West Junior High, immediately offered a contract. It was set; I'd graduate in June and begin teaching in September. Paul and I purchased a home in a newly developed neighborhood in Anaheim. We signed the contract; crossing our fingers that bankruptcy was far enough in the past to not impede us.

The end of April, I missed my period. I didn't think I could be pregnant since our sex life was almost nonexistent, and I'd used a diaphragm ever since Ron was born. When I missed again in May I was frantic.

Looking through the phonebook, I found a doctor who practiced natural childbirth. I reasoned he'd probably be one of those hippies I'd heard about, and therefore a good doctor to ask for an abortion, if need be. We'd already signed the papers for our house, and I was determined that nothing was getting in the way of my career—not now!

When I met Dr. Marchbanks, I burst into tears after only a few words.

"Well, let's take a look and see if you're really pregnant. Then we can talk about the alternatives," he mumbled.

I undressed and climbed onto the table, fixing my feet in the stirrups. I hated this examination! He probed around inside me and took a blood sample. "I'll send this to the lab for verification, but I think it's pretty clear you're going to have another child. Probably sometime in January," he betrayed no emotion.

"But I can't! I won't!" I wailed.

"Get dressed and come to my office; we'll talk about it."

I was so angry; I couldn't even cry. *How can this happen to me? Now? It just isn't fair! After all those years of schooling, I don't want another baby!*

I stormed out of the examining room, with the nurse gently ushering me to the doctor's office. Plopping onto a chair, I squirmed for several minutes, becoming more agitated with each tick of the clock. Finally, he entered the room.

"Well, now," he began kindly. "Assuming you are pregnant, what shall we do?" I stared out the window, fuming, expecting him to start lecturing. He waited patiently for me to speak.

When I realized he was going to let me talk—that he was actually willing to listen to me—I felt myself relax; my anger dissolved into tears, blurring my vision and drizzling down my cheeks. He sat placidly in his chair without moving, and let me cry. When I realized he wasn't going to speak until I did, I looked around for Kleenex; he handed me the box. I blew my nose and said, firmly, "We've sacrificed so much so I could teach. It's not fair that I should be pregnant again. I already have four children. The youngest will be seven years old when this one is born. I'm through with babies. I've got enough kids as it is."

"Tell me about your children. Are they all healthy?" he asked calmly.

"We've been lucky. All four of them are healthy, bright, creative kids. I love them dearly. I just don't want another one—especially now!" Tears began gathering again.

"An abortion is a possibility," he said gently. "But, you know—there are so many people who come here wanting to have children and can't—it seems a shame to kill one that's already on its way."

The word *kill* thundered in my head. I sat paralyzed for several minutes, unable to speak, the silence so painful my heart hurt. What could I say? He seemed determined to keep me on the hook—or was it giving me space?

"Bonnie," he finally continued. "You have perfect, healthy children. You might consider having this baby. After it's born, if you don't want to keep it, I can find a home for it like that," and he snapped his fingers.

"I don't know what to say," I stammered.

"Just trust!" He looked me square in the eyes, "If it's a matter of money, whoever adopts the child will pay the bills. I can assure you of that. Only, don't cut a life short. You'll regret it the rest of your life!"

My tears had become warm and soft by now, anger replaced by feelings of helplessness and disappointment. I looked up at him for the first time. "I know I couldn't have an abortion—not really. I'm exhausted from all the stress of school and all! I don't know how we'll manage financially, and I'm just so tired!"

"I know. And I'll be here for you through the whole thing—if you want me," he added since I had not come to talk about a birth.

"Of course," I said gratefully.

"When the tests come back, I'll give you a call and we can discuss your decision." He stood, indicating my time was up.

I left the office grateful for such a sensitive doctor. *It will all work out,* I assured myself. *I know it will!*

Paul's career was moving forward, after a rocky start. He'd taken the job having little background in instrumental music, and there was no place to hide one's shortcomings in Southern California where band is so competitive. His first music festival brought a "five" rating, the worst possible score. This year, the kids received a "two" with accolades from judges who praised their rapid improvement. He'd also taken the band to parades, learning about marching as he went. His principal was encouraged by his progress.

With early morning marching practice, competitions on weekends, plus moving into a new house, Paul was seldom home and refused to talk about my missed periods. It was my problem, and I faced it alone.

The day of my exam, I waited until we'd finished dinner before telling Paul I wanted to talk to him when the kids were in bed. I still clearly remember washing the dishes, my mind dazed. Lynne helped by drying and putting them away; it was our special time together.

Setting aside my concern, I asked about her final day at school. She was eleven now and ready for her last year of elementary school; her eyes were downcast, and I wondered if she was holding back tears.

"Did they have something special for the last day?" I asked brightly.

"Not really. Just the same old stuff." Placing a stack of plates in the cupboard, she looked at me wistfully. "It's hard to leave my friends again."

"It must be! Lynne, I'm sorry we've been so unsettled. But at least you've learned how to make friends."

"I've had a lot of practice," she replied. "Sixth grade will be my fifth school."

I dried my hands on the dishcloth and pulled her to me. "You've been such a good student in all of this, even though it's been hard." Looking into her eyes, I promised, "This will be our last move as long as you're in school."

"Really?" Her flat voice was unbelieving.

"If I have any say about it, you'll graduate from high school with the friends you make next fall."

Her eyes brightened. "I hope so," she replied in a low voice, and we finished doing the dishes and putting them away, each of us lost in our own thoughts.

I tucked the kids in bed, nearly forgetting our nightly routines.

Lowell leaned over from his top bunk so I could kiss him, but when I turned to leave he reminded me, "Sleepy bear!" He was nine years old and still wanted me to sing his favorite song: "Sleepy bear creeps in his cave, curls up like a ball. Goes to sleep and does not move, does not move at all."

I loved singing to the kids; they were the only ones in the world who appreciated my voice. I couldn't get in the high school a cappella choir, even when my friends petitioned the music director.

I bent over to kiss Ron good night. "Best things," he reminded me.

"What was the best thing that happened to you today?" I asked. The question was a nightly ritual since we'd moved to California.

"We had a party at school, and the teacher told everyone I won't be back next year. They were real nice to me."

"What about you, Lowell?"

"I walked home with David and saw our old house again. I guess it was the best thing but also the worst."

I kissed him again and said confidently, "Maybe David can come and spend the night sometime this summer. Would you like that?"

He turned his head to face the wall. "Sure," he sighed.

"I think you're going to make lots of new friends here." I repeated what I'd told Lynne. "It's the last time you'll have to move until you're out of high school. I promise!" He didn't move.

When I went into the girls' room, they were waiting for me. Lynne had already told Annie that I promised they wouldn't have to move again. "Is that true?" she asked, only half believing the news. "If I can help it, darling, I don't want to move again either!"

When I asked her about the best thing that happened to her, she told me about a kitty that had followed her home. "She's the cutest thing! Can we have a kitty in this house?"

I kissed her goodnight and promised I'd talk to Paul about it.

When they were settled, I combed my hair and put on fresh lipstick, summoning all the confidence possible.

Paul was relaxing in the new recliner I'd gotten him for an early Father's Day surprise. I bought it from our neighbors, the Maxwells. They'd been married only a few weeks when they moved into their new home. They had two households of furniture from previous marriages and gave me a great deal on the chair.

It was good to see Paul so comfortable, smoking his pipe, lazily thumbing through a magazine next to our new fireplace. I hated to disturb him; he didn't need my stressful news. Remembering my angry response at the doctor's office, I wondered how to tell him.

"What happened with the doctor?" he began, before I'd had a chance to sit down.

"I'm pregnant."

"It figures," he scowled. "Just when we're finally getting settled, and I thought the stress was over. We shouldn't have bought the house. How will we pay for it?"

I was silent, knowing he had to speak his concerns, before we could discuss options.

"What about an abortion?" he asked.

"It would be the easy way out, I guess, but the doctor helped me realize I couldn't do it. We'd be killing a baby. We'd regret it all our lives." I waited a few minutes to allow the "k" word to penetrate his anxious mind. "Besides, Paul, I've been thinking—if God wanted us to have this baby enough to make me pregnant in spite of the diaphragm, how can we possibly do anything but welcome it into our home?"

"You didn't use the diaphragm the night we bought the house. You probably don't even remember. We were so carried away about getting the loan and thinking about the house and the future we drank a whole bottle of wine. I think you were drunk. I don't remember you going to the bathroom to take care of yourself."

I was stunned. *He's probably right. It's my fault. I shouldn't drink. I'm only getting what I deserve! How come every time we have a problem, it's my fault? It just proves what a bad person I am. Like the Elder said, I've let Satan into my life and these are the consequences.*

Wait a minute, I argued with myself. *Do I think the child is coming from Satan—or God? God, of course, but he must have wanted to send the baby badly enough that he used the first and only opportunity I gave him.*

By the end of this soliloquy, I realized the child must be very special. As far as I was concerned, it was as close to an immaculate conception as a woman could come.

Paul smoked his pipe, calmly. I wonder if he enjoyed the confusion his words created. I sensed he'd mastered the art of making me doubt myself. But these insights had already slithered under my conscious awareness. I'd save them for another day when I had time to sort them through.

"So what do we do?" His question was a statement. He clenched his jaw.

"We have the baby, of course." I answered emphatically.

"And how do you propose to pay for it?"

"Doctor Marchbanks said if money was a problem, and we didn't want to keep the child after it came, he could find someone to adopt it, and they would pay all the expenses. We don't have to make up our minds until the last minute."

"And you think you could have a child and the other kids would accept giving it away?"

I hadn't considered what the children would think. *They'll be thrilled to have a baby in the house!* I answered decisively, "Of course, we won't give it away. We'll have to come up with the money. Doesn't your insurance cover maternity?"

"It probably does," he answered coldly, and I sensed he'd already checked it out and just wanted me to squirm. "What about the house payments? You can't teach for another year. That is, if you can get another contract." He almost sneered.

"I'll substitute as soon as possible after the baby comes. It will all work out, Paul. I'm certain of that."

"Of course, it will—if I get another job."

"Oh, Paul, I'm sorry! How will you ever do it with all you've got on your plate now?"

"It means I won't take the summer off. I've already lined up a job to clerk at the Broadway. I was going to use the money to buy furniture so you'd finally be happy, but it will have to go toward the mortgage. It's that simple."

"I should have known you'd have a plan. You've always supported us with everything we've needed. I'll make it up to you. I promise."

☠

In my brief study of the Hebrew Scriptures, I was drawn into the story of the Exodus, and how, every year at Passover, the Jewish family—to this day—remembers how

God brought them out of Egypt. I was particularly intrigued by the description of Moses meeting God on the mountain. He is a fugitive from Egypt living in the desert with a wife and a child. He's tending his father-in-law's sheep when he spots a bush that is burning but not consumed. He climbs up the hillside to investigate, and a voice comes out of the bush saying that he should take off his shoes for he is standing on holy ground.

The voice identifies itself as the God of his ancestors and tells Moses that he must go back to Egypt and free the Israelites who have been there four hundred years living in captivity. Moses is shocked. Who is he to go back to Egypt, where he is wanted for murder, and convince the Pharaoh to let his people go? Besides, how does Moses know the voice is God's?

My interest in this story was personal since I'd asked the same questions of the "voices" and conflicting thoughts I was hearing in my own mind. How does one know whether a voice is coming from God or Satan? Or is it one's own ego? How does one discern between good and bad, right and wrong?

Moses asks the mysterious voice how he can be certain it is God who is speaking. And the answer is that after he has done what he's told, he will bring the people back to this very spot and worship God on the mountain. Only then would Moses know who had been guiding him.

Great! After it's all over, when he looks back at what has happened, only then will he know he made the right choice. My pregnancy taught me the truth of this lesson. It's only in retrospect that we can discern meaning in our lives. Only then do we have the perspective to understand. That is, if we take the time to *try* to understand.

When I look back on my pregnancy in 1963, what seemed to be a disaster, brought blessings unimaginable, not only from the precious child, but from the pregnancy itself. It was as though I was pregnant also with myself. Something in me wanted to be born along with the baby; my soul had been in *labor* for a long time.

The due date was sometime in January, seven months after graduation. Although I'd given birth to four previous children, this was the first pregnancy I could fully experience. When Lynne was born, I was too sick to notice the miracle occurring in my body and lacked awareness to appreciate the miracle. When I was pregnant with the others, I was too busy with all my babies to pay attention to myself at all. But this time, I could be fully aware of every moment and every miraculous change.

A sense of appreciation for the mystery of life arose from my womb permeating my whole being. Our home was on the outskirts of Anaheim, the subdivision surrounded on three sides by orange groves. For the first time in our marriage, we had plenty of space so that it took only a few minutes to keep things spotless and picked up. With all the kids in school, I had plenty of time to do the things I enjoyed—sewing, walking through the quiet neighborhood, and spending hours touching my belly and contemplating the mystery of life.

Once the disappointment of not teaching waned, I was able to relax into the peaceful contentment of having realized my dream. I'd been successful in attaining my goal, and a new confidence was emerging. I felt sorry Paul had to have a second job, but I'd make it up to him. There was no way I could work since we lived on the outskirts of town and there was nothing available within walking distance. Sometimes I felt guilty having so much free time, while he had none, but mostly, I remember feeling gratitude for how hard he worked to support us. I did everything I could to have a good dinner for him and look nice and make him happy. I could now be the perfect wife and mother I'd been taught was the purpose of my life.

We didn't have money to buy furniture, and we especially needed a refrigerator since one hadn't come with the house. We tried getting by with ice chests for a few weeks, but it was impossible, as days grew hot. A small savings account had been set aside for Christmas, and when our next-door neighbors told us they would sell us one of their refrigerators—cheap—the only money available was the savings account.

Shortly after we moved in, we called a family meeting.

Paul explained, "The Maxwells offered to sell us one of their refrigerators, but we have to pay the whole amount when we get it."

"We've been putting money away every month so we can have a nice Christmas," I told them. "There's enough in the account to buy the refrigerator, but if we do, we probably won't have money for presents."

Without a pause, Lynne said, "Then the refrigerator will be our Christmas!"

Paul and I looked at each other in awe. *How did we ever deserve such wonderful children?*

Finally, Paul said, "We're not kidding, you know. There really won't be money for Christmas if we do this."

"We know, Daddy, but we need a refrigerator more," Lowell chimed in.

"We can make Christmas presents for each other," Annie added, already knowing how much fun it was to create surprises for people.

"Won't Santa come?" Ron asked, still hanging on to his belief.

There was a long silence as we collectively wondered whether this was the time to break the news to him.

Lowell finally said, "You never can tell. We might have a miracle! But I say, let's buy the refrigerator with the money."

Paul took charge, "OK. All those in favor say 'aye'!"

The assent was such a loud shout they probably heard it next door. Everyone hugged each other, and Paul took the four kids with him to buy the refrigerator stored in the Maxwells' garage. They brought it home that night, and it stood proudly in our kitchen as long as we lived there, a symbol of family priorities.

I don't remember going to the local ward, although Lynne and Lowell were baptized when they were eight years old by my father. Annie would be baptized in October when she turned eight. Shortly after we moved, in some women from the ward offered to take the children to Primary, but Paul and I stayed away from church. He now worked Sundays at the Broadway so he had a good excuse. I don't remember even worrying about attending although I still considered myself to be a good Mormon—only temporarily inactive.

Love for the new life growing within me increased daily. I remember an extraordinary fall afternoon, sitting in Paul's recliner in the living room, feeling my baby moving under my hand and being filled with a sense of awe. God seemed very near, although I had long since shut him out of my life—at least in a formal sense. But that connection was real and although I didn't know how to articulate my feelings or thoughts, I felt I was participating in God's creative mystery. And I knew all would be well. A peace came over me that carried me through to her birth.

Another blessing was the luxury of long days to watch the TV coverage of President Kennedy's assassination. I was glued to the TV set—my baby and me. I cried with JohnJohn and consciously embraced the child in my womb as I witnessed little Caroline standing mournfully, her small hand in Jacqueline's, their grief transmitted throughout the world, even into our living room. They were like family, and I was one with them in their mourning.

I watched the Requiem Mass and remember sitting in fascination, listening to the priest incant Latin phrases, absorbing the chanting—transported by the power of the procession. I didn't understand what they were doing, but I remember feeling gratitude that the rituals could make wordless sense of the horrible tragedy. The mass was as mysterious as death itself, and the pathos of the suffering Kennedy family encompassed our own through the miracle of television.

Years later, the memory of that mass would reawaken, but for now, it was an experience so outside anything I'd ever known that I absorbed it into my deepest consciousness—without judgment or a need to understand.

My parents sent an early Christmas gift, a check for several hundred dollars. It came the first of December, in time to buy gifts and store them in Paul's band room. We said nothing to the kids, but all of us followed Annie's suggestion and made something for everyone in the family. Lynne had learned how to knit and crochet in Primary and she taught Annie. They wrote poems and made cards for each of us. Lowell showed his lifelong resourcefulness by befriending an old man who made unique birdhouses, selling them from his front lawn. "Grandpa" allowed Lowell to peddle them door-to-door in exchange for our family gift. He sold so many that he had money to spare and kept his job for months after Christmas.

Paul made a short tape-recording that Christmas Eve. The four kids sang their favorite carols, which they knew by memory.

On the tape, I can hear my younger voice ask them: "When was the first Christmas?"

Lowell answers, "When Jesus was born in Bethlehem."

"How do we know that?" I ask.

"We learned it in Sunday School." "From church!" "It's in the Bible," were the various answers.

"Where in the Bible?"

Lynne replies, "Matthew, Mark, Luke and John."

"Really?" I challenge her.

"It's in Matthew and Luke," pipes up Lowell, our budding theologian.

They take turns reading from Luke's Gospel, and when they read about Joseph going to Bethlehem with his *espoused* wife..." Annie asks, "What's *spoused* mean?"

Lynne informs her, "It means she's pregnant, like Mommy."

"She was even bigger than I am!" I add.

The tape is priceless, and helps me realize that our children were not totally bereft of religious education.

When Christmas morning arrived, I was up at 5:00 AM. I thought they'd never wake up. Finally, about 6:30, they began to stir, and we went through the living room together. Family tradition demanded breakfast before opening gifts.

There was an audible gasp on the way to the dining room as the children realized Santa had been there after all; Lowell's prediction of a miracle had come to pass. We'd been blessed again, through the intervention of my god-like earthly father.

I was allowed to sit in Paul's chair while the kids opened their gifts. It was the only place I could be comfortable. The baby was due in two weeks, and I was so big I could hardly move. Visions of corpulent Aunt Loni floated sporadically into my brain, but I deftly dismissed them. After all, I *was* pregnant. I'd lose the extra weight after the birth.

Dr. Marchbanks made me feel as though I were his only patient. I wanted a natural childbirth, after being drugged on ether my previous deliveries. All I remembered about birthing was how sick I was fighting my way back to consciousness. When Ron was born, the experience of going under the anesthetic was frightening. Spiraling circles diminished into a pulsating, incessant dot. I was caught in the spiral and thought I would die when the dot quit beating. The nightmare repeated intermittently for two weeks after his birth; I'd awaken screaming, drenched with sweat. I did not want to go through it again. I wanted to be awake and fully engaged in the birthing process.

In 1964, Lamaze classes, which teach husbands to coach their wives through labor, were not yet available. Being one of the pioneers in natural childbirth, Dr. Marchbanks coached me himself, the entire six hours of labor, showing me how to breathe, reassuring me with his calm presence, squeezing my hand to let me know I was not alone in the pain. I wanted so much to have the baby without anesthetic of any kind although I knew my doctor was waiting with an epidural injection if I needed it. The last contraction brought an unbidden cry, and he injected me just minutes before she was born.

How amazing! I had no nausea, in fact, I was exhilarated—a spiritual high as well as physical orgasm. Later in life, I would recognize a blissful experience in meditation akin to this, but at the time, I knew nothing about spiritual union. They placed Wendy in my arms before cutting the umbilical cord. Kissing her and holding her to my breast, I dissolved into tears of joy, reluctantly releasing my embrace for the nurse to wash and weigh her.

I was sitting up in bed holding her a few hours later when Mom brought the kids to see us. As they shyly touched the baby, I realized that without this pregnancy, I'd never have known the full miracle of giving birth. How sad to have been drugged and unable to participate in the labor of the previous births!

When Dr. Marchbanks came into my room that evening, Paul was with me. We were playing with Wendy's fingers, counting her toes and ooohing and ahhhhing, grateful that we again had a perfect child.

"Well, have you decided if you're going to keep her?" the doctor grinned.

I could scarcely breathe as his words sank into my consciousness. "Oh my goodness!" I cried, remembering we'd considered abortion! Tears of shame and gratitude poured down my cheeks as I hugged my precious daughter giving thanks to God for her life and for Dr. Marchbank's sensitive counsel.

At that moment, I was standing on holy ground, not unlike Moses. I remembered the voice telling him he would know it was God after he'd obeyed and stood on the same mountain looking back. Only then could he accurately discern divine guidance. I firmly believed Dr. Marchbanks had mysteriously been sent to lead me to this moment.

There were other lessons to learn from Wendy's birth; lessons that came as I relished the quiet time we spent together: nursing her, giving her baths, changing her diapers and dressing her like a doll. It all seemed new to me, even though I'd performed the same actions with four other children. What was the difference?

I began to understand how passive I'd been in those days. Throughout my childhood, I did what I was told. I wasn't allowed to form opinions or ask questions. I'd simply reacted to life and sleepwalked through events.

As I was conscious during Wendy's birth, I wanted to be conscious in everything I did. When given ether to block pain, I depended on the doctor to do the work. This time, I'd been fully awake, participating in the birth, laboring instead of sleeping through it. This awareness changed the way I lived the rest of my life.

During my pregnancy and her birth, the whole world looked different to me. My senses were heightened, especially the awareness of touch. It was as though I watched myself love this child whom God had sent; I was taking care of her for him!

Why hadn't I experienced this before? These were questions I needed to ponder. How had my eyes been opened? How could I keep them from closing again?

☠

210

CHAPTER SIX

Dr. Robert Kevorkian

In 1968, when Steve challenged me to remember my years at Chapman and Wendy's remarkable birth, she was four years old. We'd built the swimming pool, and she'd learned to swim. The financial predicament had worked out, and now, Paul, after successfully building a band at Sunkist Junior High, was moving to a position as band director of Madison High School, less than a mile away. Life seemed settled, and I was preparing for a challenging assignment to teach Family Life and Sex Education to junior high students.

An article in *This Week Magazine* reported:

> In 1965 the Anaheim, Calif. High school introduced a voluntary Family Life and Sex Education course, and until the summer of 1968, school officials were gratified at its smooth acceptance. Over 99 percent of the students attended. The course itself drew national recognition as a model for scope and candor. Then suddenly and savagely, the roof fell in. A handful of parents complained in August that sex education was corrupting their children and demanded the course be abolished.[1]

Among fears that the course would "cause a breakdown of modesty and lead to promiscuity," dissidents feared reports of "sensitivity training" for teachers. Interestingly, in an article in *Redbook,* the evangelist Billy Graham recommended that sensitivity training be used for this purpose.[2]

My classes met in a Quonset hut, leaving my classroom free to teach English and Reading, while keeping sensitive materials away from inquisitive kids. I wanted to arrange the chairs in an oval so that students could see each other, but I didn't dare because of the controversy. The subject proposed for discussion each day was written on the blackboard, but their questions superceded my suggestions. A question box was provided for anonymity, but in my class, it was seldom used. The kids became comfortable talking to me and to each other. Everything spoken during the class was confidential. I would not report what they said to parents or principal, or anyone else, and they agreed not to gossip outside the room, although I encouraged them to talk to parents about *what* was discussed, while avoiding *who* said *what.*

We practiced listening to one another and being polite so everyone had a chance to participate. Their words were addressed to the entire group, not to their neighbor. Since the class was theirs, it was up to them to enforce the rules they'd agreed upon. When they realized I was there to listen and help them talk to each other, discipline was never a problem. If someone acted out, other students brought him or her into line. My first groups were seventh graders. The discussion for seventh-grade boys focused on menstruation. Since they had lots of questions, I brought Kotex to show them and explained how tampons were used. Most had seen the products at home, but didn't know what they were for.

They mostly wanted to talk about relationships with parents and siblings, marriage roles, and pressure from peers to smoke and use drugs. Once they realized I wouldn't be directive, they came alive. They wanted to talk. They wanted to hear from each other.

Sally Williams, R.N., the coordinator of the program explained:

> We do not give them a specific moral code, but
> teach them to weigh alternatives…The course

was originally designed out of the district's concern for present day morals, the increase of pregnant unwed teenagers and the effect on the family and community at large of an unwanted child…In essence, the course teaches them to stop and think about the consequences before they make a moral decision whether it is about sex, marriage or life in general.[3]

In the teachers' training group, once we satisfied our need to talk about sex as activity, our conversation turned to sex as identity—gender. What does it mean to be a woman or a man?

I remind my reader again that this was 1968. Most average white Americans paid little attention when the Equal Opportunity Commission was established two years earlier to prevent job discrimination, not only on the basis of race but also of sex. The country was hearing a few strident voices from women, but the threat of communism still hung over our country, black uprisings were dominating headlines, nightly television was bombarding the country with images from Vietnam where we saw hundreds of civilians killed each week, and Walter Cronkite told viewers the war was not winnable.

Most average American women hadn't considered themselves a persecuted minority. Even so, an inordinate number of early feminists found their way into our Sex Ed training group. They baited me into talking about my Mormon family, and I was baffled by their derision. My family was *perfect*. My father was *God*. My mother was a perfect wife, perfect mother, a white-haired angel, a smiling, happy, receptionist in the Salt Lake temple.

When they asked if she visited often, I had to admit that I dreaded her visits since I couldn't live up to her high standards. She wanted a beautiful, popular daughter, but I was plain, overweight, and not concerned about popularity. As a teenager, I was a disappointment; as a mother, I failed, especially in keeping my house up to her standards. When she visited, I spent hours cleaning to win her approval.

Well, maybe my mother wasn't perfect, but my father was. I worshipped him. No matter how they probed, I could find no fault in Jimmy Myers, president of the largest advertising agency in Salt Lake City.

One day, after several sessions where the fixation on my parents had surfaced, one of the social workers in the group said I was a perfect example of the "Electra Complex." The group agreed. When I asked them what that meant, they told me to look it up for myself.

Another time, Steve asked if I could see myself equal to my father. The visceral reaction was intense: blood drained out of my face, my hands shook and I wondered if I was going to faint. Instead, I muttered, "Are you kidding? Me? Equal to my father? That's not possible!" The faces of my colleagues showed their exasperation, and they changed the subject.

After that encounter, no one talked to me; even Steve turned his back and hurried away. My companion, *Death*, still on my shoulder, helped me find my car and drove me home, defying the confusion that fogged my brain. *I need help! Something's very wrong with me. If only I knew someone to call for counseling. I'll ask Dr. Stevenson next session.*

With this resolution, the fog began to dissipate.

At the December meeting, one month later, it was announced that we'd have a guest speaker in January, Dr. Robert Kevorkian, a psychotherapist. I wondered if Dr. Stevenson invited him because he recognized my need for help. He was the only outside speaker we had during our training.

Dr. Kevorkian discussed how detrimental a lack of self-esteem was to human development. Experiencing a magnetic bond with him, I knew he was the therapist for me. I made an appointment to see him on February 20, 1969. I can be specific about this date because I began keeping a journal. I wrote: "My decision to keep a journal is motivated by my desire to remember in detail what I feel will be a rebirth."

☠

I will never forget that first meeting. Kevorkian was a six-foot-four Armenian, ex-Baptist minister who had been head pastor at a large church in Riverside. After a bout with meningitis, which precipitated a mental and/or emotional breakdown, he sought healing at Esalen, an avant-garde teaching center at Big Sur on the California coast. He began attending classes shortly after Fritz Perls, cofounder of Gestalt therapy, began his iconoclastic work. Bob had participated in the revolutionary encounter groups that relied on confrontation rather than the "hand-holding" approach of traditional therapists. By the time he left Esalen, his whole perspective on God, himself and the church were radically challenged. His pastoral demise came when he told his congregation that they were all "prostitutes, trying to buy God's love and favors."

His dismissal from his pastorate allowed time to finish a Doctorate in Sacred Theology (STD) and become a licensed Christian therapist. We weren't told about his religious background when he spoke to the group. My understanding was that he was a secular therapist. Whether it would have made a difference in seeing him, I'm not certain. As it was, he was exactly the person I needed at the time—my issues with religion being what they were.

Kevorkian was unconventional, to say the least. When I entered his office, I was surprised to find it decorated like a formal drawing room. The décor created an atmosphere of unabashed elegance. I noted the dark wood casings around the doors and windows, richly carved antique furniture and red Persian carpet of intricate design. Two oversized high-back chairs were centered in the spacious room, their

215

cushions of red velvet. They reminded me of thrones, which is what he called them.

I felt small and insignificant as I sat in the huge chair, my feet so far from the floor he graciously placed a matching stool beneath them. He said nothing for several minutes while I absorbed the unexpected grandeur and tried to feel comfortable in my spacious seat. Sitting comfortably in an identical throne facing me, his shoulders rested against the high back, his long legs stretched out in front. He seemed perfectly relaxed, his velvet padded armrests accommodating his elbows while his hands touched each other in a position of prayer, his fingertips kissing his lips.

I looked up tentatively, but seeing him watching me was so uncomfortable I lowered my eyes and looked at my hands, tightly gripped in my lap. Still he said no word. When I looked up again, compassion in his dark eyes enabled me to hold the gaze for a few minutes. I willed myself not to look away, but couldn't resist lowering my eyes, once again. When I looked up a third time, he finally spoke—in a slow, deep voice.

"I consider this to be a birthing room. It is holy space. When people come here, they are looking for a new life. If you come back, you will discover who you really are. Just as physical birth takes nine months; new birth will take nine months to a year. You are expected to come once each week and make this appointment first priority in your life. If you're willing to do that, I'll be here for you. If you're not willing, I'm not interested in spending time with you. I'll expect a commitment before you leave today."

I'd never encountered such candor. His honesty kindled hope in the depths of my heart. As we sat in silence for several long minutes, I felt engulfed in a presence I can only call Love—a sense of being accepted just as I was. There was no question about trusting this strange man, and the promise of new life, like a spark buried under the cold ashes of disappointment, was ignited into flame by the breath of his words.

Finally, I whispered, "I will do as you say!"

"Then let us begin," and with these words, he rose to his full stature and slowly, with deliberation, strode across the room and picked up a large, ornately carved, full-length mirror. He set it in front of me, carefully adjusting the angle so it reflected my full body and the throne upon which I sat. Without words, he returned to his regal seat and, with deliberate, focused motion, lowered his long body into place across from me, his face discernible next to the mirror.

I watched every move he made; no word was spoken. With great effort, I moved my eyes to the reflection in the mirror. *Why is this so difficult?* I wondered. But once I focused on my own gaze, I withered, right there on the spot. In horror, I seemed to become smaller and smaller, seeing myself as a cringing old woman, slouched into the corner of the huge chair—filled with self-loathing. I could hardly breathe and still he said nothing. I tried to form words, but all that came from my throat was a pitiful cry. Closing my eyes, I wept. When I finally opened them, he had moved the mirror to its place against the far wall.

Finally, he spoke, "When we finish our work, you will look at yourself in that mirror with awareness and acceptance. In the meantime, we have work to do."

He asked if I'd had any previous therapy; I told him about the psychiatrist I'd seen in 1958 when I had Meniere's disease.

"Tell me about it."

"I remember telling the doctor that I felt guilty, but I didn't know why. It was about this time that I quit going to church. I didn't feel worthy; I didn't seem to belong. I had some questions about why Negroes were discriminated against, and my father took me to see one of the General Authorities. He told me it was Satan who was making me doubt the teachings of the Church. He commanded me to go home and be a good wife and mother and let my husband, who had the priesthood, do the thinking for both of us. My questions would only lead to more sorrow."

Bob again was silent. And then he asked, "Bonnie, do you ever pray?"

The question might have come from another planet. Stunned, I had to admit I hadn't prayed for years. In a flash, I realized that in my mind, the Mormon Church was God. I had taken vows to believe in and obey the Mormon Church. If I was so sinful that I couldn't be comfortable in a Mormon ward, how could I possibly pray? I'd never thought about people who were not Mormons praying. As I verbalized these insights to Bob, I realized how stupid I was.

"You're not stupid," he thundered. "You're a very intelligent woman. But you are misguided. God is not the Mormon Church. Other people pray—and they're not Mormons. Some pray who don't even believe in a God they can describe—but they know the power of prayer."

So many conflicting thoughts swirled inside my mind, I could form no words. He waited silently as I tried to assimilate what had been revealed. And then he spoke again. "When you go home, I want you to kneel down as you've been taught and say a prayer. It doesn't have to be long; there are no right words to say. Just talk to God as though you know him. I suggest kneeling because it will remind you that what you're doing is prayer—not just talking to yourself. Do this once a day all week long, even if it's just five minutes." Again, we sat without speaking, allowing the import of his words to root in my mind. He ended the session by reiterating his instructions and asking for my promise to do as he said. I agreed.

Leaving his office was like sleepwalking. The interview had been so intense I hardly knew what to think of it. But I felt such hope. What he said made much sense! *Why couldn't I look at myself in the mirror? Why had I stopped praying?* I was aware that it was *Death* on my shoulder, guiding me home.

The house was quiet; no one was there. I went into my bedroom, closed the door, knelt down as I'd been taught as a little girl, and all I said was, "Heavenly Father," and the tears came. I sobbed and sobbed—right there, kneeling beside my bed, I cried my eyes out. Finally, calmness came over me. As the tears ceased, I became aware of a presence more tangible than anything I'd ever felt. It was more tangible even than *Death,* who had become my friend. It entered my body and filled my whole being, at the same time, it encompassed me. It was both outside and within. It even swallowed up *Death.* I was one with the presence, but it was more than me. I knew it was God, and I knew I was loved. It was as though God had wrapped arms around me and entered my body in a union beyond sexual intimacy.

The remarkable thing about this experience is that it had lasting effects. I felt cleansed; I felt beautiful. *Death* never again sat on my shoulder, but I knew she was with me—that she was part of God. After this, she lived in my belly, sorting out the dark feelings that caused the fog. At my next meeting with Bob, I easily looked into his mirror.

☠

When I met Steve and he noticed I wasn't wearing my temple garments, I'd felt like the Samaritan woman Jesus met at the well. "He told me everything I'd ever done" as Jesus had in the biblical encounter. Now, the same story applied to my experience with Bob. But it was a different connection with Kevorkian. He was Jesus, and I was begging him to "Give me that water!" The water of abundant life that I realized God wants for all people. I became Bob's true disciple.

I listened to every word he said and wrote everything I could remember in my journal, although much of what happened in that "birthing room" was beyond words. Still there were teachings and they became my *credo*—what I set my heart on.

He taught that our greatest desire is for intimacy, but intimacy is also our greatest fear. "We marry the person we can live farthest away from up close." The only way one can have a true relationship is to be emotionally honest. Feelings must be expressed as they occur rather than held back. He warned me that practicing would create awkward situations because others wouldn't understand why I wasn't following the usual script. He also said that if I followed my feelings I was going to make mistakes, but that's how I'd learn. I wrote down the following:

1. Act out feelings without rational intervention.

2. When you sense pain, walk into it. Don't back off. Don't seek safe solutions.

3. Be aware of actions and feelings as coming from *Bonnie*.

It was obvious to Kevorkian that I'd never practiced being in touch with feelings, let alone expressing them. My goal was to be perfect, which meant continuously monitoring my reactions, being careful never to hurt anyone. I judged myself *bad* when I felt anger. I had never seen my parents fight—ever! It was not nice. In both the Sex Ed training with Dr. Stevenson and my sessions with Bob, I couldn't tell anyone what I was feeling. All I experienced was a mishmash of internal anxiety, which I'd never allowed myself to examine. When asked to be specific, I'd respond, "I'm so stupid!" but none of my *adversaries* in the program would let me off the hook. If I didn't know what I was feeling, how could I interact with people authentically? I came to realize the uncomfortable fog I experienced as nothing more than all the emotions I had not allowed myself to feel. My assignment was to shine light into that darkness and face what was there.

Now, my friend, *Death,* who'd been my companion since my intended suicide, was once again internalized. The fog of suppressed emotions had become so intense I had disassociated from them, and she had safely carried them for me on my shoulder. She was now deep within my consciousness, a friend whom I could rely on to sort through the disparate feelings. By facing death, I could face fear; and without fear, other unwelcome emotions were distinguishable. I realized that *Death* was one with *Life*. Acknowledging her was to embrace Life itself.

☠

This was all new to me. I remember as a child asking my mother, "What should I want for Christmas?" "What is my favorite color?" The idea that I could think for myself and be praised for speaking *my* truth was totally new.

Believing the closeness I craved with Paul and my children depended upon my honesty—being in touch with what I felt and expressing it—I gave myself completely to the practice. I had no idea where it would lead; I only knew that I was asked to be courageous and risk everything I held dear—even my marriage and family, realizing that neither was based on the truth of who I am. Since Paul had been indoctrinated the same way, we seldom experienced conflict; we hardly tried to communicate. I suspected he was most true to himself when he was hitting someone, and his pent-up hostility erupted. I perceived the truth meant by "marrying the person we can live farthest away from up close."

The first major incident had to do with housework. We were both schoolteachers. He spent many hours outside the classroom in rehearsals and marching practice, mostly early morning and on Saturday. As an English teacher, I had a class load of thirty to forty students in each of six classes. Close to two hundred students each day. I not only had preparation, but compositions to read and papers to grade. Every day I came home from school, usually to a house strewn with clothes, and dirty dishes piled in the sink because everyone left early each morning. There were five children to care for and dinner to prepare. The kids helped as much as they could, but they were busy with Little League and band and school assignments. Besides, they were children and needed time to play!

Paul was the patriarch of the family. Mormon men didn't do housework. He had his electric train set, and creating intricate model cars gave him immense joy. And he had his roses, which demanded a great deal of time. But in our entire marriage, he'd never dried a dish or helped cook a meal. It was not part of *our* consciousness.

When Bob realized how much pressure I was under, how little Paul actually helped, and more importantly, how much resentment I'd stored up over the issue, he quietly asked, "Have you ever asked for help?"

The idea of making such a bold request shocked me, and we spent the rest of the session dissecting my reaction. My whole identity of "perfect" wife and mother demanded that I do all the housework and fix the meals. I wrote in my journal:

February 26, 1969 (2nd session with Bob)

> Am I afraid of the closeness of scrubbing floors with Paul? Could this be connected to my fear of his being feminine? Mother again—perfect housekeeper. I think of house as duty. My feminine role. I recognize strong emotional reaction to allowing *anyone* to help. In fact, I think I even resent the kids' help. Why?
>
> I remember a beautiful day—how many years ago—when we all worked happily together. Work should be a source of closeness. Attitude is most important. It feels like *submission*—an intrusion into my feminine world. I wonder if Paul has similar reactions to my working. Does he fear intrusion of his masculine role?

Bob says, 'The most demanding person is the one who demands nothing.' Why can't I ask for help? Why do I *fear* conflict?

February 26 (evening – after session)

Walked into confrontation with both Paul and Lynne. Fantastic results.

Lynne came into the kitchen expecting me to be mad at her. I asked her why I should be. We talked it out. She was so involved she cried. I told her to tell me to 'go to hell' if I was unfair. Terrible 'fight' but no resentment afterwards. No guilt in me.

Paul had me flustered this morning because breakfast was late. I'd expected him to (verbally) pound me about being late. We went to school without nagging. I was so relieved. After school, I found out the reason for the pressure letup was that he didn't *have* a band sectional this morning but hadn't told me. I was furious and left for Kevorkian saying only that 'I was mad.' Afterwards—ice!

After dinner, I went into the living room with him. I knew he'd start (verbally) pounding. He did. I followed Kevorkian's advice and reacted to my feelings—fully. Kids could hear us. Different kind of fight. I told him how I felt about him not helping around the house. I *need* his help. I *want* him to be involved in the family and house.

He was hurt—but it was not a vicious confrontation as it might have been. I wish he'd see Kevorkian with me. We could accomplish so much more together.

We had a fire in the fireplace. Everyone was together for a portion of the evening. Lynne and her boyfriend joined us when they returned from the library. In spite of the 'fight' with both Lynne and Paul, which usually leaves a bitter taste for days, it was beautiful. I know now it can always be beautiful, if I only have the courage to be authentic!

The next session, Bob focused on my parents. He said, "Every girl becomes her mother and marries her father." I objected because there is no way Paul is like my father, and I have done everything to not be like my mother. But that's the point, isn't it? Who we are and how we judge ourselves are according to the standard of who we *think* our parents are. The fact that I had chosen someone so different from Dad was simply marrying Dad's opposite. The fact that I worked so hard to be different from Mom meant that Mom was still dictating who I should be. As we talked it through, I came to see the truth in what he said.

He asked me to describe my mother. I told him how beautiful she was, how she was always dressed immaculately and in elegant taste. How everyone loved her. How she worked in the Mormon temple as a receptionist. "She has beautiful, white, naturally curly hair which she wears like a halo. People are always telling me how her appearance contributes to the holy atmosphere when they enter the place."

He pressed harder, asking what she was like at home. "While I was growing up, she lived through me. I'd come home from school, and she'd always be in bed. I'd get Fudgsicles from the freezer and take one to her, and we'd lie there together, talking about my day. Everything! Dad worked at night so we took long walks together. I felt pressure to have something to tell her. She often made remarks about how jealous my friends were of me. She insisted I wear expensive clothes so that everyone would admire me. She thought I was too fat."

He asked about her being in bed. "She was always tired, often sick. Dad worked nights and weekends. When he got religious, she tried being active in the Mormon Church, but she always quit any assignment she had, usually because of headaches. She went to lots of doctors, but there was never anything wrong with her."

"How did she spend her time?"

"She had a couple of bridge clubs, but other than that, I don't know what she did. She never read anything except women's magazines—occasionally. Mostly, she just slept and waited for me to come home and talk!"

When he asked about Dad, I told him without equivocation that he was the most perfect, the most holy man I had ever met, and that everyone who knew him would say the same thing. He was always doing kind things for people. He was successful in his work. He spent a lot of time in the temple. He was a perfect husband and father.

"Tell me about your relationship with him."

"I didn't really see him that much because he was so busy, but when we were together, it was very special." I told Bob about the lunches we often shared at his club downtown. About how I'd try to stay awake until he got home from the newspaper, after midnight, because he always brought Rocky Road ice cream home with him, and if I was awake, he would share it with me. It is my favorite ice cream to this day. We had many special times together like this."

"Did he ever touch you? Sexually?"

"Oh no. Dad would never do that! He has such respect for girls and women. Why did you ask? The other therapist asked the same question."

"The relationship you're describing sounds incestuous is all."

"What do you mean? Incest!" I was incensed at his remark.

"There doesn't have to be sexual intercourse to have an incestuous relationship. You talk as though your father is the love of your life—that's all."

"Well, of course, he IS!" I exploded with tears. "He's the most wonderful man in the whole world. He is God to me! He's high on a pedestal, and no one will ever take him down!"

I remember the softness in Bob's voice as he assured me he didn't want to pull Dad down from his pedestal. "There's no lonelier place in this entire world than on a pedestal. Especially when you have to stay there, even with your own wife and children. It sounds to me like he isn't involved much with the family, except for his special times with you. You can't remember a single fight he had with your mother?"

"The only fight I ever remember is when they argued over bills for my clothes. I didn't even want them; I longed to dress like everyone else! Their argument only added to my guilt."

"So your father was not involved, and your mother was always tired—or bored. It would be boring being married to an impotent God who could never come down from his pedestal."

"Yikes!" Those words still sting, even all these years later!

☠

After this session, I realized that when I try to think about Mom in the context of my life, she gets short shrift, and when I consider her as one of my parents, Dad takes center stage. But Margie was a woman in her own right, and I loved and admired her and wanted to be like her for most of my early life. I think the relationship started going sour when I found myself competing with her for Dad's love. I now know that our triangle was a classic Electra complex.

But, I couldn't compete with Mom; she was beautiful and vivacious. I remember once being with her in an elevator. I noticed a man staring at her, who finally said, "My, but you're a beautiful woman!" My mother blushed slightly and replied, "Thank you." His retort came quickly. "Don't thank me lady, thank God!"

She always had beautiful clothes and wore them with grace and style. She was never seen in public without being perfectly groomed. Margie was one of those people who *make* a party, without dominating in any way. She was quietly there, her presence known in the little things she did to make you feel comfortable. Conversation usually centered on whomever she talked to as though that person was the most important in the world. She had so many friends she regularly received over a hundred birthday cards.

When Mom died in August 1995, I remember sitting at the mortuary with my father and two brothers, helping the mortician write an obituary. It was revealing. I was the only one who knew anything about her personal life. Dad saw her as an extension of him and kept talking about all of his achievements. I interrupted him twice reminding him that we were talking about Margie—not Jimmy. He added little to the information, and my brothers were silent. They'd forgotten that after my marriage, she'd gone to nursing school and graduated top in her class as an L.P.N.

Once she achieved her license, she began working in doctors' offices, as a receptionist. She was so warm and personable; everyone loved her. She worked a few years, having several experiences where men were "fresh" with her. Being sensitive to any kind of sexual innuendo, she took everything seriously, so how much abuse was real and how much was what most women, at that time, took as positive joking, I don't know. But the story goes that she refused to put up with it and quit her job. She told me privately that Dad didn't like her working because it reflected negatively on him as a provider. One of his advertising accounts was the Utah Medical Association, and he was uncomfortable that his wife worked for doctors he represented. Perhaps, both explanations are valid to some degree. Whatever the reason, it was disastrous for Mom. After she quit, she had little to fill her days.

She had no intellectual interests. She and Dad refused to watch anything on television except sports and Lawrence Welk; she couldn't stand anything that went against her moral principles. They never went to movies except an occasional Walt Disney film, even after Dad retired. She had low tolerance for any kind of violence and sex beyond an innocent kiss; none of this open-mouthed stuff! In her later years, she got interested in the Utah Jazz basketball team, and especially loved watching John Stockton, a white man, run circles around the "black bullies."

Her funeral was revealing also. Each speaker mentioned of her beauty and grace. Many recounted never seeing her look less than a fashion model. She always had a smile and was kind to everyone. What they didn't know is that she slept most of the time and would not go out unless she was in a happy mood, which was less frequent as she grew older and her "pep pills" lost their effect. *I now know that in Utah, which is seventy percent Mormon, antidepressant drugs are prescribed twice as often as in any other state. In addition, Utah leads the nation in the use of narcotic painkillers such as codeine and morphine-based drugs.*[4]

Mom was a hypochondriac. One year, she saw twenty doctors with one ailment after another. For twenty years, she told me she expected to die within months. Both she and Dad refused to explore psychological help, right up to the time she died of congestive heart trouble, which doctors said resulted from her refusal to exercise.

Since she was a nurse, she had access to all kinds of drugs. Her refrigerator looked like a pharmacy. She believed Vitamin B12 shots made one feel better, and she gave the shots to all her friends. If you had a cold or a sore throat or some other ailment, Mom offered to give you just what you needed from her refrigerator. It was scary. She had many different antibiotics and refused to believe the common knowledge that one should take a full dose or immunity would build up. She was her own doctor because the ones she consulted didn't know anything.

After we moved to Anaheim, Mom visited us once or twice a year. It was an ordeal because she didn't like to leave "Daddy" alone, and she hated being with Paul. She loved the kids and wanted relationships with them, but she was uncomfortable being with us, and especially tense with me. I tried to be the perfect wife and mother she'd taught me to be, but it was impossible while teaching fulltime. The housework often suffered. Since I couldn't keep the house as clean as she expected, when I knew she was coming, I'd spend days getting things in tip-top shape. I'd be exhausted when she arrived—all to avert the inevitable comparison with my sister-in-law.

My brother, Eric, married his wife, Doris, shortly after he returned from his Mormon mission to England. She was blond, petite and absolutely devoted to being a perfect Mormon. Her house was immaculate; she was naturally thin and dressed like a model. Mom admired her greatly, and when she came to see me, it was Doris that she talked about—all the time. Over and over again, she'd tell me how Doris was such a great housekeeper; Doris was the best cook in the world; Doris put on the best parties one could imagine. And it was true. She was talented and organized; she was Super Mom!

A major focus for Mom's visits was to remind me how far from her standards I had fallen. To find something amiss, she'd even check the top of the refrigerator for dust. Once, she took it on herself to clean my refrigerator, and because I was so defensive, we had a terrible row. She called "Daddy" and left a few days early. I was glad to see her go, but then felt guilty at my failure to be nice.

While I was seeing Kevorkian, Mom was a big issue. One day, she called to announce she was coming for a visit. The floor of our home was regrettably covered with white asbestos tile in the kitchen, dining room and large family room. It was nearly impossible to keep clean and easily marked by black rubber soles and heels. For Mom's visits, I'd spend hours removing those black marks off the floor. I remember being on hands and knees, with a scouring pad, removing every mark, taking out my hostility on the floor, or on Mom who was the reason for the pressure. By the time she arrived, I was so tired; a fight was inevitable.

I hadn't lost the weight I gained during my pregnancy with Wendy. I felt ugly but also helpless about tackling the problem, along with everything else. Bob kept telling me not to diet because, he assured me, when I dealt with the real issues, my body would stabilize at the weight it was supposed to be. In the meantime, I needed help with the crazy relationship I had with Mom. I knew it was time to stand up to her and invite her into my world as an equal adult.

On the second day of her visit, we were in the backyard, washing down the deck around the pool. She was talking about Doris and what a wonderful mother she was. Then she suddenly changed the subject. "Bonnie, you've got to do something about your weight. How can you possibly be happy looking like you do?"

My body contracted; I gritted my teeth and snapped, "I've never been happier in my whole life!" Screaming inside, I tried to smile and appear calm.

"You must get more exercise. Is there a spa nearby?" she asked sweetly.

"I don't know," I muttered. "If there is, I certainly couldn't afford one."

"Let's go tomorrow and find one," she suggested. "It will be fun!"

I reluctantly agreed.

What I remember of that experience was standing in the weight room wearing polyester slacks and seeing myself in the mirrored wall. It filled me with loathing, and I recognized my reaction as the identical experience I'd had at Bob's the first time I went. I couldn't shake it off; there I was, a fat slob whom I hated!

She was understandably upset, when I broke into tears, and we left the gym. *I've blown it again. She's only trying to help me. I should be more appreciative.* I didn't trust myself to say anything to her, so we drove home in tense silence.

The next morning, while we were again washing down the deck, she asked, "Are you taking the diet pills?"

"No, I gave them up a long time ago. How could I tell students not to take drugs when I was taking them myself?" I could barely control my anger.

Her lips compressed into a thin line as she held back her words. Unable to endure the silence, she gushed, "Bonnie, you need to do something about your weight. How can you go out in public looking like you do? I want to help; I'll pay for the membership myself if you promise to use it."

I could barely breathe. My throat constricted, and my seething voice came from my belly. Measuring my words, I replied, "Mom, I appreciate your offer. I know you mean well, but I don't need your advice. In fact, I'm learning in therapy that some of my current problems come from the pressure you've put on me through the years. I can't live up to your expectations. If I learn to accept myself as I am, perhaps I will then be able to release the weight."

"How dare you blame your problems on me!" she flared indignantly.

"Please quit criticizing me. Must you always compare me to Doris? Why do you come here looking for faults?" My voice was deep and had raised several decibels.

"How dare you speak to me like that!" she fumed.

I thundered, "Just shut up!" As she turned to go into the house, I reached out my hand, intending to stop her, but pushed her into the pool instead. She was fully dressed.

She struggled out of the water, and scampered to the bathroom, crying and dripping wet. Astounded by my actions, I slumped onto a deck chair staring at the water. She changed her clothes, and soon, I could hear her calling "Daddy," telling him she was coming home on the first plane available. She never visited me alone again, which was, frankly, a relief.

☠

Bob helped me see how lonely she was; I came to realize what little freedom she had to be herself. When he'd asked me the questions about Dad's involvement in the family, I realized how little there was. The matriarchy in my own family was the only pattern I knew. I had become my mother. Just as Paul had become my father; although I would never see Paul as God. Dad was a spiritual giant. He was high on a pedestal, omnipotent and omniscient. Untouchable, except for the special times I had with him alone. Perhaps that's why they were so special.

On the other hand, Kevorkian had characterized Dad as an impotent God who had no real authority in the family system. All must stay in their proper places. Mom's control was tacit—unquestionable power by default. No wonder there was so little interaction.

Empathy began to grow. *Does Mom's tiredness come from boredom? Or is it depression? Maybe it even goes back to the loss of her mother who died before she was married, as well as to the stillborn child she's never grieved. Was her need for pep pills a coping mechanism for depression?*

I was compelled to write a letter to Dad trying to explain my insights and telling him that if she didn't find some interests beyond herself, she would likely end up a depressed hypochondriac. I wrote the letter out of my love and concern and begged him to get help for her, as well as be aware of her need for his companionship.

I mailed the letter and immediately got cold feet. If I could have retrieved it, I would have, but it was mailed; the deed was done. I couldn't sleep all night, and the next morning I called and told him I'd sent a letter and was afraid he'd misunderstand it. I told him I wanted to come to Salt Lake and talk to him about it, and asked if he'd pay for the plane fare. He assured me that he'd wire the money, and they'd look forward to seeing me.

By the time I got to Salt Lake, he'd had the letter for a whole day. He met me at the airport, his face like granite. We hardly spoke the entire drive. I squirmed in my seat, not knowing how to open conversation. When we got to the house, we went straight to his study, where we always had our important, serious talks. I'd never seen my father so angry. How dare I write such terrible things to him after all he'd done for me? How could I slap him in the face when he and Mom had given me unconditional love all my life? He went on and on. I was amazed that we were actually talking! He seldom talked about anything important.

When he finished, I told him that I loved him very much. And I loved Mom. I told him I was seeing a psychotherapist who was helping me with my own depression, which was how I recognized the things I wrote about Mom. I said I was aware that I didn't really know what they were experiencing, but I wanted to share with them what I was telling the therapist, out of loyalty, if nothing else. I'd written the letter in concern and love and did not mean to hurt either of them.

Dad recognized my sincerity, and I could feel his anger give way as I talked. When I finished, we sat together for a long time—neither of us moving, neither of us speaking. I could scarcely breathe. Finally, he picked up the letter and tore it into a dozen pieces. Then he said, "As far as I'm concerned, you never sent this letter. Do you understand?" I said I did, and he took me in his arms and held me in the most intimate embrace I'd ever received.

The incident was never mentioned again; however, years later, after his death, I found numerous references to it in his journal. He referred to it as the first "poison" letter I sent him.

When I talked this over with Kevorkian the following week, he was surprised at what I'd done. He assured me I'd been courageous to "walk into the pain" by confronting Dad with my concern. He explained that one could say anything to anyone if one was "speaking the truth in love," and I certainly was doing that. Bob also suggested that the next time my parents were in town, I should bring them to a session. I'd already brought all of the children, except Wendy, who was too young, and it had worked out well.

I wrote to Mom and Dad to tell them about Kevorkian. I explained how I'd been extremely depressed and that I was doing my best to work through my problems, but much of my fear and worry was connected with my relationship to them. I asked if they would come to Anaheim and go with me to meet Bob. To my surprise and delight, they agreed to come the next week. I was overwhelmed by this show of love, especially since they had no use for psychology or any kind of therapy. I guess it was OK if I was the one trying to get fixed.

Bob was amazed they agreed. He thanked them for coming. "You must love Bonnie very much to do this." They assured him they did.

I don't remember much of the interview. I know that Kevorkian talked about general family dynamics and about the problems that arose from low self-esteem. What I do remember was when he picked up his huge mirror and set it in front of my father. It was awful! Dad reacted exactly as I had. He could not look at himself, but scrunched down in the corner of the throne, looking like a frightened old man. Finally, Kevorkian mercifully took the mirror away; Dad was ashen-faced.

Then Bob turned his attention to Mom. He said he had a feeling that she desperately wanted to be held. She didn't answer, but I could see that he'd hit a nerve. He pulled a large ottoman out from under a table and sat on the cushion—all without speaking. Then he motioned for her to come over and sit on it with him. I was amazed that she actually walked over to him. She sat on his lap, and he put his big arms around her and held her like a little girl. At first she was rigid, but soon relaxed, and before we knew it, she was crying into his shoulder. Dad sat on his chair without moving a muscle. When her sobbing began to abate, Bob took his arms away from her and let them fall to his side. He asked if she was OK. She regained her composure and, realizing what had happened, scrambled off his lap.

Dad jumped up, grabbed her arm, and they headed for the door. He told Bob he'd had quite enough, and they were leaving. I followed. The long drive home was silent. No one said a word until we got to the house, and Dad informed me they would fly back to Salt Lake early in the morning. I agreed to take them to the airport.

The next morning, we had a nice breakfast. Very pleasant. Not a word was said about the session. It was as though nothing had happened. We never discussed it.

Dad wrote about Kevorkian in his journal, many years later, although he didn't mention having met him. He said all of my problems "started with Kevorkian, a disciple of the Devil."

I never saw my parents in quite the same way after that. Here I was, nearly thirty-six years old, a mother with five children of my own, and for the first time, I realized my parents were fallible human beings—just like me. It reminded me of how I'd believed in Santa Claus until I was seven years old, defying all my friends because they would never deceive me. When Mom told me the truth, I felt betrayed and embarrassed that I had trusted so much. Now, I felt like Dorothy in the *Wizard of Oz* when the Wizard was revealed to be nothing more than a silly old man. My human god had toppled from his pedestal. My mother's longing for intimacy had been affirmed. I felt like an equal to them at last. We were all just ordinary human beings with ordinary human needs.

---

1. *This Week Magazine, July 13, 1969*
2. *Redbook, September 1969*
3. *LA Times, Orange County, November 26, 1967*
4. *LA Times, February 20, 2002*

CHAPTER SEVEN

Facing Conflict

God's love, which enfolded me in prayer, impelled transformation of my inner life. *Death*—who'd been my companion, sitting on my shoulder—found residence within my being, somewhere in my abdomen. She took with her the undifferentiated emotions that had called her to my aid: fear, anger, jealousy—the dark feelings I'd spent a lifetime denying. Now when I felt their presence, I concentrated on my belly and let her sort through the morass. Simply acknowledging her often changed my perspective. I was no longer stumbling through life trying to protect myself or play it safe, knowing I had a friend within who would come to my aid. Through Dr. Stevenson, I learned that this *pause* was a well-known method of bypassing the limbic brain to access my rational faculties.

Later in life—much later—I became interested in Jungian psychology. I recognized that *Death* was my dark shadow. Jung teaches that we must make friends with our shadow. *Death* had miraculously befriended me.

Without debilitating fear, I became an active participant in my life. When the world was gray, I recognized an opportunity to investigate the feelings and give them names. More often than not, in this simple acknowledgement, the world came alive with color and beauty. People came into sharp focus as unique individuals ready to be discovered, rather than mere extensions of my own needs, desires and projections. The passive child I'd cultivated for thirty-six years was slowly evolving into an adult capable of making intentional choices.

I loved teaching, especially the Sex Ed classes. I was amazed at my students' wisdom and how, when a classmate made a flippant remark, someone in the group would counter them with positive advice they'd received from their parents or church. My desire to avoid preaching and not put my values on them was much easier than I'd anticipated. Young people who hadn't been taught positive values were able to hear from their peers the hopes and dreams that motivated their lives—dreams they may never have considered without such sharing. It brought joy to my soul as boys and girls articulated life-giving values, which strengthened others. I loved the class! It was relevant!

At our teachers' training in February, we were warned about a growing movement to undermine the program. The John Birch Society, an ultra-conservative Christian organization that had worked on anti-communist projects for the previous five years, had turned their attention to the Anaheim Sex Ed program, seeing it as an instrument of Satan and a communist conspiracy. A large number of citizens had gone to board of education meetings, stating objections that had no relationship to what we were teaching. It seemed that Mr. Jensen's fears were being realized. An upcoming board election in April could be crucial. Three of five seats were up for change.

☠

One of the issues I wanted to deal with in therapy was my relationship to the Mormon Church. My discussion with Steve made me realize how much I longed for relationships with people outside the family and band. In my prayer experience, I found a connection with what I believed to be God, but I didn't know who or what God is. The chapel services at Chapman had exposed me to ministers from many denominations in the area. I enjoyed attending on Fridays and found the sermons stimulating and the music inspiring, but the idea of going to one of the churches on Sunday was dismissed as disloyalty to the "only true church."

Since moving to Anaheim, the family had visited a Baptist Church near our home. Lynne's boyfriend was a Lutheran, and she sometimes went with him to youth activities, while also attending Mutual, the Mormon youth organization. The rest of the children were not interested in religion. Band was their church.

Less than a month after I began therapy, my desire for a church heightened. The practice of responding to feelings demanded attention to the insistent longing—without worrying about consequences. I did so on Sunday, March 8, 1969. Here is my journal entry:

> We went to the Baptist Church this morning. Paul agreed to come, and Annie, Wendy and Lowell went also. Annie was reluctant; Lowell was eager. Lynne went to Sunday School at the Ward. (Ron was not mentioned.)
>
> I was strangely excited all morning, and I knew I'd walk down the aisle when the pastor invited people to come to Christ. I had an intense desire to respond. I knew it was irrational, but the longing in my heart could not be denied.
>
> Thoughts kept running through my head such as: *If I walk down that aisle, I'll break Mom and Dad's hearts. I'll be turning my back on them. What will the kids think?* I knew if I did it, I would stand alone—totally—for although I hoped Paul would follow, I knew he wouldn't. I also knew that such an action would be turning my back on my own religion.
>
> As I looked up at Pastor Hoover, I had no desire to step forward to him, but the need to step forward and walk that long way down the aisle was insistent, and somehow I found the courage

to move my feet. My brain tried to make me listen to the foolishness of my action—but the pastor represented the pain Kevorkian spoke of. I was compelled to walk toward it. Almost numbly, I found myself in front of the congregation, shaking hands with him.

I experienced joy at my honest expression of feeling, and I felt exhilaration in the awareness that this was the first time in my life I can remember acting for myself alone without considering the consequences. My action was an acceptance of myself even if it meant denial of the Mormon Church, my parents and my family.

I'll never forget the feeling I had while standing at the front of that church. Another woman joined me, but she was a stranger and I did not want her there. I had a terrible aching desire for Paul to come and stand there too. Pastor Hoover seemed to read my mind and asked the congregation to close their eyes and acknowledge with a raised hand if they wanted to come forward but lacked the courage. I hoped Paul had raised his hand, but I knew he hadn't. I didn't even bother to ask him afterward.

My experience ended when I was shown into a small room, and the woman who'd stood beside me told me to sit at a table. She bumbled through her Bible, glancing at references written in the inside cover, and then, turning to the Gospels, she read something.

The pastor's wife entered and sat down also. She had more scriptures, and it was all very clumsy. She asked if I wanted to join the church, and I said I didn't know. At her puzzled expression, I said I guessed I did—of course— but I knew at the time I didn't. The two women took turns praying, and they waited until I also said something. I waited a long time and then the words came out: "Father, forgive the hardness of my heart, and forgive me for the hearts I am breaking today." It was sincere, but it was a benediction rather than an invocation.

The remainder of the day was beautiful—and very peaceful, in spite of the teasing from Paul and the shock of the kids. We went to Laguna Beach. It was a crystal clear day. Paul and I went into the art galleries. I loved being with him when we are both relaxed. We sat on the rocks watching the ocean and the kids and the black silent cormorants, and I tried to explain myself, but couldn't. Perhaps it isn't necessary. Only one problem disturbed my serenity—the pastor. It will, of course, be necessary to talk to him. Is it possible to explain? Is it truly possible to react to one's emotions in the real world?

Paul asked what I expected the people in attendance would think—many were band families. But for the first time in my life, I didn't care what they thought. It's between me and God—and no one else can understand it. I won't even attempt to explain to anyone—except Bob Kevorkian. But one thing I know: I am no more a Baptist than I am a Mormon!

Wednesday, March 12

The power of emotional honesty should be self-evident. Yet, I believed I was honest before Kevorkian. The difference is not intent—but rather seems to be an openness that allows a clearer view, or understanding of a problem. The mind is not allowed to jump to conclusions. By reacting feelingly, rather than rationally, action occurs before defense mechanisms can be mustered.

Before, when I have reacted emotionally, the emotion seemed to hamper me. There was a kind of tightness, and later I would go over my irrational actions and be embarrassed and experience guilt.

This was not so on Sunday, or the confrontation with Paul or Lynne or even yesterday with another teacher over a school activity. I have felt no need to justify! No need to explain! What freedom. And what power!

As for the tightness? None. Is it that although rationality was present, it was preceded by feeling; feeling was somehow underneath— supportive rather than restrictive?

☠

By befriending my dark shadow, *Death,* my feelings were freed from fear. Although my desire to walk down the aisle was not rational, something in my mind was guiding me as I responded to the desire. I was fully conscious and fully responsible, hence no guilt or feeling stupid. I began to recognize a rational self that could help moderate my decisions. *Would Jung call that self the Animus?* A number of sub-personalities were developing in me. *Am I going crazy?*

☠

On March 3rd, five days before the Baptist Church incident, Paul went with me to see Kevorkian. We shared the time together. My journal records how pleased I was. I believed we could accomplish much more if we went together.

242

Bob talked to him about pain, and Paul's reply was: "The church, with its belief that God is all protecting, serves as a buffer between individuals and pain." *What does church have to do with the fear of acting on his true feelings? This is one of the ways he loses me when we try to communicate.* Bob explained that Paul intellectualizes emotions whereas I distort them. He called it "pseudo-emotionalism." *I need to understand what he means.*

☠

In response to Bob's questions about his childhood, Paul said, "I grew up in a house full of women. My mother, Ella, was a schoolteacher who married a beer-drinking coalminer named George, who smoked Bull Durham cigarettes, not an auspicious marriage in Salt Lake City where drinking and smoking were forbidden by the Mormon Church. My grandmother, a widowed, second wife of a polygamist, resented George, who had married Ella outside the temple, and eventually drove him from the house."

Once he was gone, the grandmother moved in to care for their three children while Ella taught school. Paul's father, William Harris, came along years later, disappearing before his child was born.

When Kevorkian heard this history, he was harsh. He said that when the female authority turned against George, they castrated not only him but also all males. Bob made Paul admit that he had been deserted by his own father. *Is this the source of his ambiguity in taking authoritative roles, at home and school?*

On March 12th, after the Baptist Church drama, Paul and I made separate back-to-back appointments with Bob. Paul went first, while I waited in the office. Here is my entry:

> I am sitting in Kevorkian's office. Paul is talking to him now, and I am alone. Music is blaring. I wish they'd turn it off. I've learned to

243

enjoy silence and the companionship of my journal.

I wonder if I can possibly explain Sunday. I'm afraid it will sound silly. Why should I be afraid? Whom am I worried about impressing? Kevorkian? How stupid! I wish I could get over this need to appear OK in other people's eyes.

Strange how anxious and nervous I am right now. I keep wondering what they're talking about. Will he make Paul hate me? I keep hearing Kevorkian shouting at him, and it scares me. I'm really frightened, more scared than I can ever remember being. Perhaps because I know I will face myself through Paul. I should have considered this before. I should have gone in first.

This is terror! I fear the face I'll see when Paul comes out! How romantic Sunday seems. How insignificant! How safe!

<u>Later that night</u>—I learned so much about myself during today's session. First, I realized how frightened I am of losing Paul. I have never lived through such agony as I did while he was talking with Kevorkian alone. I fully expected to see hatred in his eyes—or else find him gone. I must somehow feel that I've hoaxed him all these years and the sudden realization that Kevorkian would reveal my real self to him was terrifying.

At my first appointment with Kevorkian, he said that walking through his door took real courage—that it was a delivery room for a second birth—and birth is always accompanied by pain. The fear and trauma of walking through that door today was much greater than my momentous decision Sunday. Why?

I believe it's because Sunday I was facing the question of the past—my parents—my religion—I was saying "Amen." But facing Paul meant facing my present self, and I discovered that self cares for him—very, very much! The glow of self-realization was carried back home. We went out to dinner, and I felt *so open—so childlike*!

Afterward, we had a fire. It was then that my feelings for him became too much to bear. Tears came to my eyes. I was *totally* open! Totally defenseless! But he was not.

I tried to tell him about the horror of that waiting room. Of the depths of my caring. Of my fear that he would leave me. His reply? That I feared social disapproval. He doesn't understand. This has never been even a part of my fear. How unbelievably anguishing to find love—and not have him understand!

March 18, 1969

I have noticed an increased sensitivity—not only to myself, but also to other people and the world in general. It often—not always, of course— seems that I am seeing and feeling for the first time. As I search for the essence of my being— as I feel myself becoming *Bonnie*, I also seem to be discovering an increased pleasure in existence itself. The sun seems more golden, the air sweeter and I feel taller. My classes have been so smooth it is amazing. It seems impossible that one's effectiveness could increase so rapidly—almost overnight—but I think the students sense my new self-confidence and this seems to inspire their confidence. My classes have been more open—more honest.

☠

Bob was not the only stimulus for new understandings. Throughout my sessions with him, I was also attending Sex Ed teacher training. As I learned to relate to Bob—to be less flustered at things he said and did, calculated to shock and break down defense mechanisms—I became better able to hold my own in the group sessions with Dr. Stevenson. I often found myself parroting Bob's teaching and received surprised admiration from my colleagues. It felt good.

Kevorkian never minced words, especially in our discussions about sex when Paul and I met with him together. In my journal, I recorded how he'd said that Paul intellectualizes emotions and I distort them—"pseudo-emotionalism." I'd been pondering what that meant, but I suddenly realized it had to do with my disappointment when I told Paul how much I loved him. I understood that my "childlike openness" on Sunday night came from fear of him leaving me, rather than love. No wonder Paul saw through my pseudo-emotionalism. Apprehending that truth made me increasingly aware of emotional distortion and helped me understand how Paul intellectualized his emotion by equating my fear of losing him to social disapproval.

☠

Kevorkian showed me that I had created a structure of reality from which I was seeking freedom, but I didn't want Paul or anyone else to disturb things as they were. I was a Mormon matriarch. I wanted freedom, but feared giving Paul the same right. I didn't like it when he reacted in new ways that threatened my control. The same went for the kids. Seeing the tension in terms of freedom was helpful. I wrote:

246

It is necessary to be free enough to allow myself
the expression of emotion. And others the same
freedom. Do not try to be happy or pretend to
be. Trying is prostitution. I'm going to have to
learn patience—with myself as well as with Paul
and the children.

One night, Lynne and I were doing dishes together. She
had seen Kevorkian and was dealing with her fear of
standing up to me. I don't remember what the issue was, but
she defiantly contradicted something I said. I was shocked,
and before I knew it, I responded with the programmed
script: "How dare you talk to your mother like that!"

When she stubbornly stuck to her position, I slapped her
face, saying, "How could you say such things after all I've
done for you?" I actually hit my beloved daughter. It was
the only time I can remember treating her so badly, but I
realized I'd kept her in line with the tacit threat. My need for
control graphically exploded into my awareness!

☠

As I slapped her, I felt it wasn't really me doing it. I
was aware of being two different personalities at the same
time. The matriarchal self was using the same words Mom
had said to me. The slap came from my fear of losing
control. Another self was coming into being through my
work with Bob; she was getting stronger with every such
encounter. The Bonnie who was struggling for ascendancy
was amazed and happy that Lynne finally found courage for
the confrontation.

The encounter of these two selves was not like the
neutral encounter that came from *Death* when she was on my
shoulder. Neither of these personalities was neutral. Both
had their own agendas, and each was struggling for
supremacy. In addition, there seemed to be another
awareness that was watching the struggle. Both Lynne and I

were shaking when it was over, and she ran to her bedroom, crying.

☠

Before she went to sleep, I went into her room and lay down beside her. I put my arms around her and wept. She hugged me back, and her wet pillow was evidence of how much I'd hurt her. I told her she'd been courageous to stand up to me; I promised I'd never strike her again, and that we'd talk it over with Kevorkian the next appointment. We hugged, and I whispered, "I love you, Lynne." To my relief, she replied, "I love you too, Mom."

Kevorkian emphasized: "All growth is through pain. If it is real, it will be *slow!*" I remember going to my appointment bewildered. I was horrified that I had reacted to Lynne as I had, but during the session came to realize that the shift in family dynamics was affecting every one of us. We were shaking the very foundation of how we related to each other. My biggest challenge was to relinquish my matriarchal role.

Bob reminded me that there are two Biblical mandates that applied to our situation. We are commanded to "honor our father and mother," as well as "leave our father and mother." There is built-in conflict in the relationship itself. Here I was, at thirty-six years of age, still tied to my parents and trying to break free. *How much better for Lynne to accomplish this task as an adolescent!*

Lynne forgave me; now, I must forgive myself, hoping that the pain we were experiencing could save her from even greater pain later on. The difficulty for me was learning how to release parents and children at the same time. I came away from the session committed to the necessity of seeking freedom for everyone. "Seek ye the truth and the truth shall make you free." I'd learned that in Mormon Sunday School, but only now was I beginning to understand what it meant.

I wrote: "I feel uncomfortable because I'm moving closer to 'Bonnie' and away from 'Mother.' My relationship with Paul is confusing because I'm recognizing him as 'Paul' and not 'Dad,' just as I'm recognizing my daughter as Lynne, a person in her own right."

☠

Kevorkian told Paul to "stand up—to feel giant. Then you can look people in the eyes. When you're small, you can only kiss their ass and take their shit!" His language still jolted me. It emphasized my resistance to the forbidden words, some of which I still couldn't say. But as we listened to Bob and realized how right on he was, the repulsion of such words receded a bit. The statement, about Paul standing up, perfectly fit his role in the family as well as his current problems at Madison High where parents were giving him a bad time. And it fit my situation in the training group with the Sex Ed teachers. Seeing myself as a "giant among giants" and spiritually standing taller made a big difference in my ability to enter into discussions.

Paul and I kept returning to the sex issues. Just as he judged my breasts too small, he had his own hang-ups. I felt sad to learn that I hadn't been an adequate partner for him; I'd never thought of him having a secret sex life. I'd assumed I knew everything he thought and felt without asking him. *How is it possible to know so little about a man I've lived with all these years?* Bob recommended a book on sexual technique that was helpful to both of us!

We discussed Annie's intrusion in our bedroom when Paul was washing himself after we made love. She saw him naked, and he hid. Embarrassed, she ran from the room. Bob asked why he had to hide from his own children. I wrote, "Bob told us that our greatest beauty is our nakedness. Children need to know their father has a penis! We slept nude all night. He made love to me again in the morning— with the door open!"

249

As the children found their voices and began standing up for themselves, I began to differentiate my own needs and projections from theirs and realized what a challenge it was to honor the individuality of each person. I now understand that healthy human development can bring this awareness to an average person in their late teens and early twenties. But the choices I'd made, beginning with the decision to get married in the Mormon temple rather than go to college, had led to further choices in which I surrendered my own sense of self to what others told me to say, do and feel. I was emotionally retarded.

☠

The increased awareness of the uniqueness of others directly impacted my teaching. The students in my class were no longer there to be good and allow me to teach, but were there to learn who they were and discover their own purposes and desires. I was there to serve them. My job became not one of discipline, but of listening.

The Sex Ed classes offered amazing opportunities to practice what I was learning and to develop skills in facilitating group discussion. It impacted all of my classes. I was fascinated at the wisdom of the kids when they had a safe place to talk. I'd always had good rapport with bright students who wanted good grades, but now I found myself drawn to those I'd previously seen as losers.

Malcolm was a ninth-grade boy with a high IQ who was in a low English class because he would not apply himself. He didn't cause trouble; he was just bored. He came alive in the Sex Ed class. I remember one particular session where boys and girls met together. A couple of boys planned ahead to shock us by saying it was OK to have sex before they were married. The rules of the class allowed them to say anything they wanted—and these boys pushed the limits. They referred to girls as *pussy* who were in this world to give pleasure to guys. It didn't matter whom you had sex with; sex was about feeling good.

I was extremely uncomfortable. It was the first and only such conversation in my class, and I knew that my interference would make a mockery of the free discussion we had nurtured. After the preplanned slurs were spoken, the class fidgeted silently for several minutes. I was about to step in when, to my surprise, Malcolm came to the rescue. He was a tall, older looking boy, much admired by the rest of the students, who wore his hair long, ignoring school rules. He told the boys who'd spoken, "You're all full of shit. You've probably never had sex with anyone and don't know what you're talking about. Girls are to be respected just as you want respect."

When he finished, other members of the class discussed their feelings about premarital sex. I didn't have to say a word. To my relief, several of the students—boys and girls—said they wanted to wait until the right person came along before having sex.

How I wish some of the skeptical parents had been there. I'm certain that discussion had a positive influence on the lives of the young people present, but the program was being attacked by people who had no idea what we were doing.

The John Birch Society had organized a grassroots movement to get rid of the "filthy Communist conspiracy against our children." As the opposition grew, each of the teachers sent personal invitations to churches in our school area, inviting them to send representatives to the classes to sit in with us to observe what was being taught. I wrote twenty-five letters to groups in my area, but had no reply, nor did a single parent visit a class.

Dissident people showed up at the board of education meetings *en masse* with prepared speeches. Many were Mormons, following the lead of Apostle Ezra Taft Benson, whose son, Reed Benson, was head of the John Birch

Society in Utah. The parents ranted about how immoral the classes were, and yet, they would not come to see for themselves. The superintendent asked teachers to attend as many school board meetings as possible so we'd understand the situation. Because of the needs of my family, one meeting was all I could manage—and that was enough.

A stunning young mother, dressed in a fashionable robin-egg blue suit, her golden hair gleaming in a beehive hairdo, talked endlessly about a plot by humanists, which was undermining the family. She called on everyone present to join the crusade to rid Anaheim of this devious program. She ended by saying, "Jesus is standing at the door—knocking. Will you open the door and let him come in and save us from this peril!" I left the meeting, bewildered.

A few weeks later, the teachers were invited to a luncheon given by the superintendent for people spearheading the opposition. He hoped we could convince them their fears were unfounded. I sat at a table with very intelligent people who politely asked me questions. I answered as best I could, stressing the innocence of class discussions. I explained how I'd talked about menstruation to the seventh-grade boys—without the girls present. I described briefly the excellent movies that informed kids of the biological issues. I expressed my surprise that although the films were meant to generate discussion, students generally took them matter-of-factly and seemed satisfied just to get the information. What they really wanted to talk about was how to react to peers who wanted them to drink and smoke. They wanted information about drugs and dating, and they enjoyed the freedom of talking to each other in a classroom.

The *Anaheim Bulletin* elicited editorials from dissident people. Most disturbing to me was that Steve, my Mormon friend, was accused of having a girl demonstrate how to douche in class. It seemed ludicrous that anyone would believe these accusations, but they kept being printed and teachers had no recourse; to respond would make accusations more credible. We agreed the best response was no response. An article in *Redbook* reported:

> As the nation learned during the rampages of Senator Joseph McCarthy, refutations can scarcely keep up with accusations. An attack on the celebrated Anaheim, California, program contained the news that "as part of the sex training, little children fresh out of their mothers' arms are taught to model sex organs in clay." Sex education in Anaheim begins in the seventh grade and modeling of sex organs is not on the agenda. "It's completely untenable with our philosophy," says Sally Williams, who heads the Anaheim program. The latest charge involving Anaheim is that 50 percent of the girls in last year's graduating class were pregnant. The fact is that there were 37 pregnant girls among the 10,281 girl students in the Anaheim high-school district.[1]

In April, John Birchers won two of three seats on the board of education. In May, the program was in serious jeopardy. A public presentation was planned at the high schools in which junior high students joined high-schoolers to offer simulated classroom discussions. I was asked to choose two students to participate. My first choice was Malcolm. He was amazed to be invited. As far as I know, it was his only honor in three years at the school.

When I checked with the vice principal, he said no student would represent Fillmore Junior High with long hair. I learned that Malcolm was no longer on the football team because he refused to cut his hair. I pled his case, hoping to get some concession because I believed it would be a positive experience for the rebellious young man. The vice principal finally gave in; Malcolm could participate *if* he cut his hair.

When I told Malcolm the next day, he glared at me and said he was not surprised; he didn't care anyway. The next morning, when I met my students before the demonstrations, to my surprise and delight, Malcolm was there. He had cut his hair!

☠

In August, Sally Williams was demoted to school nurse. We received word from the district that Superintendent Paul Cook had stepped down and that Sex Education classes had been canceled. Dr. Cook had been with the district since 1939, except for his military service during World War II. Today, the Anaheim Sex Education program is touted as the first victory of right-wing ultra-conservative groups to successfully dominate school policy.

We were all tenured teachers. Some resigned; some waited for classes to be reinstalled in a new format; some had already found positions in other districts in anticipation of the inevitable. On July 24th, the *Anaheim Bulletin* reported that the Board "left vacant 24 teaching positions in case the sex instruction is abandoned and teachers of this subject are assigned to other work."

As far as I know, those of us who stayed were all given unrealistic assignments. I was placed in a junior high school at the west end of the city, where our poorest students lived. I had six classes of remedial reading, each class between thirty and thirty-five students. There was no attempt to group the classes according to ability, so I had young people in each class reading from first to sixth grade levels. In addition, the school was known for its lack of discipline. It seemed to be a position designed for my resignation. I couldn't see any way to teach these kids anything, but I did my best.

The situation was magnified when they provided special classes for academically challenged students. A month of testing ensued while they identified those students who most needed special help. A portable classroom was brought in and equipped with the most up-to-date materials. The Special Education teacher would have only ten students plus a teacher's aid. Those ten students were taken from my classes. I had at least thirty more just like them, but was allowed no help, and had to beg for reading materials since the enrollment was so high. I was depressed. An excerpt from my journal of October 17, 1969:

> I am aware of definite physical changes since beginning teaching at Washington Jr. High. How are they related to the job and kids?
>
> 1. I feel heavy inside—Puffy.
>
> 2. Poor elimination. Nearly always constipated.
>
> 3. Sexually dead. I feel heavy and dull. Ugly.
>
> 4. No energy to swim, exercise, or do anything physical.
>
> 5. Constant headaches.
>
> 6. Actual pain in neck and shoulders.
>
> 7. Constant nail picking.
>
> Want to diet—but don't! No effort to fix meals or clean the house. No communication with Paul. Little or none with the kids and what is said is forced. My students are a threat. Terrific fear of losing control—or of having any. Constant nagging. I interrupt because they are noisy. I'm the worst offender. I am exaggerating the difficulty of the assignment. Why? I am making problems. Why? I shouted at them—they laughed. I hate the school, I hate the kids, I hate my colleagues. Blaming principal and administration.

I am very angry! Take out my anger on Paul with a messy house and poorly planned meals. I get along with the bright kids. I can appeal to them intellectually, but the others can see through me. They want the real thing. They want authenticity, and I can't give it to them. I'm too exhausted, and they are too many! I think they threaten me because they see through the phoniness. They don't believe in school and books and rules, etc. Do I? When I think about my own schooling, I also thought it was a farce after eighth grade. I went to school to find boys. Their interests are sexual also. Their hormones are jumping. The school system has screwed them, and they know it. And there's nothing I can do.

I resigned after one semester. I'll never forget my last day. The kids had a party that they planned themselves. There were banners and crepe paper streamers and refreshments and cards. I thought they hated me—but they didn't. They *knew* I had done my best.

---

1. *Redbook,* September 1969

CHAPTER EIGHT

Where Is Love?

March 3, 1969

> If Kevorkian is right about conflict being necessary to closeness and love, it is understandable why I have so little feeling toward my brothers. It's often amazed me that I didn't care more about them. When Eric was on his mission, I must have written sometimes, but I don't remember doing so. It's strange, but I can't remember being moved by either his departure or his homecoming. My brothers' marriages meant no more to me than would a wedding of a friend. Even Dick's divorce did not really touch me deeply. Would we have more empathy had we been allowed conflict? Mom would not tolerate even an argument. Perhaps *involvement* is the key here.

In June, my brother, Dick, and his wife, Pat, were sent to Anaheim by his company. Dick is ten years younger than me. We hardly knew each other because I was married when he was eight years old. They rented an apartment two miles from our home. It seemed miraculous they'd move close to us at this particular time. Was it mere coincidence? Here I was, trying to understand my relationship to my birth family, and Dick suddenly showed up! *Would Jung call it synchronicity?*

Dick married right out of high school—to get away from the family. His first wife was a Mormon, but they were not married in the temple. She was immature—I guess they both were—and the marriage lasted only a few months. He met Pat soon after. She was of Italian descent and attended Catholic schools all her life. My parents were upset and worried; however, rather than express their disapproval openly, they tried to swallow their fears and be as kind as possible to make the best of a bad situation.

Pat's Catholic priest refused to marry them because Dick was divorced. She was incensed, and didn't know where to turn. They finally decided on a secular ceremony to be held at the chapel at Fort Douglas near the University of Utah campus. Wanting to establish a relationship with our parents, they asked Dad to find them a Justice of the Peace who could perform the ceremony. Dad chose a Mormon bishop without telling the bride or groom of his religious affiliation. After the wedding, when they learned the truth, Pat, who gives full vent to her emotions, confronted Dad with his deception. Although our parents learned to love Pat, the breach was never completely healed. He talked about it up to his death.

Dick and Pat arrived in Anaheim just as the weather turned warm, and the evenings were comfortable enough to sit outside. All four of us were trying to understand Mom and Dad and how to establish a relationship with them while maintaining the freedom to live our own lives.

Soon, they went to see Bob and began therapy also. We spent many wonderful nights swimming, barbecuing and sitting around the fire ring in our backyard, talking about what we were learning, bad-mouthing our parents and the Mormon Church, and quoting Bob as though his precious words were our new Bible.

☠

I wish I'd kept journals during the year after I quit teaching, but I'm more likely to journal if I don't have anyone to talk to. The eighteen months that Dick and Pat were in Anaheim, I had a real family—people to talk to who were interesting and excited about life. We'd often have Sunday dinner together, swimming before the meal and relaxing around the fire ring at night. Lowell learned to make great martinis and margaritas, and the kids enjoyed the relaxed atmosphere as much as we did. It was wonderful to be free from teaching with its time-consuming lesson plans and papers to grade. I drew out my retirement funds to fill the slack in our budget and bought a piano for the family to enjoy and give me something to do during the long days when the rest of them were in school. I loved taking care of the house, and even got into cooking a bit.

I do have a couple of journal entries dated February 1970, which was right after I resigned. Bob explained, "Love and hate are not opposites. The opposite of both is apathy—lack of feeling. In fact, *love and hate* are not even separate feelings but are intensity of caring. Hatred is love distorted by fear."

I remembered the scripture "Perfect Love casts out Fear." This teaching seemed to be a clue to the morass of emotions I used to encounter when someone asked me, "What are you feeling?" I would return to this statement over and over through the rest of my life as I sought to distinguish feelings. It also reinforced my understanding of the role of my dark shadow, *Death*. When one lives with the reality of one's own death, fear loses its power. *Death* had been swallowed up by God's embracing love; fear had been cast out.

☠

We were still seeing Kevorkian, but since I wasn't bringing in a paycheck, I felt I must quit. When I first began therapy, I'd asked him how I'd know when I was through. He said it almost always took nine months to a year, but I would know when I could "tell him to go to hell." I'd been seeing him weekly for sixteen months and certainly wasn't ready to tell him that, so we agreed I'd see him once a month—just to check in.

Not working meant being home all day, alone with little to do but think. This led to eating and preparing lavish meals in order to feel I was doing something worthwhile. In May 1970, I wrote the following:

> I'm terribly uncomfortable being alone. When all is said and done, all we've gone through comes back to the same problem. I hate myself. I've gained fifteen pounds. Clothes don't fit. I feel gross! Can't even move comfortably. Have exercised every day—until today. Tried to diet. Went all day yesterday eating only what the diet called for and then had tacos for dinner—and it was *my* idea.

> Terrible guilt feelings about Mom and Dad—but I realize they are false feelings. I think I must keep going over everything so I have something to think about. I haven't done a thing. I feel guilty for not doing anything. Think I should accomplish something. I've been taught to base my total worth on looks and doing. But what else is there? More tied up than I've ever been.

All the progress I'd made seemed lost. At a monthly meeting with Bob, we zeroed in on my ubiquitous feelings of guilt. He asked about my problems with the Mormon Church, which we'd never fully explored.

I explained—a bit annoyed at having to repeat the story, "We became inactive after the bankruptcy about a year after Ron's birth." I reminded him about the New York Life problems. "We were filled with disgust about how vicious the elder was to us. He was an authority in the church whom we had trusted. I think this is when we fell away."

Bob didn't buy it. He asked me to talk more about the birth control issue.

I responded, almost in a singsong manner, "We were told in the consultation in the temple before our wedding that we were never to use birth control. In my mind, that promise was connected with my wedding vows. When Ron was born, January 1957, he was my fourth child; Lynne was only four at the time. My doctor told me that I must use birth control, or I wouldn't live to raise the children I had—something about a back problem." I stopped speaking for a minute, scrutinizing my wedding ring. I looked up at him and said with wavering voice, "I agreed to use a diaphragm."

Bob didn't move or speak for several minutes while I felt the full impact of my passionless disclosure. And then I burst into tears, realizing that the guilt I'd suffered all these years was about breaking my promise to God. In my adolescent mind, I'd broken my marriage vows. "No wonder I felt dead when we tried to go to church," I was speaking more to myself than to him.

"Make yourself talk about it, Bonnie," he encouraged.

"The problem was my determination to be perfect. If I followed the commandments, I believed God would always take care of me. When I took measures to keep from having a child, I was directly defying God. After all, is there any event in our lives where we can see God's involvement more than having a baby? To prevent God from sending a child must be the worst sin one can commit."

"How did you feel when you began using the diaphragm?" His voice was gentle but insistent.

"I didn't feel anything. I just put the matter out of my mind, but I've just realized that it was only a few months later that I got Meniere's disease with the fainting and all."

"Is it possible your ear infection manifest the guilt you were trying to deny?"

"I've never thought of it that way, but the timeline fits, doesn't it? I think I believed I had given myself over to Satan. That's why I was so uncomfortable going to church.

When I questioned my father, he twice took me to general authorities who listened to my questions about the theology."

"Tell me again their reaction to your questions."

"I felt as though they were patting a child on the head when they told me to go home and let my husband do the thinking. And I remember that both of them warned me it was Satan who made good Mormons question the validity of the church. It is Satan who lures us away from Truth. Satan must be denounced. I must believe, even if it seems to make no sense.

"I came away from those meetings believing I was filled with Satan. The darkness I was experiencing in Meniere's disease was my own evil. The guilt was springing from some unknown sin I could not even remember."

"Tell me again about the conversation you had with the therapist at that time."

"I told him I felt I was guilty of something, but I didn't know what it was."

"And what was it?"

"I see now that my sin was using birth control." As I spoke the words, my heart broke open with warmth.

"You've also been taught that God is a loving father who does not want you to live in darkness, but in light." Bob said softly, "God is love, not guilt. God would never ask of you something impossible."

After a long silence, in which I allowed my burning heart to inform my mind, Kevorkian reminded me of our first visit. "Remember when you came that first time, and I asked you whether or not you prayed? You went home and experienced God's love. Surely you haven't forgotten that!"

"Of course not. I couldn't have done this work without knowing God was here with us in this room. I've felt the presence many times since. God was with me when I walked down the aisle at the Baptist Church, even though I knew I wouldn't join. Even before I met you, I experienced

His love at Wendy's birth. And I experienced God's presence when I was a teenager, telling me the Mormon Church was true. I felt the burning in my heart."

"How did God talk to you?"

"Well, He didn't actually speak, but I knew it was God…I felt *him*."

"Was it the same God you experienced when you had your vision of Joseph Smith, and when you walked down the aisle of the Baptist Church, and when you gave birth to Wendy, and when you prayed after I told you to? Was it all the same God—or were there different gods?"

"It was all the same God. It had to be. I think I must have *understood* the experience in different ways."

"When you had your vision of Joseph Smith, did he tell you his name?"

"No. Nothing was said, but I felt it was he."

"Why did you think it was Joseph Smith and not God?"

"I'd just been reading about him." A sudden insight flared into my mind. "Oh my goodness! Joseph Smith's first vision was seeing a light over his head, which descended to him. He said it was Jesus and God, but my light never became a personage, only a presence." I closed my eyes and took my breath deep into my belly where *Death* lives to ask my friend if it was Joseph Smith or God.

After some minutes of deliberation, I told Bob, "I probably thought it was Joseph Smith because I had just read the book and wanted it to be him."

Bob leaned toward me with full attention. "Does this take anything away from your vision?"

"Not really. I know the presence was real, and I felt called to do something important with my life—if not for the Mormon Church, maybe for God."

"The vision you had is not uncommon. People have experienced God's presence at all times and in all places.

But when we try to understand experience, we have to use words and concepts. If you had been Roman Catholic, you may have thought the presence was Mary. If you had been Moslem, you'd probably say it was Allah. But whatever we name it, the vision is the same, and it is real." He allowed time for me to digest this insight. And then he gave me the greatest challenge of all. "Maybe it's the God you've experienced that you need to believe in, rather than equate God with the Mormon Church. Remember, the first commandment is 'Thou shalt have no other gods before me.' Isn't it *idolatry* to believe that a church is God?"

☠

Bob Kevorkian was the best possible therapist for me at the time. I'm not sure he was the best for Paul as we attempted to work through years of a programmed relationship.

What a pair we were. My father had taught me to "See no evil; hear no evil; speak no evil." When I noticed something amiss, I'd ignore it and erase it from my mind. Paul, on the other hand, learned how to talk his way out of anything, saying whatever sounded good without worrying about the truth. When I was threatened, I cried and left the scene to replace the discomfort with happy thoughts. When Paul was threatened he talked, faster and faster, until his problem was buried in a mountain of meaningless words.

I took vows during our temple marriage that I would always obey him. When I died, my resurrection was dependent upon him calling my secret name, and I believed that if he didn't, I would be consigned to eternal death.

He ruled our family as his harsh grandmother had ruled his. He was the sole authority; his word was to be obeyed. At times, he was full of fun and spent hours playing with the kids. But when his attention was on anything else—listening to music, working in his rose garden, playing with his trains, reading or driving the car—no one was to disturb him.

Period.   In addition, he was possessive with what he considered to be his.   No one touched his records; no one touched his roses; no one touched his car without permission or his HO gauge electric train.

His anger surfaced often in our marriage, often enough that the kids and I were terrified that some day he would really blow up. My anger was sublimated in self-righteous suffering and self-loathing.

He'd been humiliated as a child and treated me the same way.   My small breasts were the object of jokes beginning after the bankruptcy in 1958.   I tried to understand his cruelty by realizing he'd been terribly hurt and needed to project it onto someone—and I was the closest person.   After reading an article about the revolutionary new breast implants, in 1962 while I was at Chapman, he told me I should look into it—as though we could afford such a frivolity.   His favorite nickname, "Bonnie Big Boobs," was a constant reminder of my inadequacy as a woman.

My other anatomical defect is my large hips. Sometimes the taunt would be "Bonnie Big Bum." The BBB endearment, always said as a joke, was his private means of cruelty; any objection on my part labeled me overly sensitive.

When we had company, he almost always told his favorite joke.   "A man went into a lingerie department to buy his wife a bra.   Not knowing her size the clerk tried to be helpful.   'Are her breasts like grapefruit?'   'No.'   'About the size of oranges?'   'No.'   'What about lemons?'   'No.'   'Could they be the size of eggs?'   'Yes,' he answered, 'sunny side up.'"   He'd laugh uproariously each time, checking out my silent humiliation from the corner of his eyes.

After Wendy's birth, I could not lose the weight I'd gained.   I kept trying to diet, but teaching all day made dinnertime the main family event.   They loved desserts and potatoes and pizza and spaghetti.   How could I possibly lose weight on such a diet?   It wasn't worth trying.   On the one hand, he'd taunt me with BBB, but on the other, if I tried to diet, he'd inevitably show up with a handful of chocolate candy bars as a gift. I'd explain I didn't want candy; I wanted to lose weight, and he'd say, "Well, I'll tell you what, I'll hide them, and when you change your mind, you can go looking for them."

The kids would laugh, knowing I'd do just that; the only thing I could think about was the hidden chocolate. Unable to stop myself, I'd hunt through the house trying to find the candy, while he sat in his recliner, smoking his pipe and laughing with the kids at my stupidity. This scenario was repeated more times than I want to remember.

This game we played so embarrassed me I never discussed it with Kevorkian; we never dealt with Paul's methods of control—only mine. Criticizing him was against my temple vows.

I loved fixing dinner, and I enjoyed setting a lovely table. Once, when I asked Ron what he wanted for his birthday, he requested, "Candles for dinner." We had a round table, large enough for ten people. Someone's friend was almost always staying for dinner. When we had company, Paul was a model host. But when we didn't, we never knew what to expect. When I tried to teach the children table manners, such as which fork to use for the salad, he'd pick up the other fork and tell them to pay no attention to my high-falootin' ways.

☠

When Paul went to Madison High, the band continued to be the center of our family life. There were parades, half-time shows, toilet-papering of our house followed by Sunday pancake breakfasts. We had numerous parties for the band members, and our house became a second home to many. The pool offered a safe place for kids to hang out, including our own. It was a spectacular success.

During my post-Sex Ed year, when I was no longer teaching, I took on the role of mother completely. I was the best possible mother to my five children and also remember feeling like a mother to Dick and Pat. In October, Pat was pregnant. I introduced her to Dr. Marchbanks, which gave us an even deeper connection. She shared her experience of that first pregnancy with me as she'd have done with her own mother, had she lived nearby. I was so completely into the mother role that I saw Paul as another of my children, and I was mother of his band students as well.

Actually, I loved the role. When I was in high school and played Mama in the play *I Remember Mama*, the image stuck. Now that I wasn't teaching, desire for something more began to gnaw at me. Restlessness increased, and even though I loved being home, it wasn't enough. I remember spending long hours trying to imagine some way to augment my life.

I tried to pray, but didn't know how. I'd outgrown the concept of God I'd had as a child, but I didn't know who or what God was, and I didn't know how to articulate my questions. The growing emptiness inside me was often filled by cooking and baking for the family, and then gobbling up the goodies myself, so that I gained even more weight. I felt ashamed of how I looked and went out less and less.

When I saw Bob, I tried talking to him about weight, but he warned me that dieting never worked. He assured me that if I'd concentrate on being authentic with all my feelings, even the ones I judged to be negative, eventually, I'd understand who I was, and my body would reflect my authentic Self.

I desperately hoped this would happen, but in the meantime, the Kevorkians included us more and more in the parties they held at their beautiful home in Irvine, California. I loved the Greek food they served as well as the alcohol. Dick and Pat also enjoyed cocktails, and alcohol became a big part of our lives. This led to more guilt about my parents and the Mormon Church. And the guilt increased the importance of alcohol because it became a symbol of attempted independence from them and the church.

During the summer of 1970, Paul took the family to Yosemite National Park. It was the first and only vacation we ever had. We stayed in the campground, cooked outside, hiked the trails and enjoyed the lovely waterfalls. I was so out of shape I couldn't keep up with the kids, making me vow to do *something*, regardless of what Bob said.

As my struggle with identity continued, Bob's influence began to wane. I knew he'd been the perfect therapist for me. Having a serious church background, he had a context through which he understood my Mormon issues and my unhealthy relationship to Mom and Dad, but I wondered if he were really helping Paul deal with his suppressed anger and his inability to communicate. Also, Bob had his own unresolved hang-ups, especially with diet and church. I never felt comfortable revealing my deep spiritual longing to him.

One of the most memorable times we spent with Dick and Pat was an evening when we listened to *Jesus Christ, Super Star* on the record player. None of us was religious. In fact, a mutual antipathy to church was primary in our relationship, encouraged by Bob. But *Super Star* had a great impact on all of us. I didn't know much about Jesus. My experience in the Mormon Church centered on belief in the church itself. I'd memorized passages from the Bible, but I didn't really know the story. All of us were mesmerized by the play, and we spent hours talking about it. Pat contributed a lot, having gone to Catholic schools and knowing much more about Jesus than the three quasi-Mormons.

I was amazed to think of Jesus being an actual human being. Because we'd listened to the recording, Christmas was more meaningful than it had ever been. I loved the carols and spent much time contemplating the words and pondering their significance for my life. During that

Christmas season, the focus of my thoughts subtly shifted from trying to solve my relationships with my parents and Paul to questions about the meaning of life and what my relationship with God really was. I wasn't hungry enough to begin reading the Bible, but I knew I would some day.

Bob had told me the day would come when I would tell him "to go to hell." That day came in January when I decided to join Weight Watchers. I told him my intention at a party he held at his home. Shirley, another of his clients, surprised that I wasn't drinking or eating the rich food, asked what I was up to. I explained that I'd decided to do something about my weight. She was surprised, knowing Bob would be against it. She confided that she'd recently defied him by going to a psychic named Edith Gable. Bob was against anything like this also. Shirley chattered about the positive influence she was in her life. I didn't believe in psychics, but I listened politely, mentally rejecting everything she said.

The next Sunday afternoon, Shirley called saying she had an appointment with Edith, which she couldn't keep. It was on Monday; would I like to go in her place?

"Why would I want to see her?" I asked, wondering why my heart was pounding.

"She's amazing, Bonnie. I think you'll get a lot out of it."

"How much does she charge?"

"There isn't a charge, but you can leave a donation if you want."

"I don't know; it sounds pretty weird to me."

"It'll be fun. She doesn't know anything about you. I won't tell her I'm not coming. You'll be amazed at what she'll tell you about yourself, and you'll know that she has no prior information. Be a sport and try it!"

Edith lived only a few blocks from us, and I walked to her house on January 11, 1971. I don't know why I went, except I was intrigued and wanted an adventure.

Apprehensively, I knocked at her door, which was answered by a small lady, about sixty years old, dyed red hair, penetrating gray eyes. She was holding a drink of much diluted Scotch, a constant companion, and was surprised to see me instead of Shirley.

"Mrs. Gable?" I began. "My name is Bonnie Harris. Shirley called yesterday and said she couldn't keep her appointment; she thought I could come in her place. I hope that's all right with you."

"Of course," she said kindly. "Come in."

Edith's eyes sparkled as she showed me into the house, leading me down a hall to a small room containing two chairs, a desk and a couple of lamps. The walls were covered with photos. She pointed to several, telling me who the people were and sharing memories they evoked. We sat down; she kept on chattering, almost to herself. I wondered when she'd stop and ask about me. After all, that's why I was there. I didn't care about all the people on her wall.

Suddenly, she stopped talking. After a few seconds of silence, she looked at me with her piercing eyes; her whole manner and even her appearance had subtly changed. Her voice was lower, and she spoke slowly and deliberately.

"Your grandmother is here; she has sent for you."

"My grandmother?" I asked incredulously. "Grandma Myers?"

"No," she seemed to be listening—"No, it's your mother's mother."

Grandma Etta died three years before I was born.

Edith continued. "Your grandmother's glad you came; she sent for you."

I froze. I could feel a presence in that room, but I didn't believe in such things. Edith went on, "Your grandmother wants you to know she loves you very much. She is your guardian angel and has always been with you."

Tears sprang to my eyes. I recalled how, as a young girl, I had used her name, Etta, as a middle name since I didn't have one of my own. I'd always felt close to her because my mother talked about her so often when I was a child. Mom had never gotten over her mother's death.

"There are two men with her," Edith continued. "One has a black mustache and is carrying a lunch bucket. He'd like to share his lunch with you."

Immediately, I knew it was Grandpa Myers, who had lived with us the last few years of his life. I loved to sit at the kitchen table and talk to him. He had a strong English accent and worked as a guard at the golf course where my high school friends played and worked as caddies. They all loved him. Again, I responded with tears, now allowing them to run down my cheeks. My mind was bombarded with memories of crazy things, such as how he loved pickled pig's feet and beer, and my heart glowed with love for the grandpa I'd missed so much after his death. I don't remember who the other man was, and my journal says nothing more about him, only that he was there.

Edith continued, "Your grandmother wants you to realize that all mothers meddle. You take Margie too seriously. She has you knotted up in a tight ball. You need to release her. She's very unhappy. She was jilted when her first love married her best friend. She's lonely with your father and feels guilty about it. Your mother's afraid of death and uncertain of her Mormon beliefs. Your grandmother wants you to talk to your mother and tell her she shouldn't fret about her imperfections—that life is a school—a progression, and that seeing one's faults makes progress possible."

After a few seconds of silence, Edith went on, "Your grandmother is worried and wants you to know that your mother really loves you."

The above conversation was recorded in my journal, or I wouldn't have remembered it. Reading it now, so many years later, my eyes again fill with tears as I realize how amazing the conversation was. I'd never tried to take my mother's point of view. Grandma wanted me to befriend her, and her message proved to be a turning point in our relationship.

After a pause, Edith continued, "Your grandmother knows you'll doubt she was really here when you get home. She wants you to call your mother and ask her about her mother's Kennedy rocking chair. She'll tell you something about the chair that will help you believe."

Finally, Edith said she was happy I'd decided to change my eating habits, that it was a good decision. When I told her I was thinking of joining Weight Watchers, she affirmed the choice. She also knew about Kevorkian and told me that he had been a valuable guide for me, but now was the time to let him go. "There will be other teachers who will come to your aid," she assured me.

Again silence. It seemed her mood shifted to a more somber note. "You're going to go through some difficult times with your husband. Is his name Paul?"

I nodded, amazed that she would know his name.

"He's having problems at work, but no matter what happens, remember that he loves you in his own way. Everything will work out for the best."

She continued, "You will take two trips and come to see things very differently. Everything, even the trees will be more clear. One will be a trip of revelation. You will become less analytical and reach out more to others—to help others."

When I stood to go, I was a bit shaky. There was no charge for the session; Edith said it was God's work. She walked me to the door, and before I left, she looked me in the eyes with great kindness and said, "Remember, God holds the answers no man can give. Seek his guidance. Listen to him." Then she hugged me and whispered, "Bonnie, turn to God."

I left her house, walking on clouds the three blocks to our home, feeling that my grandmother was still with me. Going into the kitchen for a drink of water, I suddenly sensed she was sitting in Paul's recliner. I froze. I literally could not move. Fear gripped me. *Why? Where does the fear of "ghosts" come from anyway?* I stood motionless at the sink, unable to move, trying to force myself to go into the living room to see if she was really there. When I finally willed my legs to move, I tiptoed slowly into the room expecting—what? *I don't believe in ghosts. I don't believe in psychics. I don't believe in any of this!* And yet, I wanted to believe. Once I realized she wasn't there, I felt I'd cheated myself. *Did I cause her to go away? Will I ever have another chance to see her? Am I going crazy?*

I went directly to the phone and called my mother in Salt Lake City. She was surprised to hear my voice since our conversations had been few, far between and very guarded. But now, I was totally present to her, and I'm sure she could sense the difference in my tone.

"Mom," I began, "this is going to sound really crazy, but I want to tell you what just happened." I told her about how I'd gotten the appointment. How Edith didn't even know I was coming, let alone have a chance to find out anything about me. And I told her about her mother being there, instructing Edith to tell me she had been my guardian angel all these years.

Mom surprised me by saying in a knowing voice, "I think that's right, Bonnie. She would have loved you very much—I've always known that."

My eyes watered spontaneously. "This is all very confusing because I don't believe in such things, but Edith said Grandma told her I wouldn't believe it so I was supposed to call you and ask about a Kennedy rocking chair. She said you would know what she was referring to. Does that make any sense?"

Mom was silent for a few seconds and then seemed to get her breath. "Well, as a matter of fact, it does. My mother had a rocking chair in the living room, which was very deep—one like President Kennedy's. When men sat in it, they often lost the change from their pockets. She called it her "club chair" because she used the money she found to pay dues for her club. Otherwise, she couldn't have afforded them. It was our secret. Only I knew about it."

Sharing this mystery united our hearts—even though long miles separated us. I felt closer to my mother in that moment than I had since before I was married.

Before I hung up, I told Mom I was joining Weight Watchers; I was determined to lose weight. Her happiness and encouragement became another bond between us. Grandma Etta's visit accomplished exactly what she'd intended.

☠

CHAPTER NINE

Chrysalis

The fall of 1969, the same year I began teaching Sex Ed at Fillmore, Paul moved to Madison High School. The move reminded me of when he left his successful insurance job for a better position with New York Life. In both cases, he saw himself as upwardly mobile. The word my parents used both times was that he was "cocky." My goal in our marriage was to help him be successful. That's what wives do when discouraged from careers of their own. Paul's success was my success. What my parents called cocky, I celebrated as self-confidence.

In the insurance move, when he realized he'd misunderstood the contract, he had no coping mechanism to deal with the situation. It was the manager's fault, period. There was no attempt to negotiate anything other than bankruptcy. We were young, and although I hoped we'd learned something from the failure, we still saw ourselves as victims.

When he went to Madison High from Sunkist Junior High, Paul was ebullient. He'd built a prize-winning band from scratch, and he knew he could do it again. He was determined to succeed and would soon have the best band in Southern California.

Paul expected to walk into the music program as a hero to students who were fortunate to have him. And he *was* their hero—at least to those who'd graduated from his Sunkist band. But there were other band members who came from other junior highs. Some had competed against

Sunkist. Some had been in the Madison band the year before when, as a first year school, they had done very little.

He was frustrated from the first day because he encountered opposition to his plans from non-Sunkist students. Having few listening skills, he was as authoritarian in the classroom as he was at home. Consequently, he created bitter opposition among those who did not share his expectations.

One night, Pete, one of his faithful Sunkist boys, warned Paul that the "bad" kids were planning to break into the band room and spread mustard all over everything, hoping to ruin their new black-fur shakos, the tall, elegant hats worn in parades. Pete even knew the time of the planned mischief.

Paul was waiting for them when they broke in. He locked the door, turned on the light and called the police. Caught red-handed, they were taken to the police station where parents were called to come for them.

Paul had been decisive, as Bob told him he should be, but his action did nothing to improve relations with the boys or their parents. The principal was furious that he'd used such extreme measures to forestall the prank.

I now realize the growing tension with parents was the main reason he agreed to see Bob Kevorkian, whose advice to him was to "stand up to the bastards and not take their shit." Just as I practiced confronting my parents and the family, Paul practiced confronting his adversaries in the band.

Bob stressed two issues with him. The first was the necessity of facing conflict through honest dialogue, and the other was letting go of his obsession to win.

Paul misunderstood the necessity of discussing problems openly. He missed the point that speaking one's truth and revealing one's feelings—even if it meant saying hurtful things—could lead to a more honest marriage and family. He thought Bob was teaching that we should vent hostility for its own sake. His inability to engage in conversation with me about our problems was similar to his inability to engage his rebellious students and their parents. Kevorkian was trying to help him understand that winning competitions was not all there was to life, that if he'd let go of his obsession to win, the kids would do it for themselves. But he could never "let go" because winning was about self-glorification, and the kids were his pawns.

The problems seemed to abate his second year at the school as seniors graduated, and his students from Sunkist Junior High became the majority of the band.

At the same time, I was depressed. Sex Ed had folded, and I was teaching at Washington Junior High and working with Kevorkian on my own issues. I tried to be supportive of the band, but we hardly talked about what was going on. Later, I learned that although the band was having a winning season, he had persistent problems with the principal and some of the parents. A group of them took him to dinner after the band had won a sweepstakes award, and told him it was a good thing they had won—otherwise they were going to ask him to resign!

Just as I didn't know about his problems with the insurance company until it was too late, he kept his band problems to himself. When I went to see Edith, I was puzzled when she said he was having trouble, until I remembered how, a few months before, some of the older students had climbed the cinder-block fence that surrounded our backyard and dumped several bags of horse manure into the pool, causing considerable damage. Paul found out who'd done it, contacted their parents, and demanded they pay damages.

He couldn't understand why his principal was furious at him when the kids had vandalized his property. The possibility of sitting down with the boys and their parents to work through the problems was never considered. He'd heard Kevorkian's advice to "stand up to the bastards," but had not grasped how conflict could invite closer relationship if faced with respect and a willingness to listen. How different it might have been had he listened to their complaints and sought solutions to the problems together. Knowing those parents, as I did, I'm certain they would have made financial restitution without Paul's uncompromising demands.

☠

While Paul was dealing with his problems at school, I committed myself to Weight Watchers. It's not easy changing one's eating habits when you're a mother of six— counting Paul. I was determined to eat according to the prescribed program and adjust the food for the rest of them as best I could. I reasoned that we could all benefit from eating less red meat and desserts; it was a unilateral decision, but I was determined. If they wanted something other than what I fixed, they'd have to fix it themselves. They were old enough.

We struggled throughout January. I ate only what was on the diet and tried to make meals as enjoyable as possible for the rest of them. There was a lot of kidding—especially from Paul who ridiculed me mercilessly. He didn't believe I was serious, and I didn't blame him—I'd been on so many diets before, why should this be different? I don't think he saw how cruel his jokes were. He played the game of hiding candy bars, which he'd done before, and although it was difficult for me to resist searching for them, somehow I managed to ignore him. He could make me the family laughingstock if he wanted, but I was not going to give in.

Eating fish was a real challenge. At that time, three to five meals of fish each week were required, and I had to learn how to cook it. Once, I heard Lowell call to Ron asking where I was. His reply, "She's in her aquarium fixing dinner." Ever after, when I saw the window in the oven, I couldn't help chuckling at the remark.

For our anniversary on February 7, Paul brought home ice cream and cake along with a dozen roses. It was a family celebration. How could I refuse to take part? But I did—and with grace as I remember, telling him how much I appreciated his thoughtfulness, but explaining I did not want the sweets. If he really cared for me, he'd understand and help me succeed.

The next week, Valentine's Day, offered another excuse to celebrate. I fixed the family baked chicken and mixed veggies, with potatoes and rolls for the rest of them. I carefully weighed my portion so that I could stay on the program. After dinner, he went out to the car and brought in a gorgeous Boston Crème Pie—chocolate, with loads of whipped cream. My favorite dessert! I was devastated.

Sitting at the table, I stared at the pie, trancelike, until Paul handed me the silver pie server and plates to serve them. Sudden anger flamed inside me, filling me with rage, and then, being true to my feelings, I put down the cake server and thrust both hands into the cloud-like whipped cream, squeezing it between my fingers. My fury dissolved into tears. I sobbed and squeezed, and when I looked up, the whole family was staring at me in disbelief. I hurled some of the cake at Paul and seconds later, a full-blown food fight erupted, with Paul, the kids and I all lobbing handfuls of gooey ammunition. I still smile remembering our hysterical laughter and the horrible mess I had to clean up afterwards. But that ended the teasing. I finally got their attention, and, even though the family continued to complain about the menu, I realized I'd established a new kind of respect.

As I began losing weight, it became easier to fix meals they wanted and not be tempted myself, but I still had to watch desserts. I tried to find sweet alternatives to cake and pie and cookies. One day, I relented and heard Wendy tell her sister, "You'll never guess what Mom's doing. She's making a cake, and it isn't even anyone's birthday!"

An important insight from my struggle with diet came through noticing two selves inside my head, each with different agendas. One firmly told me not to diet because I'd never be successful; why not enjoy myself and eat what I wanted? The other begged me to stay with my program and lose the weight. Back and forth they'd go, until I was worried again that I was going crazy, hearing voices in my head. Then one day in the midst of an internal argument over a cookie, I realized there were not two selves but three. The third was aware of the other two—watching them argue. I'd noticed her before when I slapped Lynne. She was calm and neutral and didn't take sides. I wondered if the detachment I'd experienced when *Death* hopped onto my shoulder had anything to do with her. I came to call this witnessing self, my Soul. She lives in my heart.

☠

In the months preceding their baby's birth in July, Pat and Dick took Lamaze classes, which were now a routine preparation for natural childbirth. I was intrigued when she talked about their lessons, having experienced the power of focused breathing when Wendy was born. Pat also went to see Edith, who predicted they would move to Seattle and have two other children there. Dick was transferred a month later, and they left Anaheim in February. I'm grateful for the time they lived near us; we had bonded as family and friends. Our friendship would withstand many difficulties, but last the rest of our lives.

I'd noticed a yoga studio within walking distance of our house, and remembering that Lamaze was based on yoga breathing, I signed up for classes shortly after they moved. I hoped it would help fill the void of their absence.

My heart warms as I remember Marley Stevens, my yoga teacher. She'd been a Broadway actress in her earlier years. When I met her, she was probably in her sixties. Her voice was strong and mellifluous, and I knew from the start

280

she was one of the teachers Edith said would take Bob's place.

With no understanding of the process of spiritual growth and lacking the vocabulary to think about it, I knew Marley was taking me to a place inside myself that was sacred and true. I especially remember the day she taught us the "cobra." We lay on our bellies, tucking our chins into our necks, slowly lifting our heads until we needed our arms. Slipping our hands in front of our chests, fingertips forward, we raised our heads as far back as possible, holding the posture while breathing slowly, eyes closed, no tension on the face. While I was doing the posture, I felt graceful for the first time in my life. I had always experienced myself as awkward and clumsy; as a child, I'd never taken dance lessons for that reason. But now, lying on the floor in a yoga studio, I was an elegant swan, my neck stretching up to the sky.

I began doing yoga every morning—at home when there wasn't a class, and three days a week with the group. Sometimes I'd practice relaxing postures before going to bed at night. I remember peace filling my soul, deeper and more profound than I'd ever experienced.

In February, Edith invited me to a meditation class she was teaching in her home one night a week. I didn't know what meditation was, but I trusted Edith. I learned to center myself with breathing, realizing it was the same practice that *Death* had taught me when she left my shoulder and moved to my abdomen. She'd taught me to distinguish specific emotions, and name them, and once I knew what I was feeling, my responses became more appropriate. My acceptance of *Death* removed much of my fear and proper response eliminated guilt.

Edith taught me a whole new concept of prayer. Instead of petitioning God for what I wanted, I learned to become still and await divine presence. I began meditating using a simple breathing pattern, which was added to my daily routine.

One night as I was meditating in her class, I experienced an unusual degree of stillness. I observed a circle forming itself and whirling downward. My witnessing *Soul* recognized the spiraling energy as that which accompanied Ron's birth. Making a split-second decision to trust, I relaxed into acceptance, watching dispassionately as the spiral hit bottom, becoming the pulsating dot I'd feared before. The dot opened up into a tunnel, revealing a light at the other end, which beckoned me forward. Unfortunately, Edith brought us out of the meditation before I could respond, but my *Soul* holds the image in my heart. I realized the dot I'd feared in the recurring dreams was an invitation to explore a deeper part of myself—fourteen years earlier. Had it also manifest itself in the swirling vertigo of Meniere's disease? I opened wet eyes with a glowing heart, unwilling to share the sacred revelation, meant only for me.

Little by little, the empty space in my life filled with amazing energy, all coming from within—not dependent upon a job, or Paul, or Kevorkian, or even my children. The image of the caterpillar retreating into the chrysalis is an apt description of my new life.

☠

In April 1971, the tension in our marriage increased dramatically. Paul often left the house after dinner and was gone until very late; when he came home, he would not talk. I begged him to communicate. Thinking his behavior was due to problems with the band, I longed to share them with him, and yet, I also wanted to give him space.

His unwillingness to communicate was agonizing. I kept falling back into self-accusation. *It's got to be my fault. How often has he called me a bitch? How often has he gotten upset because I nagged him to talk to me? He just wants to sit in his rocker and smoke his pipe and be left alone. Why can't I leave him alone?*

I tried to sleep and not worry, but ended up pacing the floor—back and forth between kitchen and bedroom. Determined not to break my diet, I somehow found the will not to eat, knowing that the program was my lifeline to sanity.

I'd lie on the bed, wondering where he was. *Is he OK? What if he's had an accident?* He said he sometimes went to Laguna Beach to listen to the waves hitting the cliffs. I asked why he didn't take me with him. He just sneered, saying he didn't need my questions.

For several months, we'd planned a band trip to San Francisco. We'd not had a vacation together since early in our marriage, and even though we'd be with students, there were enough parents chaperoning that we'd have evenings free. For my birthday, we went to an Armenian restaurant, wanting to experience Kevorkian's world. The food was wonderful; the evening a nightmare. Somehow I'd upset him and I didn't know what I'd done. He was gloomy and sad and absolutely silent. I tried tactfully to invite him to tell me what was wrong, but he clenched his teeth, anger glaring from his eyes in obstinate silence.

A week later, Jane, one of his banner carriers, came to the house to swim. She and Lowell had dated, and they seemed to like each other. Paul and I had taken them with us to the Shakespeare festival in San Diego the summer before. I fixed tacos and salad, and while I was cleaning up, I could hear the three of them outside, sitting around the fire ring, laughing and talking. How I wished Paul would be like that with me. I rejoiced that her company could bring him back to himself!

One night, sometime in May, he came home at 2:00 AM. I'd gone to bed at midnight, worried about where he was, feeling helpless and scared. When he came home, he tiptoed down the hall, trying not to wake me as he slipped into bed. I was staring at the ceiling, wondering where he'd been, concerned he was depressed. I snuggled up against him and stroked his face. He was like stone.

I begged him to talk to me, but he turned over and would not speak. Beside myself with frustration, I could no longer stand the silence so I scratched on the pillowcase. He told me to stop. I said I wouldn't stop until he told me what was going on. It went on like this for a few minutes. He raised his voice and again told me to stop. I refused. The next thing I knew he'd thrown me off the bed, face down on the carpet and was sitting on my back, pounding me with his fists. I cried out, but he wouldn't stop. I could hear the kids crying in their bedrooms, and then suddenly, Lowell yelled that the police were driving down the street. Fearful silence descended. Paul swore, whispering that neighbors had probably called the police because I'd screamed. I was so scared I couldn't breathe. I remember feeling guilty I'd made so much noise! It would be a disaster for the police to find us that way. No one made a sound.

Finally, Lowell came to our closed bedroom door and told us the police car had gone. He whispered angrily, "When will you two grow up?" Paul helped me onto the bed. I was dazed. He made love to me; we both cried and held each other all night.

The next morning, I could barely move. I didn't know whether anything was broken or not, but my whole body was swollen and sore. I turned black and blue and didn't dare go out of the house. I recalled how he'd beaten Lowell when he was in junior high. But foremost in my mind was hope that the release of tension might lead to openness and authenticity.

☠

In June, Lynne and Jane both graduated from Madison High; the band played at the ceremony. Paul came home with three corsages: for the two girls and me. I wondered why he'd give one to Jane, but he explained that we were taking her with us because her parents were not going. It felt like another double-date. I loved being part of Lowell's life, and Jane was like my own daughter.

The stress let up for a couple of days, but then the late nights began again, and Paul moved into Wendy's bedroom so that he wouldn't disturb me when he came home. I wondered if he was still going to Laguna Beach to meditate and sort things out. I don't remember the sleeping arrangements for the girls, but assume they were all three in Lynne's bedroom. I'm sure they didn't want a repeat of the terrible night we'd experienced a few weeks before.

Now that the school year had ended, Paul was teaching summer school, and even though the pressure was gone, his moodiness continued. Our kids were in his summer band, and they assured me he seemed happy at school and more relaxed than he'd been for several months, but when he came home at night, he brought gloom with him. I was beside myself.

One night, he didn't come home until 3:00 AM. I was so worried; I even wondered if he'd committed suicide—he seemed that depressed. I was waiting in the hall.

"Paul, where have you been?" I demanded, trying to conceal the irritation from my voice and express only concern.

He glared at me with absolute hatred. "Leave me alone, you bitch! Do you hear me?"

Worried he'd hit me again, I returned to my bedroom, shutting the door, leaning against it, frozen with fear and rage. I remember shaking so hard I fell to the floor, sitting there crying, trying not to make any sound that would further intensify his wrath. Crawling to the bed, I buried my head in the pillow to stifle my sobs and finally fell asleep. When I awakened, he'd already gone to school.

What should I do? How can I help him get through this terrible time? I cleaned the house extra carefully and fixed a salmon salad, making it as attractive as possible. Then, setting the patio table, I waited for him to come home for lunch. I swam, did my deep breathing and meditation, willing myself to be calm and centered, determined to be happy and make him love me again.

I was sitting outside when he came into the house. "I've fixed lunch on the patio. Come and join me," I called to him. He looked more relaxed as he sat down; I was careful to not speak throughout the meal. I just sat there trying to bring up happy thoughts about how much I loved him.

When he finished, he stood to leave. I panicked. "Paul, can't we talk? Can't you spend a few minutes with me and tell me what's bothering you?"

His eyes glared. "I thought maybe you'd learned how to be quiet—but that's too much to expect, isn't it?" All the feelings I was trying to repress surged upward through my body. He must have seen the rage in my eyes because he seemed frozen midway between sitting and standing. I grabbed the nearest thing, my own uneaten salad, and in slow motion, dumped the slimy food on his miserable head.

"How dare you!" he softly thundered. Horrified at what he might do, I dashed to the other end of the pool. He came after me; I streaked back to the table and grabbed a saltshaker. As he came near, I hurled it at him, missing by a good yard. It crashed into the side of the pool, and we both froze, watching the shattered glass disappear into the water.

We stared at each other, rigid as statues. Finally, he announced he was leaving and not coming back. I watched him march into the house. Annie was there—I don't remember who else—but she was furious I had attacked their father. She ran into the bedroom where he gathered clothes from the closet and stuffed them into a suitcase. I sat on the patio, paralyzed by what I'd done, ashamed of my behavior, crying over my lack of patience. *I'm no good. Just a selfish bitch. No wonder he's leaving me!*

The following days were difficult, especially since the kids were so angry at me. I'd carefully withheld from them what I was going through, not wanting them to worry. It was my obligation as his wife to never say anything that questioned him. That was my vow in the temple. The children didn't know about the intolerable nights and his lethal attack on my soul. In their eyes, it was my fault; I had erupted and driven their father from our home.

I worried where he was, concerned that he might be living in some fleabag apartment, but the kids saw him at school and soon became more relaxed, letting me know he had a furnished apartment and seemed very happy. They'd promised him not to tell me where he was. I wondered how long he'd had the apartment—if that was where he spent the late nights, but firmly dismissed the suspicion. I told myself he just needed time to be alone and think things through; the situation at school was difficult, and he certainly didn't need me pestering him with my paranoia.

I didn't know enough then to question the collusion of silence and secrecy with the kids. I was now the enemy, and they were protecting Paul from the bitch. In desperation, I held on to what Edith had said six months before, that when things got difficult, I was to remember he really loved me— in his own way!

Through it all, I stayed focused on my program. I didn't have a car, but one of the women in my Weight Watchers class lived in the area and gladly took me to the meetings. The yoga class was a couple of miles away; I enjoyed walking and welcomed the additional exercise. I swam in the pool—sometimes several times a day and was consistent in doing my yoga and meditation.

In the evening, Wendy and I and any of the kids who were home, walked to the shopping center for a treat of some kind. I found a shop that had sugar-free licorice; it became my reward for staying on the program. The weight continued to drop off, and I felt more alive physically than I could ever remember.

I was lonely, of course. I remember standing on a street corner on Sunkist, watching cars go by, almost all of them with a couple in the front seat. Everyone seemed so happy! I wondered if I would ever have a partner again. Would it be Paul? And as the time went by, I began to think about the possibility of meeting someone else—someone who would love me and appreciate who I was.

The inner grace I'd felt while doing the cobra/swan in yoga class became more and more present to me. I had lost so much weight my clothes no longer fit so I began sewing again to fill the empty hours.

One night, I got a call from the principal at Sunkist Junior High telling me Ron had stolen liquor out of our cupboard and given it to an eighth-grade girl. She'd ended up in the emergency room of the hospital and had her stomach pumped. I felt so helpless! How I wished Paul was there to handle the crisis. But he wasn't, and something needed to be done. I told the parents we'd pay the hospital bill, but they assured me they had insurance. I could see concern in their eyes when I explained that Paul wasn't home, he was living by himself for the summer—needing solitude. I remember their compassion and how my situation seemed to override concern for their daughter.

I explained to Ron he must be punished. He was looking forward to a drum major camp in July, and I told him he didn't deserve to go—his behavior was not that of a drum major. I requested the principal to withdraw his name. It was a severe punishment, which I regretted for many years, wondering if I'd been too harsh—somehow taking out my frustration about Paul on my son. Years later, Ron told me the incident was pivotal in his development. Before that, we were so lax about his whereabouts he wondered if we really cared. He thanked me for doing the "just and right thing." We never know how our decisions will affect others in their lives.

The first of July, Paul showed up with a check for groceries. He was so hostile and cold I was glad when he left, and began to relish the possibility of life without him. I should have looked for a job, but how could I without a car? Besides, in the one interview I'd had, I was informed they were not hiring anyone who'd been involved in Sex Ed classes. I decided to enjoy my summer and worry about getting a job later, clinging to the hope that our situation would work out.

The end of July, Paul invited me to go to the band concert, which he'd been preparing all summer. It was good to get out of the house and do something, and I thought our problems might be over. We had such a good time that we went to a movie the next night. The following evening, he came over to the house and said he wanted a divorce. I wrote this letter to him:

Dear Paul,

Last night we had a lengthy discussion about divorce, and I was surprised at my strong feelings against legal action—especially since I've held equally strong desires in favor of an immediate settlement. I could not express my feelings to you yesterday because they were only vaguely formed, but I've been awake all night, again—and have come to several understandings which I'd like to share with you—realizing of course, that feelings change, and I might think differently at the very minute you are reading this.

I recognize three distinct reasons for not getting a divorce at this time. I will try to explain as well as I can.

<u>First</u>—I don't think either one of us knows exactly how we feel at this point. If my feelings

289

vary so greatly from day to day, and if your feelings also vary as much as your manner indicates, I certainly do not think we are ready to come to a conclusion as final as divorce. I am not ready. Give me a few months, and I will probably know and understand myself better.

Right now, I am enjoying a welcome release from hostility. In the past few weeks, I have gone through the hell of my fear, jealousy, self-pity. I have tried to hate you—but there is no reality to the hate because the hostility hate feeds upon has long since disappeared. I can't even be angry with you—but neither do I love you. There is only a tremendous emptiness inside of me, which can best be described as a question mark. Until the question is resolved—as long as strong feelings toward you remain, whether negative or positive—I do not want a divorce.

<u>Second</u>—I have the curious feeling when you're talking to me about myself that we are discussing a third party! The things you say would have wounded me several months ago. Your cutting remarks would have made me bleed last year—but not today because you curse a Bonnie who no longer exists.

You told me last night that I was more beautiful to you than I've ever been. You were speaking about my physical self. The change here is considerable. I am simply a different "looking" person than I was a year ago. What you fail to realize is that the change has been internal and spiritual, and that the physical appearance is only an outside manifestation of what has taken place inside me. If you had called me a fat slob a year ago, I would have been crushed by the insult. The same remark today would mean nothing because I know it does not apply. Likewise, when you call me a "domineering bitch," I recognize that once it might have been true, but it no longer describes who I know myself to be.

The last few months have been remarkable— ever since December. Something happened within me that released hostility, and for many months, I've experienced inner growth that has transformed my life. Mrs. Gable foresaw it and recognized its occurrence. The weight loss and the change of appearance were a result of concurrent spiritual growth. For the first time in my life, I'm experiencing peace with myself and a capacity to love.

How ironic to realize that all this time when I was glowing with new life and hope, you were sitting in the rocking chair, judging me, wallowing in self-pity, picking your nose and scratching your hands from the tension of hostility. It seems strange that I didn't realize— but I truly didn't. You have been like this so often during our marriage; I simply attributed it to the pressure of the band festival and your unhappiness in your job.

Last night, you said I could never change—that I would always be the "domineering bitch." I already have changed, Paul, as surely as my appearance. The hostility in you is not gone. It glares out of your eyes; it closes your mind; it distorts your vision. You also can change. I believe you will.

I do not want a divorce until we can face each other as we truly are. When the ugliness and anger and hostility have gone, then, if we can look each other in the eyes and say there is nothing between us, at that time, we will be ready for a divorce.

<u>Third</u>—The least important consideration to me at this time is money, but nevertheless, it is a consideration.

On the practical side, neither of us knows where we stand financially. Your job is a question mark, and I don't have one yet. To make a financial settlement at this time is ridiculously premature. If you insist on such a decision, I will be forced to get from you every penny I can, simply because I have no source of income and am responsible for five children—we must live. On the other hand, in a few months, the entire picture could change. Even Bonnie the Bitch was never out for your money.

A divorce would accomplish nothing that I can see except strap you with a premature obligation and attorney fees, which we certainly can do without at this time. How much better to use that money for Lynne's schooling!

Money has been a source of fear for me all our married life. The biggest struggle I've had in the past weeks has been going through the hell of that fear. But I have gone through it! For the first time, I feel that I can put my life and the lives of our children unconditionally in your hands. I trust you completely. You know our needs better than I do. I know you love them and will do all you can for us. What more can I ask?

It is a wondrous feeling for me to experience this trust and confidence. How much better to end our relationship like this, than with the bitterness of a legal financial obligation.

Affectionately, Bonnie

A few days later, I received a letter from Paul telling me that he loved me and wanted to start fresh. I wrote back:

August 4, 1971

> Dear Paul,
>
> Thanks for the beautiful letter and the welcome revelation of the depth of your feelings. I am confused by many of the things you say, but tremble with joy at the current of electricity I felt while reading your words.
>
> How can I reply on paper? I am simply not that gifted with words. Besides, the very act of writing seems to distort meaning and where such personal matters are concerned I cannot take a chance on distortion. Perhaps some day, we can speak frankly and openly face to face.
>
> You say you would like to court me and fall in love, etc. But you kill the possibility of real courtship by assuming we will fall in love. That is the unknown; that is the future. But an evening together, Bonnie and Paul with no obligation or demands or pressure, that is entirely possible. It would be part of the present, and it is as intriguing to me as it is to you.
>
> The one constant in this world is change. You are changing. I have changed. Our situation also has changed—totally. Our relationship must also change. We will never again be able to relate to each other in the old way.
>
> The excitement of the future lies in the present possibilities. Your companionship is a possibility I find very desirable.
>
> Sincerely, Bonnie

The actual letters were lost long ago, but luckily, I'd drafted these two in my journal. What a gift it was to discover them. Mainly because I realize how much I'd changed in eight months. The cringing, self-hating Bonnie seems to have vanished, and I actually *like* the woman who wrote these words while in such chaos. One of the greatest lessons of my life was learning that real transformation demands acceptance of pain and loneliness, and discovering I could move into it—like moving into the pain of a good stretch in yoga—taking a few deep breaths and finding I could stretch much further than I'd ever thought possible.

CHAPTER TEN

Betrayal

The two months of separation from Paul were preparation for the traumatic events about to unfold, and I'm grateful for that precious time. I was like a caterpillar that had crawled into my chrysalis and was about to be reborn. The actual birth happened like this.

Several nights after I'd written the August 4th letter, Lowell awakened me from a deep sleep. He burst into my room, breathing heavily. "Mom, wake up! You'll never believe what just happened!"

Still groggy, I sat up in bed. He came over to sit next to me, his whole body shaking with rage. I reached out and touched his arm, waiting for his breathing to slow. "Now then," I whispered. "What could possibly be so terrible?"

He sat silently; his body gradually relaxing a bit. I reached up to touch his face, surprised to feel damp tears on his cheeks. I couldn't remember Lowell crying since six years before when bullies beat him up on his way home from junior high. The tears got my full attention. I was now completely awake.

He was working at A&W Root Beer on the late shift that ended at midnight. He said that Jane was now a hostess at Coco's a few blocks away, and she got off fifteen minutes later. He'd called her at home earlier to see if he could meet her after work and go out for a snack. Her father was surprised at the call because she'd told him she had a date with Lowell and would be home late. After work, he drove his motorcycle to the restaurant and waited for her to come out. When she saw him, she seemed flustered. He suggested they get a bite to eat, but she was tired and wanted to go right home. He felt brushed off.

Puzzled by her coldness and the earlier discussion with her father, he had a premonition to drive to Paul's apartment. He parked his bike on the street, walked into the apartment complex and waited in the shadows. Sure enough, in a few minutes, Jane drove up, parked her car and let herself in. He hung around for some time, waiting for her to come out, but she didn't. Finally, about 2:00 AM, he got on his bike and came home to tell me.

"Jane? Paul?" I couldn't take it in. *Why would she be in his apartment at this time of night? Oh no! Is this the explanation for all the late nights? It can't be!* My mind raced but was soon called back to my son, who cried bitterly, "How could she go for an old man over me? What does he have that I don't?" Humiliation thrust him to his feet. Silhouetted by moonlight, he paced back and forth in the room, understandably unaware of my stake in the information. Taking a deep breath, I willed myself to focus on his agony.

"Remember, Lowell, we don't know why she was there." Summoning *Death* to calm my concern, I cautiously broke the silence. "We don't have any real information. It's easy to jump to conclusions. We need to get some sleep and deal with it in the morning." He again sat on the edge of the bed. We cried together, our words disjointed syllables, for some thirty minutes. *Should he tell Jane's parents? They'd have to know eventually, of course.* He left the room; his shoulders slumped with grief, hoping to clear his head through sleep.

I lay there, looking at the ceiling, my mind blank, but surprisingly, no fog. I couldn't imagine what was going on, and I certainly couldn't think what would come of it all. About 3:30 AM, I heard Lowell leave, and wondered where he'd go. He was so angry. *Please, God, protect my son! Protect us all!*

It was then that I began to cry, softly at first, but soon my sobs engulfed me. This time, I didn't hide them in the pillow, giving free reign to express whatever emotions I had. I still remember how honest it felt, crying my heart out until I fell asleep.

The next morning, Lowell came into the kitchen about 10:00 AM. The other kids weren't around; I don't know where they were.

Sitting at the dining room table, he described leaving our house and going back to the apartment where, sure enough, her car was still there. Enraged, he drove to Jane's house and awakened her father.

"Jane didn't have a date with me!" he shouted. "She's with my old man—right now. In his apartment!"

Lowell said he felt better having done something, but didn't know how he would ever face his father or Jane again. He was too angry to hang around, so he left the house without a specified destination. "Please be careful," I shouted after him. "You're upset and that's when accidents happen."

"Don't worry, Mom. I'll be OK." And he drove off on his motorcycle.

I desperately tried to think. *How can I face him? So many unanswered questions.* I made myself a cup of tea, acknowledging the vacuous presence deep inside my gut. *What will I say to him if he comes here?* And I was certain he would come; he could no longer hide his deception. I stripped off my clothes and swam laps until I was physically tired. Clothing myself in my terry robe, I felt better able to handle whatever came.

Sure enough, early afternoon, Paul rang the bell. When I opened the door, I was faced with a desperate man who seemed to have aged ten years. His red, swollen eyes were full of fear, and his voice quivered.

"Come in. After all, this is your home." My voice was flat—certainly a giveaway that I knew what had happened.

He stood helplessly by the closed door, giving into tears. I couldn't bear to look at him, so I turned my back, sank onto a dining room chair and let him cry. He shuffled through the living room and stared out the patio doors at the pool and the fire ring and the roses. After some time, he made his way back to join me at our table, the stage upon which so much of our family life had been played out.

There were no words. We just sat there, he struggling for control, while I contemplated this man whom I'd both loved and feared and who was now a stranger. The mask had been ripped from his face; the pretense was shattered, I hoped for good. And just as I'd had a flicker of hope while he was beating me, in spite of my current pain, I sensed hope that he was finally in touch with some authenticity. It's strange how we can experience such diverse emotions at the same time!

He finally found his voice and told me that he'd been having an affair with Jane—since early spring. Since before our San Francisco trip!

"She came to my apartment last night after work. Early in the morning, the police knocked at my door and took her home."

I could barely breathe as I listened to his words.

"The police said they were calling my principal, and I could expect to hear from him. I waited at the apartment, afraid of what could happen. Finally the phone rang; he was furious. He wants to see you and me at Jane's house at seven tonight."

"Why me? What do I have to do with this?"

"Well, he ordered me to be there, and, I guess, I'm asking you to go with me. My job is on the line, you know. Perhaps if you're there, it will make it somehow better.

Please, Bonnie, come with me. We need this job. It might save me from being fired!"

My blood boiled. I thought he'd come over to admit what he'd done and ask forgiveness or something. But his only reason for being there was to use me. He wanted me to plead his case with the principal. Humiliation joined force with outrage and fear. I could hardly believe he'd sit there expecting me to help him after what he'd done.

That's when my practice came to my aid. Closing my eyes, I took a few deep breaths until I felt focused, bringing my awareness to my abdomen where *Death* dissolved fear, allowing my feelings to sort themselves. After several minutes, I opened my eyes, and from my centered acceptance said, "Of course, I'll be there. Our marriage is for better and for worse—and I suppose this is as bad as it gets!"

His whole demeanor changed—instantly! His face relaxed; relief softened his beautiful brown eyes. He said he'd pick me up just before seven, and he left, with me still sitting at the table. I walked outside and sat by the pool, marveling at the alchemy of emotion that had just occurred within me. So amazing, it was almost worth the pain that had brought it about.

I was centered and calm when Paul picked me up for the meeting. I'd spent the entire afternoon doing yoga, meditating and refusing to rehearse the scene ahead of time. Bob had shown me that when I allowed myself to imagine what was going to happen and what I would do or say, I'd lock myself into expectations and be unable to respond authentically. I didn't want to be in the way of an unimaginable solution. Every time a thought came into my mind about the coming encounter, I acknowledged it—out loud—and told the thought to be patient so that God's will could be done. I didn't believe in a God who was a person, and I didn't really think that whatever God was had a specific plan for my life, but I did believe, because I had experienced it, that there was something greater than myself which could lead me, if I didn't interfere. It was that neutral Self within me—my real Self—someone I could be if I'd trust the process. The only words I knew for the phenomenon were God and God's will.

Jane's father opened the door for us, but did not speak. Paul and I sat on the couch in the living room—alone—waiting for the principal to come. I happened to look up and see Jane in the hallway going to the bathroom. Impulsively, I jumped up and hurried to the closed door, waiting for her to come out. She turned pale when she saw me, and ducked to slip past, but I caught her arm and held fast. She wore pink curlers in her hair and a blue chenille bathrobe; her eyes glared fear as she finally looked up and faced me. My heart melted.

Putting my hands on her shoulders, I said softly, "Jane, it seems you've fallen for the wrong Harris."

She lowered her eyes, struggling to get away.

"Jane, listen to me," I heard myself whisper calmly. "Just promise you won't let this ruin your life. You've got a lifetime ahead of you. This will pass—for all of us—but promise me you won't let it stand in your way for happiness."

It was as though someone else spoke through my lips. I remember giving full permission for that *other* to say whatever she wanted to say.

Jane looked up with astonishment in her eyes. We held each other's gaze for several minutes before I added, "I want you to promise me one thing more."

"What is it?" Her voice trembled.

"That you will never see my husband again. Is that clear?"

She dissolved into tears and promised, and I knew she spoke truly.

I calmly returned to the living room, sitting on the sofa next to Paul. The principal sat on the edge of his chair, across the coffee table from us. He was staring at the floor, but looked up when I came into the room, his face expressionless. Jane's parents were seated on the loveseat to our right, her father tense with rage. Now that we were all present, they talked about what had happened, but I don't remember anything that was said; I was still experiencing the afterglow of my encounter with Jane. The conversation around me seemed unreal. I do remember reaching for Paul's arm and holding it gently. And I noticed his eyes watering as I touched him.

I remember the principal somehow becoming more gentle and compassionate, and eventually, Jane's father said he would not press charges. However, the bottom line was that Paul was fired and would never again teach in the Anaheim School District.

☠

I can't possibly find adequate words to describe what happened in that encounter with Jane. It was as though I became that illusive Self that I had experienced briefly before, but not this completely. She was magnificent! I loved her with all my heart, and I wanted her to stay and be me for the rest of my life. Nothing else mattered. Not Paul, the principal, Jane or anything—if I could be the person I had just been.

For several days, I was totally in touch with her—this new Self—and I began to believe she would never leave me. But then, one morning, the phone rang; Jane's mother was on the line. She said that Jane had missed her period, and they feared she might be pregnant. She declared that any medical expenses, including the initial examination, would be our responsibility.

It was then the truth of what had happened really sank in. Jane could be pregnant! Paul had actually had sex with this young girl! The rage returned, and my beautiful new Self was driven from my awareness. I have been searching for her ever since.

☠

CHAPTER ELEVEN

Moving On

My Mormon obsession with what the neighbors would think went out the window after Jane. Because I stayed with Paul, I was treated as an accomplice in the scandal. Why didn't I divorce him? Had I done so I'd have retained the respect of the community and might have kept our home. What different lives our children would have lived, had I not been enslaved by my marriage!

Divorce was not an option for me. I married Paul in the temple for "Time and all Eternity," and even though we were not active Mormons, my values and hopes were part of who I am. Another reason against divorce was dependency; I couldn't imagine myself without him. In addition to Paul's disgrace, Sex Ed teachers were no longer welcome in Anaheim, and in my stupefaction, I didn't consider applying at another district.

Another, more obscure reason was that Paul's affair intrigued me. After nineteen years of marriage, I thought I knew every thought in his head; I could mentally finish his sentences. His actions were as predictable as sunrise; our relationship, though boring, was familiar. Suddenly, I was faced with a man I didn't know. Paul was the least likely person I knew to have an affair, especially with a student. I'd invested two years in therapy, working on my own issues, hoping he would some day slough off the adolescent persona he'd outgrown and be his authentic self. I sensed there was an incredible person buried in all the mush in his mind, and his acting out held the possibility that something genuine might emerge. I wanted to reap the reward of my hard work and the abuse I'd suffered at his hands. I knew how much I'd changed and grown; I wanted to believe that he could change also.

So I set aside a lifetime of worrying about what others would think, and stuck with him. After an initial flurry of concern about the children and me, when people realized I was intent on keeping our marriage intact, no one called. One day Rev. Hoover came by to see if he could help, but when I told him we were trying to work out our problems, he offered to pray for me and never came again. The ostracism was painful. I'd go to the grocery store where we'd shopped for ten years and sometimes see the backsides of people I knew, but never their faces. My Weight Watchers companion dropped out of the class, and was never home when I phoned her. Even our neighbors were not around.

One day, an official from the California Board of Education made an appointment to see us. He questioned Paul about his affair, asking, "Are you aware how serious your actions are?"

"Yes, sir," Paul responded dejectedly. "I've lost my job; I'll never teach in Anaheim again."

"You will never teach in California again!" The man glared at him. "You have betrayed the trust of the parents, the California Teacher's Association and the State Board of Education."

I moved a bit closer to Paul and took his hand. "Look, we're both aware of how serious his actions are. It's been extremely painful, and we'll pay for it the rest of our lives. We know that." My voice was soft and calm, coming from that place within me that I now nurtured through my spiritual practice.

The man looked at me with surprise. I could see compassion stirring as his eyes softened.

Thus encouraged, I went on: "The fact is that the girl's father has agreed not to press charges; I have forgiven Paul; I love him and am staying with him to work this through. He knows he can't teach again; it's a terrible punishment because he has no other way to earn a living. What more do you want from us?" Tears welled in my eyes.

Looking flustered, he finally said, "Well, I guess that's all I need to know. I'll be going now." We showed him to the door and never heard another word from anyone in the school system about the affair.

It was true that Paul had no way to earn a living. His career was teaching, and it looked as though he'd never teach again. As it turned out, he did teach again in Utah, but never again in California. A band member's father, a carpenter, was influential in the union. Taking pity on Paul, in November, he helped him get a job as an entry-level carpenter. He worked for nearly a year, making more money than he had as a teacher, but the job ended abruptly.

Lynne had a scholarship to a college in Iowa. The catastrophe happened in August. I was frantic about how we could manage to support her. Mom called one night. I had been crying when I answered the phone, and there was no way to pretend everything was just fine! She gasped when I told her what had happened, lamenting that I didn't dare send Lynne to school because of finances. Dad called back a few days later and offered to help her on the condition that she'd attend Mormon seminary while she was there. She refused to go under those conditions. She later told me her real reason for refusing was that she was worried about me and couldn't imagine leaving the family when we were in such chaos. She enrolled at Fullerton Junior College and began classes in September.

Lowell was determined to finish high school and get a good education in spite of the scandal. He made arrangements to attend Madison High in the mornings and Fullerton Jr. College in the afternoons. He rode his motorcycle to FJC.

Annie was a junior at Madison. All her friends were in the band and the neighborhood. Her boyfriend dumped her because his parents didn't want him coming to our house. The district allowed her to transfer to South High about ten miles away. Ron still had a year in junior high. The Anaheim District arranged for him to attend Fillmore where I'd taught Sex Ed. He had to leave the house by 5:00 AM to be on time for band practice, riding his bike, rain or shine. In his own words:

> I almost didn't graduate from Fillmore because my grades were so bad, but on the final day, I squeaked by my algebra test literally by one point. I didn't communicate to the family about my graduation and ended up riding my bike to graduation. No one in the family attended, but some girlfriends bought me a shirt and tie to wear. You were very proud of me for winning the Bill Cook Music award and also when I played a clarinet concerto with the band. Everyone made me feel like a hero. I continued on to South High in the fall.

As for me, I lived in a stupor; my whole world had collapsed. Paul kept his apartment, and I visited him often, listening to him talk about Jane. He was writing about the affair and wanted me to listen. His writing was difficult to hear but also titillating. I wanted to know about her because I wanted to know him. I felt as if I were participating vicariously.

While I was with him, there was no doubt in my mind that the affair was my fault. I was fat and ugly and had small breasts and a big bum. He'd told me that often enough. No wonder he wanted someone else. I felt like an old coat he'd outworn and discarded. Then I'd go home and look in the mirror and realize my self-assessment was not true. What I saw was an attractive woman who'd lost 55 pounds and gone from size eighteen to eight. I wondered if his affair would have been easier to accept if it had happened while I was fat; I'd lost the weight to make him love me. What more could I do?

One afternoon, when the kids were in school, I came home from my yoga class and began changing clothes. I removed my shoes, hung my slacks in the closet and was slipping out of my leotards when Paul suddenly appeared in the doorway of the adjoining bathroom where he'd been hiding. He was nude and aroused. I screamed out. He threw me onto the bed, covered my mouth with his and raped me with a passion I'd experienced only the night he beat me.

Was it rape? We were still married. In today's world, we call it rape, but I'd taken vows to submit to this man; I was his property. I know I wouldn't have consented to intercourse without being forced. As it was, his conquest ended the formal separation, although I wasn't ready for him to move back—I still needed time.

After several days of deliberation, I told him he could come back on the condition that I could get the breast implants he'd hounded me about over the years. I blamed his affair on my small breasts. I'd no longer put up with his teasing and feeling ashamed of my body.

I sold the piano I'd bought with money from my retirement fund. This was my sole possession, the only thing I'd ever purchased for myself. I sold it and used the money to pay off bills and have my breasts enlarged. What a strange choice from this perspective. *Why didn't I sell the piano to pay for Lynne's schooling?* This haunted me for years, but two months earlier, in August, when the decision about college was made, I couldn't think clearly enough to realize the piano was a resource. Paul moved back into the house, and the separation was over.

Within a month, I found a job at a small engineering company as an office manager, filling in for a woman who'd taken maternity leave until June. Being the only woman in the office, those men gave me all the attention I could have wanted. With my new body, I felt beautiful and sexy and realized that life was not over yet!

Weight Watchers invited me to be a leader. I taught three classes at night to supplement our income and avoid being home. My self-esteem was enhanced as the women in my classes responded enthusiastically. One class, near the campus of Cal State Irvine, was attended by exceptionally well-educated, exciting women. One day, instead of giving a prepared talk, I extended the question-and-answer period, inviting them to share their own experiences and thoughts. It was so stimulating, the next week I put them in a circle, rather than the lines of chairs they were used to. Using the skills I'd learned from Sex Ed training, I structured the class on the Reality Therapy model. They loved it, and each week the class increased in numbers and weight loss. In March, a Weight Watchers supervisor visited to evaluate the results. I was excited to have her; she was horrified. I was fired the next day for not following the established format.

When my job at the engineering company ended in June, I responded to a classified ad at a Jack LaLanne Health Club. It paid only minimum wage, but was fun. I realized that although women were coming to the spa to lose weight, all that was offered were diet and exercise. I knew from experience that psychological issues needed to be addressed as they came up. Weight Watchers wouldn't have worked for me without having two years of psychotherapy from Kevorkian first; I knew that.

Remembering how effective my classes at Irvine had been, I envisioned a similar class at the spa. After putting my ideas on paper, I requested an interview with one of the directors at their office in Beverly Hills. I smile as I write this, remembering how self-confident I was. They loved the presentation, and we agreed that I'd teach the class in the Anaheim and Long Beach spas beginning in September and ending in June of 1973; we'd evaluate the results at that time and see where to go from there.

In the meantime, everyone else in the family was making decisions of their own. Lynne met a foreign exchange student from Iran while she was at Fullerton Junior

College. They were married in January 1972, only five months after Paul's affair was discovered. I was heartsick, but didn't blame her for wanting to leave the tension in our home. I made her a beautiful wedding gown and have fond memories of the hours I spent beading it with seed pearls. She was married in a restaurant by Bob Kevorkian. I prayed that she could bridge the culture gap.

Lowell, who had lived in an apartment with a friend, moved back into the house in December. In January, he began studies at FJC full-time. He turned eighteen in March and got his draft number, *three*! He investigated the ROTC program at USC, from which he eventually graduated.

The house, which had been full of life a year before, was deserted. No one wanted to be home. Paul was depressed and withdrawn. We all missed the band kids who no longer hung around. Meals were haphazard since we were all on our own.

Paul gave me a diamond for Christmas; it was our pledge to a new commitment, which I sincerely hoped would work out. We refinanced our house to pay for the wedding and to recarpet and buy new furniture for a fresh start. We began attending the meditation classes at Edith's home once a week, after my night classes for Weight Watchers ended.

In a journal entry dated March 24, 1973, I find two quotes from Edith. I don't know where she got them, or if they were her own personal wisdom, but they have been with me ever since. The first: "Question me an answer." She explained, "The answers we find are determined by the questions we can ask." When I asked, "Where do I begin?" she replied, "At the beginning. Do that which is nearest at hand."

Insights into my own situation came through sharing other women's stories in the group classes at the spa. In addition, I kept a journal. The entries show that although I was depressed and discouraged at home, I came alive when reaching out to others. Finally, on April 19, 1973, there was a noticeable shift in mood. I wrote:

> What a blessing it is to be alive. I feel that I've been living a semi-death for some time. Necessary probably for the insights have been important—but I feel life stirring once again—and know that I am reaching for a new level of consciousness. I feel that I'm completing the process of rebirth—I'm ready. Fear seems to have gone and although I know there are always other fears to face and always will be—still, I feel that my journey through life is at a turning point. I await it breathlessly.

> Last week at Edith's, I had a vision that has been increasingly meaningful to me.

> I am on a turbulent ocean. There are two small, helpless boats—mine, a raft with a sail and Paul's, a rowboat—both battling the stormy waves. Then all is peaceful. I am alone on a shore, and it is night and the moon shines on the water marking a path of light on the calm and peaceful sea. It reminds me of the lovely evenings Paul and I have spent at Laguna—listening to the surf, enjoying the peace of calm, balmy nights.

> Once again, the storm rages, but this time, I am under it all, protected from the treacherous turbulence, which churns above me. I seem to be alone, but at peace and unafraid, and yet, there is no happiness either, simply a neutral state of being. Unthreatened—a quiet knowledge that everything will turn out all right.

> Next, I am flying. There are several birds, but I'm not aware of numbers and Paul is not one of them. We are flying in a dark sky—flying toward the east. Peacefully, expectantly.

Several times we catch a glimpse of the sun's light. For an instant, the sky ahead is illuminated, shining on the clouds, silvery with promise, but then the clouds once again hide the light.

Finally, there is a brighter illumination—though still merely a promise. How I want the day to realize itself. I will it to appear. I try to force the culmination, like trying to force orgasm—but the forcing destroys the beauty that is there and darkness closes in again, heavy and deep and impenetrable.

My feeling is not discouragement, but rather a calm acceptance that the light will come in its own time, as surely as the day must break. It is impossible to force such realities.

April 24, 1973 –

My Birthday! I am forty years old and just now being born. I had another significant vision during meditation.

I see mountains, range after range. Then pine trees come into focus. Before I can enjoy the beauty and peacefulness, I am aware of falling. All I can see are vertical lines, plunging downwards. I am numb. No feelings of fear, but before I am about to hit the bottom of the valley, I hear my voice say, "Thy will be done!" Dispassionately.

The falling sensation ceases, and I am in a dark forest, groping my way, following a path blindly. I wish desperately for the light to shine through, but only see glimmers. I know I must be patient. The light will come!

☠

Paul's carpentry job lasted less than a year. He tried to make a living teaching piano lessons and developing his own course, but even that failed. I told my students at the spa how discouraged we were, and one of the women said her husband was a supervisor at a local dairy. If Paul could finance a truck, he could take over a route. He'd been a milkman while he was going to school in the early days of our marriage.

Summer was difficult. My classes ended in June to resume in September. I was trying to sell Mary Kay cosmetics to earn enough money to pay taxes in the fall; otherwise, we would have to sell the house. I made plans to fly to Salt Lake the end of August and sell them to Mom's friends. It was a long shot, but also was an excuse to have a break from the stress.

Paul retreated into melancholy, which I interpreted as guilt for having created such a mess, as well as frustration about his inability to earn a living. Because of my support with the principal and the State Board of Education, he treated me as though I were an angel. I felt dismissed to that lonely pedestal that Kevorkian talked about in terms of my father.

As I packed for my trip to Salt Lake, I mused that the most obvious reason for our disaster was our unfaithfulness to the Mormon Church. Perhaps now, I would receive the coveted testimony. After my rebellion, I would discover with certainty that the LDS Church was the only true church. I would be welcomed in my parents' ward, and because of my painful experiences outside the church, I'd be hailed as a celebrated convert. It would be a fitting climax for my life.

Edith had predicted an important trip. My dream of flying was being fulfilled. The true light was about to shine. Could I be returning to Eden to live happily ever after?

☠

In August 1973, four months after my fortieth birthday, I boarded a plane for Salt Lake City, a trip that would begin a whole new phase of my life. It's difficult to write about my state of mind because I was so conflicted. The two separate selves I had experienced before were both well defined by now, and completely separate.

One Bonnie looked out the window at the carpet of clouds beneath the plane, wondering what awaited her. Memories of losing our home twenty years earlier when Paul declared bankruptcy, like shadowy phantoms, hovered on the fringes of my mind. I recalled the anguish of loading the moving truck after dark to avoid being seen by neighbors. I wondered if we were to repeat the same trauma with our home in Anaheim. This Bonnie was going home to her Mormon parents, hoping to find a way out of the financial dilemma threatening to destroy what was left of her eternal marriage.

But there was another Bonnie—the one who'd knelt beside her bed four years before and felt the loving arms of God embrace her; the one who'd been nurtured through yoga practice and meditation; the woman who had reached out in love and forgiveness to Jane when Paul's adultery was revealed. This Bonnie had experienced a sense of competency, helping other women acquire self-esteem through Weight Watchers and her own program at the Jack LaLanne spas. The Bonnie, who lived a life unacknowledged by her husband and children, was eager to get away from the chaos of a loveless marriage and a bankrupt future with a narcissistic husband. This Bonnie had packed her favorite clothes along with the cosmetics. This Bonnie was going to Salt Lake City eager to begin a new life, if the opportunity showed itself.

So completely split were these two selves that the one who occupied my present consciousness would not admit the other even existed.

I recognized exhaustion lurking beneath my awareness. For many months, I had not allowed myself to feel pain or anger. I had seldom consulted my friend *Death* as I'd stoically weathered the long hours of loneliness, trying to survive and keep things as normal as possible in our home. It had been two years since his adultery. Being a good Mormon woman, I had stood beside him when questioned by his principal and by the State Teachers' Association, putting the best spin possible on the situation—with my parents, as well as with our children.

When Annie graduated from South High in June 1973, my parents offered to pay her expenses at Brigham Young University. She would be flying to Salt Lake a week after my arrival to begin school in Provo, and I looked forward to seeing her settled before I returned to Anaheim.

It was a tradition in the family for each of the children to visit their grandparents for a summer before their tenth birthday. This summer was Wendy's turn, and she was there waiting for me. We would fly back to Anaheim together in time for school to start and for me to resume my classes at the spas.

The Mormon Bonnie stepped off the plane into the arms of my loving parents. It was easy to spot them in the waiting crowd as we deplaned. Was it Mom's perfectly coiffed white hair and her stylish white suit that made her stand out? Or was it the Holy Spirit radiating from both of them that set them apart from the crowd? Wendy, holding Mom's hand, jumped up and down when she saw me. Dad stood a few steps behind Mom, his eyes soft; his jaw clenched. I could hardly imagine the suffering they had endured through my long ordeal. Even though I'd talked to them frequently, I'd been careful to not inflame their dislike of Paul. Breaking into tears the minute I saw them, I sobbed all the way home, feeling tears melt the hard shell of defensiveness I'd worn while living in Anaheim. When I walked into their kitchen, I once again was Bonnie Myers, blessed daughter of Margie and Jimmy. I allowed myself to dissolve into the safety of their love.

For several days, I drank in the peacefulness of their home. Wendy and I shared a bedroom suite in the basement of the luxurious condo they'd purchased five years before, shortly after Dad became president of Olson Advertising Agency. It was a bright spacious room, painted pale yellow, with white antique furniture. A large oval picture of bright daisies smiled down on me from the wall opposite the bed while high windows flooded the room with soft light and fresh air. I spent most of my time in that room, sleeping and allowing the rich aura of their love to caress me and begin to heal my broken heart.

Even though the stated purpose of my visit was to sell cosmetics, Mom hadn't told anyone about it. Dad made it clear that I was not going to exploit their friends. Without an agenda, I spent my days taking walks with Wendy, and being indulged with wonderful meals Mom insisted on preparing herself. I especially remember the childlike joy of drying dishes, as I'd done when I was a little girl. Determined to maintain my loyalty to Paul, I tried not to say anything I'd regret later as we moved beyond the catastrophe I'd temporarily left behind.

When Annie arrived, Mom and I drove her to Provo, making several trips until we found a suitable apartment, one she would share with three other freshman students. Mom opened a bank account for her and bought everything she could possibly need: bedding, towels and school clothes. Annie seemed overwhelmed and skeptical about the whole arrangement, and certainly had cause to be anxious. She'd been baptized into the Mormon Church when she was eight years old, but except for attending the weekday Primary classes, had scarcely been in a Mormon ward. Her new classmates most probably had attended Mormon seminary classes in high school; Annie had not. I am fairly certain the reason she was accepted at BYU was my father's intervention, but I don't know that for sure.

We left Annie in Provo knowing she was comfortable, had everything she needed, including money in the bank, and prayed as we drove back to Salt Lake, that she would have good roommates and find a way to fit into this challenging environment. I was confident she was resilient enough to make the transition—with God's help.

The Sunday before Labor Day, after getting Annie settled, my brother Eric and his wife, Doris, were invited for a Sunday barbecue. I hardly knew them because we moved to Anaheim in 1959, fourteen years before, and although our visits to Salt Lake had included family dinners, I couldn't remember having one significant conversation with them. Part of the problem was Mom's inordinate praise of Doris, whom she had always held up to me as the perfect Mormon woman I should have been. I admired Doris, as well as resented her—in fact, I remember feeling hatred toward her in Anaheim, although I didn't even know her. What I hated was the comparison and Mom's constant praise of her to my disparagement.

I'd been in Salt Lake ten days before that dinner, having no contact with Paul and the family, except for one phone call I made shortly after my arrival. I didn't want to run up my parents' phone bill, and Paul had not called me. Grateful for my parents' love, I found it easy to shut out everything except the present. My defenses had been discarded, and I was more at peace than I'd been for months. I remember thinking how beautiful Doris was and felt warmth and admiration for her as she confidently talked about her children and their many accomplishments. Then she turned to me with bright eyes and asked sweetly, "And how are your kids, Bonnie?"

Her question crashed into my consciousness like a torpedo, and feelings, which I'd purposely submerged, exploded into awareness. In my frustration to answer, tears gushed up from my belly, spilling over my cheeks. I sobbed uncontrollably, my family frantically trying to soothe the unexpected storm, their comforting words only intensifying my embarrassment at losing control. To my knowledge, such an outburst had never been experienced in the Myer's family. As children, we weren't allowed to fight, and we never saw our parents argue. I was not only filled with grief but now added guilt to the turbulent sea of emotions. When my tears diminished, we sat quietly for a long time, the barbecued chicken cold on our plates.

"I'm sorry," I sputtered. "I miss the kids so much and yet dread going back to all our problems. I'm so tired. I don't seem able to control myself any longer." I assumed Mom and Dad had told them about the affair.

"What are you going to do?" It was Eric who brought us back to the world of practical solutions. I felt somewhat calmed.

"I don't know," I sputtered. "I tried getting a teaching job in Anaheim, but because of the disgrace, no one wants me. I'm treated as an accomplice in Paul's crime because I stayed with him. No one knows what to say to me; I understand that. But it's lonely, and I feel overwhelmed with anger and grief." It was the first time I'd admitted this fact, even to myself. Tears leaked from my eyes again, much softer this time. "It's as though I'm being punished for being a faithful wife. I don't get it!"

After a long few minutes, Eric asked, "Do you want to stay in Salt Lake?"

"How could I?" The Bonnie speaking could not remember packing her clothes for an extended stay; she was the helpless Mormon wife who had taken vows to do everything her husband told her. But this Bonnie's shell had nearly dissolved with Doris's question, "And how are your kids?"

My brother leaned forward in his seat. "There's an English position available at Hillside Junior High." He'd taught drama there his entire career. "Teacher orientation is Tuesday and Wednesday, and classes begin the next day. I checked with Mr. Phelps, and he still hasn't found anyone to fill the position."

I could scarcely believe my ears. "Are you saying you think I'd have a chance at the job?"

"Why not?" was his immediate response. "You have a good teaching record in Anaheim. You've taught the same classes in the same grades. If you want, I'll arrange an interview. In fact, I've told him about you, and he's set aside time tomorrow morning to see you. It's Labor Day, but he's desperate to fill the position before school starts. I'll call him first thing in the morning, that is, if you want an interview."

I was stunned. *Is it possible that God has brought me here? Is it possible that Dad and Eric planned this before I arrived? It's too good to be true.*

I finally responded, "How could I pass up such an opportunity? Someone in the family needs to work." *It's not what I planned, but it would be good to have some time away from Paul and the financial pressure. Maybe then I could think more clearly.* I added resolutely, "Yes, I want to go to the interview and give it a chance."

"Shouldn't you call Paul and see what he thinks?" Mom was clearly concerned.

I pondered the dilemma for a few minutes before answering, "If I get the job, I'll call him. I don't want to get his hopes up unless it's a sure thing. If I'm hired, I'll work it out with my family—some way!"

Eric called early the next morning saying I had a meeting with Mr. Phelps at 11:00 AM. I could scarcely believe what was happening, and wondered again if God was calling me to come back to Salt Lake for good. For the millionth time, I wondered if the problems we'd faced were because we'd not been faithful to the church. *Is it possible I'm being given another chance? What will Paul say? How will the kids react?* I took a deep breath and firmly put these questions aside. I did my yoga with full focus on my body and had time for thirty minutes of meditation, which I offered to God's will. By the time I left the condo, driving my father's car, I was as open to a new future as possible.

☠

Hillside Junior High is located in the foothills of Salt Lake City. I marveled at the pristine blue of the sky and the mountains rising protectively behind the school. From the parking lot, I had a full view of the valley, which seemed to welcome me home. The front door of the school was unlocked. I easily found my way to the office where I was greeted by a smiling Mr. Phelps who thanked me for coming in, even though it was a holiday.

Sitting in the brown leather chair across the desk from his, I felt confident and at ease. He seemed open, more like a kindly father than a prospective boss.

"Eric has talked briefly about your situation, but I'd like to hear it from you," he began.

No niceties here; no preliminary lead-ins to the difficult story I had to tell. So I dove in, being as candid as possible, without touching the raw pain I feared I couldn't control.

Centering energy in my belly, willing *Death* to drive out fear, I described my teaching experience, including the Sex Ed classes, explaining the program in detail, especially highlighting my work with Dr. Stevenson. Then I carefully related the problems, which arose from Paul's affair and the subsequent lack of employment.

I don't know how much of this Mr. Phelps had heard from Eric—in fact I don't know how much of it Eric knew. The kindly man who sat across the desk showed only compassion in his warm, hazel eyes. I took a deep breath.

318

Fearing the connection with *Death* was slipping, I asked her for strength to get through the interview without crying. We said nothing for what seemed an eternity. Finally, the principal asked, "What do you intend to do, Bonnie? Do you want to go back to Anaheim—to your family?"

"I don't know," I answered truthfully, my voice coming from my depths. "I think I need some time away to figure it out. Someone in the family needs to be working; we've refinanced our house, and the money is draining away. Our oldest daughter is married, and one of our sons is going to college and will be married in January. Our third child, Annie, is here at BYU, and my youngest is with me. I'd have to leave my youngest son, Ron, with his father—that is if I stay in Salt Lake."

Again, we relinquished words. I could see him carefully weighing his decision. Finally, I added, "I can make no promise that I'll be here a second year. But I can promise that if you're willing to take a chance on me, I'll be fully committed to my students this year." Then I added shyly, "I may seem emotionally unstable at the moment, but I assure you I can handle the job—with great joy!" Even as I spoke these words, I could feel my heart open and assurance fill my being. It was as though God was pouring love into me at that exact moment, encompassing *Death* and driving out fear.

I got the job! Mr. Phelps said he'd make the necessary calls to the Anaheim School District to verify my credentials as well as my experience. If all was well, he'd arrange for me to go to the Board of Education on Tuesday afternoon— the next day—and he wanted me to attend some of the teacher orientation and be ready to meet my students on Thursday.

I left the school only half believing what had happened. With all the red tape usually associated with credentials and out-of-state transfers, how could this possibly be? It seemed like a dream, as if I were making it up. But this was no fantasy. *It really is happening. He was willing to hear my story, believe me and go out of his way to help us get back on our feet. It's a miracle!*

I drove to a nearby shopping center and found a parking space where I could see to the Oquirrh Mountains delineating the western perimeter of the valley. The day was crystal clear with a bite of fall in the air. I sat for a long time, entering into that special place in my being which I'd discovered in meditation. Everything was absolutely still, within me and without—thought suspended. I didn't know how to think; the situation was beyond thought. The peace that filled me was palpable.

Was this the "peace that passes understanding" Jesus had promised his disciples? I would call it that today; however, at the time, I did not know the phrase. I only knew that what was happening was holy. I sat in the car and welcomed the assurance that poured into my heart. A nightmare was over; a new life was about to begin.

CHAPTER TWELVE

What Is Truth?

When I entered my parents' condo, I was calm and centered. They were waiting for me.

"I have the job!" I exclaimed, setting my purse on the kitchen counter. "That is, if my credentials are verified, but Mr. Phelps is confident they will be. He's calling the Anaheim District, and if everything is OK—which I know it is—I'll begin teaching on Thursday."

Tears of gratitude filled my father's eyes, and Mom was speechless. "Is it possible God wants me to come back?" I searched their faces.

"It certainly looks that way," Dad managed.

"What will you tell Paul?" Mom's brow furrowed with worry. "He isn't going to like this."

"How can he not be relieved? This job will help the whole family! Who knows, he may sell the house and come here to join me. I told Mr. Phelps I'd commit to one school year only. Maybe I'll go back to Anaheim next June if Paul wants to stay there. But right now, this is the only job either of us has; he's got to understand and be grateful." I realized I was being defensive.

Suddenly, my confidence began draining away. I felt sick to my stomach and thought I might throw up.

"Are you OK?" Dad asked.

"Yes, I'm OK," I replied. "Just a bit woozy from all that's happened. I need to lie down for a while and think this through. Then I'll come up and use your phone, if it's OK."

"We're here for you, Bonnie," Dad said with genuine concern. "You and Wendy can stay here as long as you want. Everything will work out, you'll see."

I thanked him and hurried downstairs where my nine-year-old daughter was reading in the family room, next to our bedroom. Wendy was totally engrossed in Tolkien's *Lord of the Rings,* a gift from her father for her trip to Salt Lake. She'd hardly put the trilogy down since she arrived a month ago, making her an easy guest for my parents.

Oh, my gosh! What's she going to think? She'll be devastated not to go back to her family and friends. What have I done? What else could I do? My mind spun out of control.

"Sweetheart, I'm going to lie down for a while. Will you be OK?"

She nodded absently.

I lay on my bed for nearly an hour, unable to sleep. With effort, I slowed the spinning thoughts to a manageable intensity, until I was finally ready to make the call.

Poking my head in the doorway, I interrupted again. "I'm going upstairs to call Dad. Do you need anything?" She hardly looked up.

"I'm fine, Mom. This is a great book!"

"Do you want something to drink?"

"No, I'm fine!"

I climbed the stairs slowly. My father had retreated to his den; Mom was taking a nap in her bedroom. I gently closed her door so I'd have privacy to talk to Paul; then I dialed his number.

"How's the trip?" he seemed unnaturally cheerful. It had been over a week since we'd talked.

"Amazing, Paul! More so than I ever could have dreamed."

"How so?" he asked indulgently.

"Well, you'd better sit down because I have some important news for you."

"OK, I'm ready!"

"Yesterday, Mom and Dad had a barbecue for us with Eric and Doris. I explained how much trouble we'd had finding jobs in Anaheim, and Eric told me about an opening at his school—Hillside Junior High. He said the principal would talk to me about it, if I was interested. I didn't think it would hurt, so I had the interview this morning. Well, he hired me."

"He what? You have a job teaching school in Salt Lake?"

"Yes, it's a miracle—a blessing for the whole family. Mom and Dad said Wendy and I could stay with them for a while, and I can send you money for the taxes and…."

"You want a divorce." His voice had hardened.

"I didn't say that, Paul. No, I don't want a divorce. I want to help us get back on our feet, and this is a way to do it."

The line sizzled with silence.

"I haven't had time to work it through; I just found out about the job. But I've thought for a long time I needed a break from the pressure. It's been such a difficult two years."

Silence.

"Paul, remember when you needed time away from me? I gave you that time. I understood how much pressure you were under with the band parents. I'm asking you for the same understanding. I'll stay here and teach and come back for Lowell's wedding in January. We can see where we are then."

"You want a divorce? OK—you'll get one!" He hung up.

My hand shook so hard I could hardly hang up the phone. "Oh my gosh!" I cried out loud. Both of my parents came running from their rooms. "What's the matter?" they asked in unison. "Was Paul upset?" Mom asked. "Let's go sit in the living room," Dad suggested. Mom hurried to the refrigerator. "I'll get some Cokes, and you can tell us about it."

Barely able to comprehend what had happened, I followed Dad into the living room where I settled onto their white damask loveseat. Dad sank onto the sofa, which was placed at a right angle to mine. Mom set glasses of cold Coke on the coffee table between us, and settled into her rocking chair across from me.

"Well…." Dad urged. "Tell us."

I finally found words, although I could scarcely believe them. "He thinks I want a divorce. He didn't even listen to my explanation; he thinks I want a divorce. He hung up on me without listening."

After a long pause, Dad asked calmly, "Well, Bonnie, don't you?" To my quizzical look, he repeated, "Don't you want a divorce?"

I stiffened at his response. It was as though they'd expected it. "No! I don't know! I'm just so confused!" Tears spurted from my eyes, trickling down my cheeks. Mom got up and procured Kleenex. "I don't know what I'm doing! I don't know what I want! I'm just so tired from all of this!" The sobbing continued in earnest. I was completely out of control; my parents were not upset in the least.

Finally, Dad said, "Just wait a few days and let things settle down. If he doesn't call you first, you can call him. By then you'll see things more clearly. He needs time to think about it."

Wendy had been sitting at the top of the stairs; she came over and sat beside me. I put my arm around her and pulled her closer. Wiping my eyes and blowing my nose, I finally managed to say, "Sweetheart, how much do you know about what's going on?"

"I know you didn't sell the cosmetics to pay the money we owe. I know that Dad is mad at you and thinks you want a divorce. I heard Uncle Eric tell you about a job at his school. Does that mean we're going to stay here and not go back to Anaheim?"

"I still don't know," I looked at her squarely. "There are lots of things they have to check out first, but…the principal does want me to teach at his school."

Her muscles loosened a bit, and she sank her head onto my chest. She looked so forlorn it nearly tore my heart out.

"I'm sorry, Wendy. I don't know what to do. Someone needs to make money, or we'll have to sell our home anyway. If this works out, maybe we can go back in June and be a family again. In the meantime, there's a big sacrifice being asked of us. It looks like we'll have to stay in Salt Lake for now. If they hire me, you'll have to go to fifth grade here."

No one spoke for long time. I hugged my precious daughter trying to assure her that all would be well. And then, she looked up at me with her beautiful eyes and said, "It's OK Mom, I already have a friend in fifth grade."

"You have?" I felt hope stirring.

"Her name is Liz, and she lives right around the corner. She plays the violin and loves to read. Maybe I can go to school with her."

How did I ever deserve such an amazing daughter? She doesn't even seem concerned about her friends in Anaheim. How can she be so adaptable?

"Well, let's see what happens tomorrow, and if they offer me the job, I'll take it. School starts on Thursday." I turned to my mother who was sympathetically taking it all in. "If it works out with Granite District, will you take

Wendy to the school and get her registered while I'm at orientation on Wednesday?"

"Of course," was her ready reply. "And you can live here as long as you want. We'll be a family again."

Collapsing into bed that night, foremost in awareness was gratitude for the love that surrounded us. My credentials were verified the next day by phone; paperwork was being sent directly. "There is one problem," the gentleman working on the issue told me. "You have a junior high credential, and you need a high school credential in order to teach ninth grade in Salt Lake. We can't do anything about it before school starts, but you're free to begin teaching on Monday. We'll get the paperwork settled as soon as we can." He was so gracious to me I was amazed. *Does he know about my problems? Is it possible Dad has arranged all this? How could he? But it seems too easy.* The questions were there, but I never knew the answers. I was simply grateful for all the kindness.

That night, I called Paul to tell him the news. He either wasn't home or wouldn't answer the phone. I was disappointed.

The next morning, Eric gave me a ride to teacher orientation. I only missed one day of the meetings; Mr. Phelps was pleased. I wished I had more time to prepare for my first day; it had been three and a half years since I'd taught school, but I was confident I could wing it. To my amazement, the Granite School District gave me a high school credential, without additional requirements on my part. Such a thing is unheard of.

When I got home on Friday, after my first two days of teaching, Mom and Dad met me at the kitchen door. Their faces showed alarm. "We got a call from Annie," Mom said. "She's left BYU and gone home to be with her father."

"She's what?" I was flabbergasted.

"She said she was mailing the bank records to us and had taken only enough money to buy her plane ticket. She was very upset!"

"When did she call?" I asked.

"This morning, after you left. We've been stewing about it all day and nearly called Paul ourselves, but we decided not to interfere. This is between you and him." Dad was adamant.

"I'll call him right now." I picked up the phone and dialed his number. This time he answered. "Paul, what's going on? Is Annie there?"

"You wanted a divorce from me; you've divorced us all. You've left, and I don't want you calling here again. Do you understand?"

"What are you saying? I can't believe you're being so cruel! Paul, I never said I wanted a divorce; that was your idea. I want to earn enough to pay the taxes and save the house."

"If you've said your peace, I'm hanging up. I hope you're happy!" The phone died.

After all the tears, what amazes me in looking back on that phone call is how calm I was when I hung up the lifeless phone. I was again in touch with *Death* in my belly. My anger was too much to deny and with that acknowledgement, it was as though the other Bonnie took over. No more "pseudo-emotionalism." My energy turned to "What is the next step?" I recalled Edith's advice when I asked her, "What should I do?" And she answered: "Do that which is nearest at hand."

With a calm confidence that astounded my parents, I told them what Paul had said. The shock on their faces spoke volumes. "Well," I said with resolution. "There's nothing I can do about what's going on in Anaheim. We're here, and a new opportunity has opened for me. I just have to trust that the kids know me well enough to realize I would not desert them. It's got to work out." I smiled at Dad and reminded him, "You're the one who taught me 'everything will work out in the end.' In the meantime, what I need to do is concentrate on my classes and help Wendy adjust to a new life. And I have both of you to help me. How can I ever thank you enough?"

We hugged each other. "Where is Wendy?" I asked.

"She's down in her room reading. She's such a strange little girl. She spends too much time by herself," Mom scowled.

"Think of her as being self-reliant. Since she's so much younger than the other kids, she's learned to entertain herself. The family always reads and studies in the evening, and she loves her books." I was aware that my confident voice made Mom nervous.

"Well," she smiled, "you're the mother!" I stopped my defensive reaction before it took hold; we didn't need to clash on how to raise my child.

Turning to Dad, I asked if I could borrow the car. "I want to go to the library and get some books. I'll take Wendy with me, if it's OK."

"I'll have dinner ready at 6:00. Try to be back by then," Mom smiled sweetly as she handed me her keys.

"How can I be so lucky? You're both so gracious to have us here and fix our dinner. I hope you'll let me cook sometimes." I was genuinely grateful.

"I love to have you here to fuss over." She'd relaxed again. "Do you know where the library is?" I nodded. "Well, be careful."

It was good to be with Wendy alone. We went to the library where she picked out five books. They gave us a card based on her school registration since we didn't have a residence of our own. I knew exactly what I wanted, Kahlil Gibran's *The Prophet*.

We drove by her school, and she showed me the building and grounds. Although she could easily walk on good days, the roads were congested so a school bus would take her from the corner near Liz's house.

"I'd like to meet Liz's parents. Could we visit them this weekend?"

"Oh yes, Mom, let's. You'll really like them." Wendy's happy smile was reassuring.

After dinner, Mom and I did the dishes; I dried them just as Lynne always did for me. I felt like a child again, and willingly let go of the authority I'd had in my own kitchen. It felt freeing. Afterwards, I joined Wendy in the family room downstairs, a lovely room with green shag carpet, comfortable bamboo furniture, and pillows upholstered in a bright Pacific Island print. I remembered when Mom and Dad went to the Islands on a church assignment. Paul and I met them at the L.A. airport for a short wait between planes. Dad was exhausted so I had him take off his shoes and socks, and I sat on the floor, massaging his feet for about twenty minutes. My thumbs were sore by the time I quit, but he looked totally relaxed. Remembering that intimate moment made me smile as I realized the décor of our living space was a result of that trip.

I found Wendy busily writing a letter to her friend Mary, who lived in our sub-division in Anaheim. She wanted her to know she wouldn't be coming back, at least not until next school year. I took out my copy of *The Prophet* and turned to Gibran's passage about children:

"Your children are not your children....They come through you but not from you, and though they are with you yet they belong not to you....You are the bows from which your children as living arrows are sent forth." I sat reverently, imagining each of my beloved children being sent forth as living arrows into the world, without me. *They belong to God not to me, and I must trust that whoever God is will guide them, as he has guided me to this very moment.*

The text continued: "The archer sees the mark upon the path of the infinite, and He bends you with His might that His arrows may go swift and far." *Oh how that bending hurts! Help me, God, to be pliant enough that their journeys may take them to your ultimate destination. Teach me to be glad in my sacrifice, knowing that "even as He loves the arrow that flies, so He loves also the bow that is stable."*

I read the passage over and over. Pausing at emotion-packed words and thoughts and then going on. I allowed the wisdom to sink into my soul. I was being asked to let go of my children as well as my husband—at least for now. I knew that our separation would change our relationships forever. *When I see them next, at Lowell's wedding in January, they'll no longer be children—except for Ron. What will happen to him? I know this—he'll be better off at South where he'll probably be drum major than here with us, having to start a new school in his junior year.*

Please God, no matter what happens; let them know I love them. Let us be a family again some day. Teach me to live in the house of today and treasure the blessing of the daughter still in my care. The prayer came spontaneously. I didn't know who this God was that I was petitioning, but I was open to finding out.

☠

On Saturday, Dad let me take his car again so that Wendy and I could drive to Hillside. I checked out the books in the room, which were new to me. Taking one of each set to peruse over the weekend, I wished Paul were there to help me decorate the room as he'd always done. He was an artist as well as a musician. My sighs were heavy and deep.

After leaving the books at the condo and returning the keys to Mom, Wendy and I walked over to her friend's townhouse. The girls immediately hurried off to Liz's bedroom, and Dorothy offered me a cup of coffee, which I eagerly accepted. I hadn't had a *real* cup since my arrival, three weeks earlier, not counting the freeze-dried stuff I shared with my mother who still drank it surreptitiously in the mornings.

Dorothy enjoyed brewing the real thing for me in a real coffeemaker. I nearly swooned, so delicious was the aroma.

"I'm living with my parents who are super-Mormons. They've been wonderful to us, but oh, how I miss my coffee."

"They'll have it in the teachers' lounge at school. The way to establish your *gentile* status is to indulge. I highly recommend it," she laughed, setting the coffee cups on the kitchen table and sitting across from me.

"When I first moved to Anaheim from Salt Lake, fourteen years ago, the first day on my new job I was offered coffee in the break room. I remember self-righteously saying, 'I don't drink coffee; I'm a Mormon.' I still cringe at that memory." I savored the coffee.

"Are you going to stay with your parents long?" she asked.

"I haven't gotten that far. I didn't come here to stay, but this teaching position fell in my lap. It's a godsend, but completely unexpected. My husband is furious and thinks I want a divorce, and maybe I do, but I'm not sure. Everything will unfold in its time, I guess, but I don't want to stay with Mom and Dad so long we have conflict."

"I know what you mean." She paused a moment, leaning toward me, confidentially saying, "Bonnie, I'm so glad you've brought Wendy here. You'll find the schools are very difficult for non-Mormon kids. Liz has no friends. It's wonderful to see her and Wendy enjoying each other. I hope you'll stay close by so they can develop a lasting friendship. Wendy's going to need someone like Liz just as Liz needs Wendy."

I winced at the word non-Mormon. *Isn't there some way to avoid choosing sides?* Wendy and I walked home together, holding hands, both of us happy as clams—whatever that means!

We went to the ward on Sunday with Mom and Dad. Everyone was very kind, and I felt peaceful in the meeting. I wondered if God had brought us back, not only to my parents, but also to the Mormon Church. I tried to imagine a God who had a body, as the Mormons believe. *Where is He?* I focused on some latticework above the pulpit. *Maybe he's looking at us from there. Do I find God outside or inside? If he's outside, then the experience I have within must be the Holy Spirit. It's very confusing and seems unnecessarily complicated, but I can't deny the blessings of returning. I need to start paying tithing and get involved some way. Also, Wendy should go to Sunday School and Primary so she won't be an outsider. We need some kind of community beyond ourselves.*

September flew by. In October, my first paycheck made me feel wealthy. It was an excuse to call Paul and find out how much we owed on taxes. I needed to budget my money so I'd have enough to send him in November. The telephone line froze when he realized it was me.

"I miss you," I began. He did not respond. "How are things going, Paul?"

"We're doing just fine without you."

"Well, I'm glad for that." I lied, resolutely stopping tears. "I called to hear your voice, but also to find out how much the taxes are going to be. I just got my first paycheck and want to set aside enough money to pay them next month."

"Don't bother; the house is up for sale."

"Why the rush?"

"It doesn't concern you anymore."

"Of course, it does, I'm co-owner of the house, or have you forgotten?"

"You're not here. Not even for Annie's wedding."

"Her wedding? What do you mean?"

"She's going to marry Henry's brother, Amir, next Saturday."

"And her own mother isn't invited? You've got to be kidding!"

"Keep your precious money and don't bother me again."

"Let me talk to her!"

"You left. You're no longer part of this family." The phone went dead.

My daughter, Annie, is getting married without me. What about a wedding? Why hasn't she called and told me? And Amir? He's a nice young man, I guess, but she's so young! Tears came again. I thought I'd cried myself dry, but this was too much! *Maybe I could take a few days off and go to Anaheim.* I called back, but he wouldn't answer the phone.

In mid-October, I received a registered letter from Paul. Before I could open it, the phone rang and Mom called from upstairs, "Bonnie, it's Paul!"

I bounded up the stairs, two steps at a time. It was the first time he'd called since I'd arrived in Salt Lake. "Paul, how are you?" I asked enthusiastically.

He quickly put the damper on my excitement, "Did you get the letter from me?"

"Yes, I got it. I haven't read it yet; what does it say?"

"I'm asking you to sign the house over to me."

I was tearing at the envelope and gasped when I saw the documents. "But surely you don't expect me to sign this before we've discussed how to distribute the equity."

"You have your choice. If you don't sign, I'm walking away from the house completely. The mortgage company can have it. We've already moved; Ron and I are living in an apartment."

"You've already moved? Why so fast?"

Silence.

"What about Annie?" I felt sick to my stomach.

"They've put off the wedding—for now."

"Where is she?"

"It's none of your business. You left us."

"If she isn't with you, will you please give me her phone number?"

"No." The silence on the line was deafening. My whole body turned cold.

Finally, he said, "The choice is yours, Bonnie. If you don't sign, nobody will get anything." He hung up.

I found a local attorney in the phonebook, Alan Howe. When I called his office the next day, he agreed to see me after school. Handing him the documents, I told him my situation briefly and asked about my options.

Despair clouded his eyes as he listened. He scanned the papers and then looked at me sadly. "You can go back to California until the sale is closed and the money is distributed, or you can sign the papers."

"But that's unfair. I can't go back and jeopardize my job."

He answered gently, "You have no recourse; you left the state. You'll have to trust that he'll be fair."

After a few seconds, he asked, "Are you filing for divorce?"

The world stopped, as though I were suspended between breaths. I leaned forward, my elbows on his desk, my hands touching my lips—the attitude of prayer. I stared at the papers in his hands and finally answered, "No. At least not now. I don't know what to do. I didn't plan this, and I don't know what I want." I felt so tired I could hardly hold up my head. But there were no tears gathering behind my eyes, which gazed vacantly at the papers in his hands.

When I looked up, his eyes searched mine. Finally he said, sadly, "I'm opening a file for you; when you're ready, give me a call and I'll be here to help."

At that point, I didn't have much hope for Paul's fairness, unless we got back together. He seemed locked into a divorce. *Well, it's only money. But it's all the money we have. It's the only asset from all those years of working. It's all tied up in the house.* I signed the papers, trying to still my shaking hand. I watched the attorney notarize my signature and put the papers in an envelope with his return address, then I shuffled out of his office to find a post office. I'd never felt such desolation. *My God, my God, why have you forsaken me?*

☠

Dad was shocked at the turn of events, but agreed with the attorney that I'd just have to trust Paul. He told me he'd write him and try to bring him to his senses. We both agreed it would be foolish for me to go back to Anaheim and jeopardize my job. There wasn't even a place to stay now that he was living in an apartment. I wondered what he'd done with all our things; my mind was jumbled.

Finally settling down, I brought myself back to the present. *It seems I'm being asked to let go of my marriage, four of my children, my house and all our possessions. Ok. That will be my spiritual discipline for the present.* Every time I found myself thinking about something in the house I loved, I'd bring it into my imagination, thank it for giving me such pleasure, and then let it go. The practice brought much peace.

The next night, I went to see Paul's brother, Dwight. I told him what had happened and asked for his help. I told him I'd been going to church and felt God had brought us here. I asked him to contact Paul and help him know I was sincerely trying to make a new start. Dwight and his wife, Theresa, were the same age as my parents. They had been lifelong friends, and Dwight had been my bishop when I was growing up.

We all knelt on the floor, and Dwight gave me a blessing that God would be with us and all would work according to His purpose. I left with an awareness of the goodness of these two saintly people. If anyone could help us through this mess, it would be Dwight.

I didn't call Paul again, but there were letters. I wish I had saved them, but they have been lost. However, I have drafts of two letters I wrote to him which were recorded in my journals. My visit with his brother had been a response to a letter I'd received from Paul. After seeing Dwight, I wrote:

Dear Paul,

> I have sat down so often to answer your letter, and end up staring at the first two words. "Dear Paul"—how far away it makes you seem—how totally unreachable. I cringe when I read your words—those words which are a mockery of my own. I know only too well how often I have scoffed at the church—and at the idea of crawling back to the nest. It must certainly seem cowardly to you—as you said before—like I couldn't stand and face the strain of the problems

before us, leaving you and Ron to do the dirty work of closing the house, etc.

How could you know of the torture I feel at not being there—of not being *able* to take care of the lovely possessions we have spent a lifetime collecting. How could you know how much it hurts to hear that Lynne and Annie have done my job of cleaning? Just as a knife is turned in my heart every time I hear of a family dinner without me—and realizing I'm neither needed nor missed.

I often wake up in the middle of the night crying, wondering what I'm doing here and how this all came to be—but Paul I do not know—I have felt myself totally in the hands of God. I have been aware of acting without conscious decision—of doors opening without my knocking—of words spoken *before* I understood their meaning.

You say I have crawled back through fear, seeking "pat" answers and safe solutions. My situation is anything but "pat" or "safe." I am seeing the church in a way I've never seen it before, and it's beautifully clear. I can't see how I missed its significance—except that until now I was not forced to look.

I do not know what this is all about, Paul, except that I couldn't do anything other than what I've done.

What is God telling me? That this is where I belong? I can no longer deny the truth and beauty that are here—painful as it is to admit how wrong I've been.

What is God telling us? This is the question that tortures my soul. Has He led me here to show you the way back? Has He forced my return because this is where the solution to our dilemma lies? I don't know!!! Perhaps you do. Do you have some small feeling that this might be part of your destiny too?

When I studied Greek literature, I remember being puzzled about the sin of *hubris*—arrogant pride. To the Greeks, it was the worst of all sins. I now think I understand. It is the pride that keeps us from accepting truths—even when they are divinely revealed—because we cannot admit we've been wrong. Especially, Paul, when we've been so vocal about our own insignificant ideas, even while they've taken us over such rough terrain.

I have never felt so close to God. I've never felt so completely willing to put myself in His hands—even at the risk of losing you and my beloved children, I must be true to what has been so dramatically revealed.

Paul, there is such beauty here—friends and loved ones ready to welcome us both. Dwight and Theresa's concern is rich and sincere. Mom and Dad's offer to help is as genuine and full of love as is their forgiveness of the absolute hell we led them through during what was supposed to be "our enlightenment."

Please listen. Please hear what I'm saying. Take this letter to Edith if you must—to realize the depth of my conviction.

Life is indeed a circle—or as Yeats said "a gyre"—I have returned to the starting place, but on a much higher level. Everything looks different. We were such children when we left. I will never return to the spiritual charade which we were living—unknowingly—but in contrast to the strength of the church, it seems so to me now.

You say you will never betray yourself as I have done—and also that you "want me back." It seems hopeless, doesn't it?

May God bless you with wisdom and truth!

- Bonnie

☠

Instead of replying to me, he wrote a letter to my father telling him he had "long ago decided to return to the church." Dwight called Dad saying that Paul had told him the same thing.

Here is the draft of the letter I sent to Paul; it reveals my confusion at the time.

Dear Paul,

Dad showed me the letter you wrote. He didn't intend to, but I had a premonition that you would write to him at the office, and I knew somehow that he had received it. When I asked him, he couldn't lie, and once I knew, for him to have withheld the letter would have simply added to the senseless mystery with which you have shrouded everything. In fact, he did not show it to me until the following morning, and through that sleepless night, during which my mind tried to imagine what you could possibly have told him that I could not know, I came to an important understanding about the frustration I have with our relationship.

And that is I don't trust you! You see, it was relatively easy for me to understand and forgive your affair—I didn't feel that it involved me. It was your problem and your sin. Not mine. The

339

thing that I couldn't escape was the terrible distrust I felt—your betrayal of our relationship by bringing her to *our* home, taking her to the band banquet, thinking about *her* during our trip to San Francisco. These are wounds which I have *prayed* would heal, but somehow the scars will not go away.

A week ago, I contacted Dwight and literally confessed my sins to him and asked for his help in contacting you because you wouldn't believe my sincerity about the church. He called yesterday and told me I was wrong about you, that you had wanted to return to the church all along, and that you told him I would not communicate with you.

I'm stunned, for certainly I have tried. You have made only one phone call to me, and you remember how thrilled I was to talk to you, until I realized the only reason you'd called was to get the deed to the house settled. What a disappointment!

You won't tell me anything. I don't know where you're working or what you have done with our things…I know nothing and when I asked the last time I called, you cut me off!

Now about the church—In Dad's letter, you say I "ridiculed and reviled you." You said you'd decided long ago to return, etc. Yet, in your letter to me, you "ridiculed and reviled" me for crawling back to the nest, seeking "pat answers" because of fear. You told me that you would "seek God to the pit of hell, and even though (you) do not find him, you will never betray yourself as I have."

I am once again confused. I have read your two letters over and over again trying to understand you. Yes, and my father has read them both also. They're written by two different people. Which is the real Paul? If the one you wrote to Dad and what you told Dwight is true—and I pray that it is—why did you write to me such a senseless lie! If the letter to me is the truth, why are you taking such a stand with them? Is it that you think this will enhance the present role you're playing of martyred, perfect, long-suffering father?

Why must you belittle me to build up yourself? Why can't we break through the lies and distortions and just be who we really are? It is only in truth and "nakedness" that we can make the important decisions that are ahead of us.

You say there are other more basic factors that "drove" me away from Anaheim besides the Church. First, I didn't come here because of the church; my decision to stay had to do with earning a living for all of us. Second, I am not aware of being "driven" as much as being "led." However, I realize clearly since your letter that my frustration basically lies in a loss of faith and trust in your integrity. I find it difficult to respect your slander of me and your attempt to discredit me to make yourself look good. And when faith and respect are gone, where is love?

- Bonnie

The good thing about these letters is that they were in writing, and my father could see plainly how Paul had distorted—no lied—to all of us. Mom and Dad repeated that Wendy and I could stay as long as we wished, rent-free. However, since it was going to be a long stay, he wanted me to get a car. For one thing, Eric was picking me up every morning to take me to school and driving me home every afternoon. I'm sure it was a burden for him. Dad offered to give me the down payment. Without having to pay rent, I could pay it off quickly, if I were frugal. My father did not believe in financing anything but a home. I promised.

The issue of the money from the house began to gnaw at me. I knew I would never see a dime, and I didn't want to obsess about it. So I wrote a letter to Paul, sending copies to all the kids, relinquishing my half of the proceeds on the sale with the stipulation that he would divide my share with the kids for their education. Of course, he never did. Since I had no one's address, I sent the letters in care of Paul. Only Ron, who was living in the same apartment, got his. I was grateful in later years that he could be a witness to my request.

Years later, I asked Ron to recall what happened in Anaheim after I left. Here is his account:

> Early in September, Paul held a garage sale and sold all of our things. I watched a part of my childhood die as someone walked away with my autographed autobiography of Sandy Koufax. All I kept was my clarinet, my record collection and a JFK bank that you gave me in first grade (I still have it). A few weeks later, Paul told me that we were moving into an apartment across the street from our neighborhood. I always wondered why we didn't move closer to South. It was when we moved that he told me you were not coming back. He told me that you had called and asked for a divorce. He began to fill my head with many things blaming you for leaving him. He never once spoke to me of any wrong doing on his part. He only blamed you, completely. Not knowing all that I know now, I began to resent you very much.

I was also very busy with marching season and working at the Sheraton, trying to stay away from home. When I had downtime, I was hanging out in the neighborhood looking for trouble to get into.

I wrote back:

I can't imagine you selling your Sandy Koufax book. Why? And I wonder what the hurry was. We never talked about selling the house. The reason I went to SLC was to sell cosmetics to pay taxes in November. I had no intention of getting a job when I left Anaheim. I was simply going there to bring Wendy home from her summer visit, get Annie settled at BYU and try to earn some money. When I got the job and called him, I was excited because I thought we could save the house. I asked him to let me stay here and work so we could get things put back together. I certainly didn't say I wanted a divorce. He is the one who wanted it— evidently. And the timeline is mind-boggling. He must have had the garage sale before my phone call.

Ron's reply:

Yes, he cleared the house. I don't remember the exact day, but I was the last one to leave the house, only because I still had a key even after he turned his over. It was just he and I then. When Annie returned from BYU, she wanted to move in but he turned her away—he didn't want to pay for another bedroom so she moved in with friends. By the way, now I remember the yard sale more clearly. Annie was just leaving for BYU. It is very clear because she gave me her car, and I remember taking consolation in the car while all the other stuff was being sold…I think her toy horse collection was sold. Anyways, back to the house. I was the last one out. I went through every empty room and then sat in the entranceway crying, and then finally shut the door behind me.

☠

Bonnie:	Did I hear right? He sold everything before Annie came to Utah? Before I got the job? It's too much to take in! So Paul wanted the divorce! As soon as I was on my way, he began dismantling our lives. If I'd gone back, there would have been no home to return to, is that what I'm hearing?
Soul:	I'm not telling you how to interpret, only asking you to look at the facts.
Bonnie:	How long had he wanted a divorce? Since Sue? Since the bankruptcy, when he first threatened to leave?
Soul:	What do you think?
Bonnie:	No wonder our marriage was a charade. Playing roles; mouthing lines; but no love on either side. Just two people trapped by their temple vows and four—later five—children. How tragic!
Soul:	Not really!
Bonnie:	How can you say that?
Soul:	Think of all you've learned about adult development. Take Eriksson's model. The task of adolescence, possible at ages thirteen to twenty-one—but for many people extending their entire lifetime—is to sort through the problems with identity and role

confusion. You were so totally identified with your Mormon teaching and the definition of mother and wife that came out of that system, that you delayed adolescence until age forty. The goal that Erickson sees as possible when these two aspects are integrated is "fidelity." I had been gradually urging you to move toward that goal as you worked through the tension between who you ARE and the roles you thought you had to play. You were nearly there. The soap opera of your life has been the backdrop for a natural process leading to the next stage of your development.

Death

Letting go of the house brought peace. There was nothing I could do about Paul or the children in Anaheim. I knew I'd see them in January at Lowell's wedding and until then I turned my attention to the challenges of the present. "Do that which is nearest at hand." Edith's advice kept playing in my mind like a mantra and kept me focused on Wendy and school.

We had fun picking out a car, settling for a Toyota with four doors so we could take her friends with us sometimes. I knew we needed a place of our own as soon as possible so we shopped for an apartment. The first priority was to keep Wendy in the school she was enjoying.

We found one a mile from my parents' condo. Built a few yards from a creek, our patio looked out on weeping willows whose long green fingers touched the water. We could hear the song of the creek from our bedrooms. In Wendy's imagination, it became the home of Frodo and Sam.

We moved in November with little furniture, but didn't need much. Mom lent us a card table and chairs to use in the kitchen, and I bought a yellow French provincial bedroom set that looked like a little girl's. I intended it to be Wendy's some day when I could afford something more sophisticated; for now, we slept in the same bed. We bought large pillows to relax into while we read together in the living room. For the first time in my life, I was on my own.

I wanted to be with the family in Anaheim for Christmas, but it was impossible, since Lowell's wedding was January 26, 1974, and I couldn't afford two trips. We spent Christmas Eve with Eric and Pauline and their family. Mom and Dad invited us for Christmas dinner, and we enjoyed a small Christmas tree in our little apartment.

Wendy had brought her Barbie dolls with her when she came in August to visit her grandparents. I bought her a Barbie airplane and some new clothes to enhance her collection. There was plenty of room for the dolls to have their very own space on the living room floor.

I looked forward to the wedding, but felt sad I couldn't take Wendy with me. The cost was prohibitive and there was no place for her to stay in Paul's two-bedroom apartment.

"It's best you go alone," Dad counseled. "You need to talk to Paul without worrying about Wendy."

"We'll take good care of her, you know that!" Mom reminded me. I knew that, but I also realized she wanted to see everyone as much as I did.

"Are you going to stay with him?" Dad asked.

"Where else?" I responded defensively. "After all, he is my husband."

"I wish you didn't have to go," Mom lamented. "I don't trust him."

"I wouldn't miss Lowell's wedding for anything in the world. And besides, I hope to see Annie, as well as Lynne and Ron. I especially need to know that Annie's OK."

The wedding was on Saturday afternoon. I took an early morning flight, and Paul picked me up at the Orange County Airport for the drive to Anaheim. He seemed relaxed; I was excited to see him again. The doubts and confusion began to drop away.

"It's good to see you," I glowed. "It's been so long, and I've missed you!"

"I've missed you too, Bonnie." His eyes were soft and sincere. He looked handsome in his black tux, blue ruffled shirt and black bow tie. "You can change at the church. We won't have time to stop at the apartment before the wedding."

"That's fine," I responded, relieved that we'd have time to get used to each other before being alone.

"Lowell's OK now, but he was in a bad accident on Thursday."

"What happened?"

"He bought a 1969 Datsun over Christmas because Diana's folks worried about him riding the motorcycle. He was broadsided by a woman who ran a red light. He was not hurt, but it looks like the car is totaled."

"Thank heavens he's OK!"

"His car was crushed and lying on its top. There was glass everywhere, but except for a few scratches, Lowell was fine. Later, when he opened his luggage, it was full of tiny bits of glass. We both knew God was watching over him that day."

It was good to have something safe to talk about.

We got to the church early. I found the bride's room and changed into the floor-length dress that I'd carefully matched to the swatch Lowell's bride, Diana, had sent me. Both mothers' dresses matched the men's shirts and the attendants' gowns. I glanced at the full-length mirror, pleased with my reflection. Diana arrived with Donna, her mother. When we embraced, I felt overwhelming gratitude for this woman who'd given my son a family when his own had broken apart.

Lynne, Henri, Annie and Amir came just as the service began. I never saw Ron, and didn't talk to Lynne, since they left right after the wedding. I did catch Annie as she was rushing away. She looked terrible, her hair straight and stringy, her skin gray. Grabbing her arm, I whispered, "Can we talk before I go back?"

"I work tomorrow. When do you leave?" Her icy voice was a knife in my heart.

"Not until Monday morning. Where do you work?"

"At Carl's Junior in Fullerton."

"Could I come by for your lunch break?" I begged.

"How will you get there?" Amir was motioning for her to hurry; she tried to get away.

"I'll either have Paul bring me, or I'll use the car! I'll get there one way or the other if I can see you." I released my hold on her arm.

"OK," she said. "About 11:00AM."

"That's perfect. I'll be there!"

She scurried away. My heart ached seeing my beautiful daughter in such a state. *What is going on?* Rejoining the wedding party, I tried to enter into the celebration of Lowell and Diana's new life, but my heart was heavy for whatever Annie was going through.

After the reception, I changed clothes again and found Paul waiting patiently. He too had changed and looked more like the man I knew.

"Is there anything you want to do while you're here?" he asked.

"Mainly, just talk and get caught up and see where we are with each other."

He headed for Laguna Beach—our favorite spot. We hardly spoke on the drive, but I enjoyed seeing the palms and eucalyptus I loved so much. Camellias were in bloom and the highway was lined with pink and white oleander and multi-hued ice plant.

As we approached the beach, I hungrily breathed the delicious sea air and relished the familiar sound of squawking seagulls. I marveled at vibrant grass, so refreshing after the snow of Salt Lake. White-haired couples were bowling on the green with their oversized bowling balls, wearing sunshades. They moved in graceful silhouette against the brilliant light of the sinking sun. We walked to the edge of the cliffs and sat down on rocks we'd claimed as ours, years before.

"Tell me what you're doing," I said, finally.

"Still delivering milk. I don't want to for long, but it's better than nothing. How's the teaching going?"

"Great. I've never felt so comfortable with kids. The time away from teaching—after the stress of Sex Ed and all—has made a big difference in me. I love the students as well as the school."

He was scratching his hands. "What about the Church?"

"Wendy and I attend every Sunday with Mom and Dad. We've now transferred to our new ward. I think we're doing OK, trying to get back into it."

"I'm glad to hear that." He was subdued.

"And you?" I asked tentatively, purposely avoiding mention of his letters.

"I am totally committed. It's been a miracle."

"Tell me about it!" I took off my shoes and stretched out my legs, burrowing my feet in the sand; hungry for communication, I truly wanted to hear his story.

"I don't know if you remember Chuck Atkins. He was our visiting teacher for the last few years. He came by several times, but we more of less brushed him off. One night, when I was really down, he came by and we talked. He bore his testimony that Joseph Smith was a true prophet and the Mormon Church is the only true church. I felt moved by his words. He asked me to go to church with him the next Sunday, and for some reason, I don't know why, I agreed.

"I spent a couple of days airing out my clothes so they wouldn't reek of tobacco. The bishop reached out his hand and welcomed me without making me feel awkward in the least. The elders in the quorum gave me a similar reception—no questions asked! During the meeting, one of them bore a fervent testimony, and as he spoke, I felt a burning sensation inside of my breast. I knew he was speaking the truth.

"That afternoon, I went back to the apartment and dumped the liquor into the kitchen sink. I took my pipes to Newton Gable and told him he could have them. He protested that I might need them, but I assured him I was through with tobacco forever.

"I might have hesitated about returning to the ward, but on Thursday, Chuck's wife called. She said Chuck had broken his leg and needed a ride to church on Sunday. He asked if I could take him, and I couldn't say no. I drove him to church for several weeks until the doctor took off his cast. By then, I was a regular churchgoer."

We sat listening to the pounding surf, and watching the sun disappear on the horizon, deprived of the blaze of color I'd expected. There seemed nothing more to say.

Finally, he broke the silence. "Well, are you ready to see my apartment?"

"I'm ready," I assured him. I wasn't surprised to find it was in the same complex where he'd stayed the summer of his affair; however, I made no comment about it.

Ron hadn't come in; he was working at the Sheraton Hotel near Disneyland. Paul said he might be staying the night with a friend.

I slept with him, and we made love. It was as though I'd never been away.

I asked if I could go to church with him, but he said he'd rather I didn't. I winced, figuring he probably saw the ward as his turf and didn't want me interfering. Instead, we went to Coco's for breakfast. "What are we going to do, Paul?"

"What do you want?"

"I've thought, since I got the job, that you might decide to come to Salt Lake. You know I've never asked for a divorce; I've always hoped we could work things out. My contract is for one year only so another option is that Wendy and I come here in June—if you want us."

"I'm seriously thinking of going to Salt Lake. I want to get back to the church. I want to go to the temple again."

"What about Ron?" I asked. "He's in the middle of his junior year. It seems unfair to expect him to pack up and leave because of us."

"I can handle Ron!" he said with certainty.

"I wonder if there's someone he could stay with. A South band family, maybe. We could pay rent and he could be with us in the summer."

"I'll take care of it!" His eyes blazed, and I realized I was interfering again. "Can't you trust me to take care of my own son?"

"Of course, Paul," I answered meekly.

After breakfast, he drove me to Carl's Junior, promising to be back in an hour. Annie was waiting for me.

I bought her lunch and myself a cup of coffee. Since I hadn't ordered coffee with Paul, I needed my fix. Her dull eyes, drawn face and pinched lips were heartbreaking. She said they had very little money and were just scraping by. "I moved in with friends because Dad and Ron only had two bedrooms, and there wasn't room for me." I could scarcely believe my ears. Does this mean they moved before Annie left BYU? But it couldn't be! I told him about the job only two days before that. "Why didn't he get three bedrooms?" I asked incredulously.

"I don't know. It's OK. Don't worry about me. I'll get by." Her eyes glared defiantly.

My mind raced as I tried to comprehend her revelation. *How can I help her? I don't have extra money, and even if I did, I don't want to condone an obviously bad situation.*

"I wish I could help you, but we're on a tight budget also." After a pause, I added, "Why don't you come to Salt Lake and live with Wendy and me? We both want you!" She scowled and made a move to leave. Taking a check from my pocket, I made it out to Air West and signed my name, leaving the date and amount blank. "Here's a check for airfare. If you ever want to come to us, fill in the blanks and get on the plane. Do you understand?"

She took the check skeptically, and rushed away before I could ask more questions.

Slumping into the booth, I noted gray haze moving into my brain, but suddenly my eyes were startled by a sun-kissed, ruby poinsettia outside the window. Mesmerized by the brilliant petals glowing with light, my gaze widened with astonishment to the emerald leaves and beyond, to a mother who was kissing her baby as they ambled toward the restaurant. *Why is the world so amazingly clear when I feel so sad?* I could feel panic inching its way upward from my heart to spill through my eyes; at the same time, I sensed my friend *Death* waiting in calm acceptance within my belly. There was a clear choice between them. If I chose tears, I could escape in justified self-pity and wouldn't have to deal with *Death.* At the same time, I knew *Death* had something to teach me. It's like Wendy's birth. I can choose the epidural, or I can accept the pain—Annie is lost to me; death is real, but so is life.

Focusing my eyes on the luminous flower outside my window, I sat in perfect stillness for forty minutes before Paul arrived. I was aware of Annie's presence as she talked to people at the counter, going about her life as best she could, and I realized she'd be OK. She has to make her own way, as do I. She was talking to the cook when I left so there were no parting words. *Death* led me tentatively into the waiting world.

Paul and I stopped at a park. "Do you think we could make it if we try again?" he asked tentatively.

"I think we could, if you want to. I've never wanted a divorce. Why would I be here, sleeping with you, if that was what I wanted?"

He was quiet again. "You haven't asked about the furniture or anything."

"It's you I'm concerned about. You and Ron. The furniture can be replaced."

"It's in storage; I'll ship it as soon as we decide on a date. I'm thinking the middle of February?"

"And you'll come with it?"

"That's the plan!"

We fell into each other's arms and prayed together that God would bless us all.

When we went back to the apartment, Ron was in the living room, but scampered to his bedroom when we came in. Here is his memory of what had happened, written many years later.

> You came to Lowell's wedding. I didn't want you there because Paul had blamed you for everything. The day after the wedding he and you together told me that we were going to be a family again in SLC. I started to cry and protested and ran away. I reported for work at the Sheraton and after work got drunk for my first time. All I could see was that I was going to lose my friends again. I was going to be first chair in South's band, and I was going to be drum major in my senior year. I don't remember where I slept that night, but the next day, I came to my senses…and holding back tears, agreed to

move. We waited until the semester ended, the end of January.

Paul filled my head with hope and dreams. First that there was a wonderful clarinet teacher, Martin Zwick, who would give me lessons every week. Also a great symphony conductor by the name of Rosenstock who would teach me to conduct. And best of all that Bompa (his grandfather) had pledged to send me to the Curtis Institute! My dreams of being drum major in the All Western Band Review quickly disappeared, and I left South, and all my friends saw me as a hero—they all joked that they would want my autograph when I became famous! I couldn't wait to get to SLC.

☠

When I got back to Utah, I found a three-bedroom apartment in the same building. We moved our few things upstairs, and Wendy and I eagerly awaited Paul and Ron's arrival. Wendy was excited. She hadn't seen either of them since August.

Actually, I learned later, Paul and Ron arrived the first of February and stayed with Dwight for two weeks. The next day, he saw an ad in the paper for a music warehouse job, which he took. He did not tell me he was working.

☠

When Paul and Ron arrived at our apartment, we had everything ready to receive them and the furniture. Together, we had washed windows and shampooed the carpets. I loved the apartment. There were two bedrooms on the main floor with a bathroom and staircase between. The living room, next to a small but adequate kitchen, had space for a dining table. It opened onto a deck overlooking the

355

creek. The high, open-beam ceiling made it seem spacious. A gas fireplace reminded me of our fire ring. The master suite, an upstairs loft, was over the bedrooms and kitchen. It had its own bathroom and sitting space. My new yellow furniture seemed dwarfed in the large room. I'd made up the double bed with new sheets and a floral bedspread. It was definitely feminine; I hoped he wouldn't mind.

Wendy and I sat on our pillows in the middle of the living room trying to picture how the furniture would fit the space. We didn't know what had been sold, and we couldn't wait to see what they'd saved. It was like Christmas all over again.

The moving men must have been glad we didn't have appliances since our apartment was on the second floor. The bulkiest furniture was the sofa and loveseat, which we'd purchased when we refinanced the house. I was excited to see them again; they fit perfectly in the living room. Paul had brought the crystal, china and silverware I bought before our marriage, and he'd saved some wedding gifts. They placed a bunk bed in each of the downstairs bedrooms along with chests of drawers for each. Boxes of books, his record collection and a TV and sound system were stacked in the corner of the living room waiting to be unpacked. Wendy was disappointed when her toys weren't in the truck, but Ron told her they had been sold along with the rest. I couldn't believe they'd sell her toys, but refrained from reacting. I'd said goodbye to everything we owned in my meditations. Anything he brought was a gift; I'd promised myself I would not question his choices. Besides, we'd have fun getting new toys for Wendy.

As for personal belongings, Paul and Ron brought only what fit in their car. Once his bed was set up and made, Ron went into his room and closed the door. His eyes were lifeless and he hadn't yet spoken to me. I took Paul upstairs to see our new bedroom. There was no kiss, not even an embrace. He seemed cold and distant as he looked around, grunted, and said he wanted to put stuff away and lie down for a minute. I excused myself and returned to the kitchen to fix dinner. It was a somber beginning.

☠

Ron later recalled his ordeal of moving to Salt Lake City with Paul.

> The furniture was shipped to your apartment and we left with only what we could fit in the car. We arrived at Dwight's house and moved into his basement. My clarinet lessons started immediately. The band director at Cottonwood H.S. put me second chair and also in the orchestra. For those things, I was grateful and saw it as help in getting to Curtis. All of my new hope blocked me from even caring when Paul told me that we were not going to move in with you after all. He was very clear about telling me that you did not want us there. I never considered what your point of view might be because I was not sophisticated enough to do that. I just thought you were a very, very evil person, and I didn't care anymore. I only held onto my dream to go to Curtis.
>
> Finally, after a period of time, I don't recall exactly—maybe a few weeks?—we did move into your apartment. I never got the conducting lessons. I never asked Bompa about Curtis. It just began to dawn on me, slowly, that there was no truth in these promises. If there was any truth, then Bompa would have talked about it— especially when I went to see him all on my own. We sat in his office and that was when he himself released me forever from the shadows of the Mormon Church. He told me that although it was his hope that I would practice Mormonism, what God really wanted of me was to find my

357

way into a church—any church. The truth about Curtis was upon me, a path to God was instilled, and I now trusted nobody except my grandparents.

☠

The four of us lived together for three and a half gloomy months. Ron hated me; there was no denying that. Paul was preoccupied with his study of the Mormon scriptures. Except for a walk in the evenings, we managed to skirt past each other. I thought he was looking for a job and didn't ask questions because I didn't want to badger him.

Paul, Wendy and I went to church. I was amazed how friendly people in the ward were toward us, now that Paul was there. They asked me to help with the Primary, the weekday classes for elementary schoolchildren. My job was to teach the teachers. Primary was held right after school, and there was no way I could attend the meetings, but I could certainly meet with the teachers once a month and offer suggestions. I was pleased to be invited. The material to present was planned by the Primary Board of the Church. I didn't think I could go too far astray.

We even had Ward Teachers come visit us. I enjoyed the husband and wife who'd been assigned to us, remembering how I hated those visits when the kids were little because I always worried my house was too messy, but I didn't have to worry about that now.

I found myself staying at school as long as possible, preparing for classes and correcting papers. No matter how much I tried, I could not break through Ron's sullenness, and it became clear that Paul would be happier had I not been there—except of course, to fix meals.

After my presentation to the Primary teachers in April, Paul was informed that my teaching was not acceptable. I needed to be back in the church longer before I taught anyone else what I thought. Embarrassed by the rejection, I tried to be graceful in relinquishing my short-lived assignment. One evening, the middle of May, Paul and I walked to the shopping center two miles from the apartment. We sauntered through a cemetery on the way, and found a bench on which to sit.

"This isn't working, is it?" I couldn't stand it any longer.

"No." He sat silently staring at a nearby gravestone. "I've been praying about what to do. I even talked to Dwight about it."

"Is that why you've been fasting the last couple of days?" I asked. The air was very still. A faint fragrance of jasmine from a grave next to us caught my attention. It was a sad place, a place of death.

"Yes. I told Dwight I didn't know what God wanted me to do. I couldn't get an answer. He asked what I'd been praying for. When I told him that I was looking for a way to stay together, he suggested that perhaps I was asking for the wrong thing. 'What if God doesn't want you to stay together? Get down on your knees once more—but be sure you're willing to do what He wants. Afterward, get something to eat, because you've fasted too long. Then come and talk to me.' I did as Dwight suggested and received an answer immediately, 'Let her go!' A feeling of peace accompanied my prayer so that I felt no doubt. That was yesterday," he concluded.

"Then it's settled," I added, taking a deep breath. After a long pause, I asked, "What do we do now?"

"I don't know, but as you said, it isn't working."

"A teacher at school has a condo at Bear Lake. He offered to let me use it over Memorial Day weekend. I think I'll ask a friend, a single woman, to go up there with Wendy and me. If we're away for the weekend, you and Ron can take your time moving into a place of your own. Take anything you want from the apartment. We'll make do with whatever is left."

"I should find a place by then," he said softly.

"Then it's settled. I'll contact an attorney right away and file for divorce."

We walked home in silence and slept back-to-back, hardly speaking to each other for the next two weeks. It was over!

Ron describes his situation in these words: "I went to Paul and told him that when I turned eighteen, I would return to Anaheim and graduate from South with my friends. He told me I could leave whenever I wanted to, and so I did"

☠

Going to Bear Lake with my friend, Nancy, was a good move. She was divorced and had been a confidante during the last few months. Wendy loved being at the lake, and she also enjoyed Nancy. I took several long walks alone while they played with the Barbie dolls. I cried freely, and went over all the events of the past three years, trying to see what I might have done differently. Nancy listened to me, but wisely offered little advice. The first of June, I was ready to call Alan Howe.

"How long has it been since we first talked?" he asked.

"It was in October—seven and a half months," I counted on my fingers; my voice was flat.

"I'm surprised you waited so long."

"I never thought this would happen." I could feel unwanted tears begin their ascent and firmly pushed them back down into my heart. "I've tried to make it work, but it's impossible. The marriage is dead."

He shuffled some papers, and I could see the sadness in his eyes.

I recalled aloud, "A wise man once told me that the opposite of love is not hate; it is apathy. That's where we are. There's no feeling left, except sadness, and I think that's more about failure than our relationship. Of course, I care a great deal about the kids, and I wonder if I'll ever regain their love. They're angry at me and blame me for leaving them." I focused again on the papers on the desk. "But I do have Wendy. That's a blessing!"

"What about assets? I assume the house was sold."

"Yes, as far as I know, but he hasn't told me anything about it."

"Do you want the court to try to get something from him?"

"No. I told him to give my share to the children for their education. It's gone now. I don't want to fight about anything. It will only cause more feelings."

"But he has a legal obligation to help with you and Wendy."

"He doesn't have a job; I do. I can manage. I want him to have a chance for a new start just as I've been given."

"We'll ask for $100 monthly in child support, commencing the day the divorce is final." After scribbling notes on his yellow pad, he asked, "Does he have insurance?"

"I think he has a $40,000 policy from when he worked at New York Life."

"We'll ask that he continue making payments and keep it in your name."

"I can agree with that."

We finished filling out papers, and before leaving, I asked, "How long will it be until the divorce is final?"

"Usually six months," he said.

"Six months is a long time," I mused. "I'm ready to get on with my new life right now. I've waited so long to make the decision."

"I'll see what I can do," Alan promised, and I left his office with a feeling of relief. I was almost free.

Paul did not contest the divorce; in fact, I don't think he even had an attorney. The hearing was on June 24th. The judge questioned me briefly and then said he was waiving the waiting period. The divorce was finalized on Tuesday, June 25, 1974.

In July, I called Paul to ask how he was going to pay the child support. He said he didn't have the money but would get it to me as soon as possible.

"When are you going to see Wendy?" I asked. "She misses you."

"Oh, of course." It sounded like he hadn't considered seeing her.

"Let's set up a schedule so she can plan on it," I suggested. "How about next week?"

"Saturday afternoon," he mumbled.

"I hope you'll bring the check with you."

We repeated this scenario each month until school started. Each time I called, he reluctantly made a date to see her but never initiated a visit. I felt I was forcing him to give us the money. Remembering my mother's description of begging her father for child support while she was growing up, the situation was repugnant to me.

In October, when he didn't have time to see Wendy and refused to tell me when he'd give me the $100, I gave up. I wrote a letter telling him that she wanted to see him, but he'd have to make the arrangements. I also told him I was sick of forcing him to pay. I requested that he open a savings account in her name and put the money in the bank. She was ten years old; he was obligated to make payments until she was eighteen. This money would help with her education. He agreed to the terms. It was my last tie to him.

I walked alone to the cemetery where Paul and I ended our marriage. It was a beautiful Indian summer day with a hint of bite in the air. Golden leaves still clung to the birches and oaks, and dwarf maples blazed like small bonfires amidst the graves. Lavish mounds of asters and chrysanthemums lined the walkways; the green grass had not yet surrendered to winter's demands. Another few weeks, and leaves would carpet the ground, flowers would wither and the grass turn brown. There's nothing pretty about death—except the promise of rebirth when spring arrives to begin the life cycle once again.

Death had moved from my shoulder to my belly. The person I'd known myself to be was fading like the flowers and leaves. Who I'd be at winter's end was still unknown, but hope flickers in death's arms. I don't know what to believe about God or church or life's ultimate purpose, but I know the circle is unbroken; the end is the beginning. I await resurrection from the tomb of my heart.

☠

Epilogue

Christmas 2003 found me living in Salt Lake City once again, after many years of absence. I mailed a message to my brother, Eric Myers, to let him know I'd returned. He sent a card in response that read: "Thanks for the Christmas greeting even though the sentiment came through rather shallow, knowing of the hatred you have for me!...I still have love for my misguided little sister even though I pity you and the tragedy of your whole life."

I've always admired Eric. His life follows the pattern for a successful Mormon. He taught at the same junior high school from the time he graduated from college until his retirement. He served a mission for the Mormon Church, and has been a bishop in his ward. His wife, Doris, developed a successful pre-school at the same time they raised three lovely children. They are admired and respected by members of their ward.

In short, he has lived his life in perfect alignment with the goals of the LDS Church, and I have great admiration for him. It has been a good life, filled with many blessings.

I have lived my life in a different alignment. I *am* a Mormon; born and bred. As an adolescent, I had a testimony of the truth of the church, but as I grew, like the ugly duckling, I realized I was *different* from the others. I no longer fit. I tried with all my heart to follow the teachings of the church, and yet, my trying missed the mark. I remember praying, in great frustration, for God to renew my testimony that the Mormon Church was the only true church. I never doubted its validity for my parents or for Eric or for anyone who found inner peace within its structure, but there was no peace for me. I remember many years ago having a vision of myself as a young woman, standing outside a window where happy Mormons were joyfully having a party, but I was not welcome, and I didn't know why.

If other Mormons didn't recognize me as one of them, I asked myself, "Who am I?" Once I allowed questions to lead me, life became a journey. I was one of the Israelites, wandering in the wilderness seeking the Promised Land; I was following Jesus on the road to Jerusalem; I was Odysseus trying to get home again. So many stories spoke the truth to me, but they were not Mormon.

When we find the freedom to follow inner guidance, we release everyone else to an unpredictable future. My family is as diverse religiously as we are individually.

Lynne is the mother of five children, all of whom are faithful members of the LDS Church. I thank God for their inspiring lives.

Lowell put himself through school, became a Baptist minister and later received a doctorate from Marquette University. He's now a Lutheran pastor and teaches at a theological school. Our "budding theologian" was discernible as early as Christmas 1963. He has three children.

Annie made her way through college with two children, both natural childbirths. She earned an M.A. degree in Education and is a well-loved teacher at a private school.

Ron continued his passion for music and teaches at an inner-city school in Whittier, California. His middle school band, made up of young musicians, many from broken and abusive homes, has performed twice at Carnegie Hall; the band room is full of trophies. Ron and Annie are both Roman Catholics.

Wendy, a born-again Christian, is music director in her church. She has two boys, has just finished an M.S.W. degree, and has recently produced her first CD of inspirational music.

Taking responsibility for our actions is imperative if we are to evolve; without confession and repentance, we risk repeating the same mistakes. Paul married a young woman a few years older than Lynne seven months after our divorce. Their temple marriage ended ten years later when their four children were ages five to nine. Paul who had been teaching band in Utah, was suspended from teaching at the time of the divorce. The public record shows that the children were "in the custody of protective services" and their home was in foreclosure. According to court documents, he married his third wife in the Salt Lake Temple within days of the divorce decree; his teaching credential was suspended, but his temple recommend was not. Paul and his new wife are presently serving an LDS mission at a European temple. I grieve for his four children who face life fatherless, as had Paul himself.

I was married to the love of my life three years after my divorce. Our twenty-seven-year marriage is filled with such joy and fulfillment I can't imagine having lived without Jack. If ever there was a marriage made in heaven, it is ours. Once I gave up trying to fit into a Mormon ward, Jack and I joined the Episcopal Church, where we were embraced with unconditional love. Finding acceptance for who I am enabled me to let go of expectations impossible to fill. Jack supported me through three years of training for spiritual direction, and three additional years of seminary. After my ordination in 1988, he resigned from his federal career and we spent twelve challenging years serving Episcopal parishes, I as a priest and he as a deacon. Our adventures could be another book.

We are an ecumenical family that respects one another, knowing all have chosen religious structures to support their individual lives. Jesus Christ joins us in love. To think one church is truer than another seems absurd.

What about my mother and father? I love my parents deeply, and I honor them as *holy* people who have lived God-given lives in "the only true church"—for them.

Early in our marriage, Jack wanted me to attend another church with him, especially since Wendy was never welcome in the Mormon Church, and he felt she needed a religious community. I was adamant that I'd never join another church as long as my father was alive.

In June 1982, Jesus intervened in my meditation so unmistakably I could no longer deny I was a Christian. When we visited an Episcopal Church, I knew I was home! I'll never forget talking with Dad in his den and telling him I was going to be baptized, that I wanted a church of my own. He was heartbroken and said I was "disowning them." I reminded him of Paul's image of the Body of Christ saying, "The Mormon Church may well be the head of the body, and the Episcopal Church may only be the foot. I may be only a cell in the big toe of the foot, but it is where I authentically belong. I leave my fate in the afterlife in the hands of Christ."

After my baptism, I had a dream in which I died and went to heaven. I was asked to give the sacred handshake, but I sensed a personage standing behind the interrogator. As I fixed my gaze on him, my heart responded, and I cried out that I put my whole trust in Jesus Christ rather than a handshake. I was engulfed in light and awakened with blessed assurance in my heart that has never left.

I realize there are important differences in the two religions, but somehow I believe, in the depths of my heart, that they are united in truth. Jack says that he is a "Christian expressing as an Episcopalian." I feel that I am a "Mormon-Christian expressing as an Episcopalian." One can never completely give up the language and beliefs of the tradition of their birth.

Dad and I tried to find some common ground. It was especially difficult for him when I went to seminary. He wrote a sixteen-page epistle, outlining the sins of early Christianity and how the Gospel had been taken from the earth to be restored through the Prophet Joseph Smith. I was deeply moved that he cared enough to prepare and send such a lengthy document. In my reply, I reminded him that Jesus had promised he would "be with us always, to the ends of the earth." I could not believe He would break His promise and leave the human race alone, without his love and guidance.

Dad claimed the *Book of Mormon* was the Word of God brought forth through the power of the restored priesthood. I responded that it was through the priesthood of the Anglican Church, through which I would be ordained, that the *King James Bible* was brought forth—the very Bible that Mormons use today. It is the translation that Joseph Smith copied into the *Book of Mormon*, in "Third Nephi."

I weep as I read his journal and acknowledge how much pain I caused him. He wrote, "We feel very, very badly about our poor record because we see little chance for those who have left the church to be with us in the hereafter or have a chance for the Celestial Kingdom. We have not been very successful in this most important area of our lives, and we feel very badly about it."

How sad that two wonderful people like my parents suffered such guilt over their children seeking their own way to live productive lives.

In June 1984, Dad's anger had increased. He wrote that I was "very bitter about the church. She is really an apostate, restless and looking for something, not realizing, or refusing to recognize, that what she is looking for, she has turned her back on. Refusing to see that Mom and I have it…peace of mind and contentment. No fear for the future…happy together in the church, assured of a future *together* forever. I think basically Bonnie realizes and knows this but stubbornly continues to revolt, to fight against the church and us, to tear down instead of build up and in the process stay unsatisfied, frustrated and continually unhappily searching. It started with Kevorkian, a disciple of the Devil, through the mystic religions of the East and Protestant religions, shorn of all priesthood authority and the true knowledge of God."

The same year, I asked Dad about questions that were arising from an angry film about the Mormon temple ceremony entitled, *What's Going On in There?* People who knew I had a Mormon background were asking me if the film was accurate; I wanted to know how to answer without contributing to the intense emotion the film provoked. Dad was furious that I would ask him about the secret rites and accused me of "hitting at the temple ceremony."

Through the years that followed, I never stopped going back to Salt Lake and keeping in touch with them. We spent every vacation possible in Utah, until Jack finally refused to go because it was too painful and the relationship seemed impossible to mend. Even then, I continued my visits, and both of us prayed for reconciliation before they died.

Much was happening in the Mormon Church at this time. On June 9, 1978, blacks were granted the priesthood. This was the first issue I tried to resolve with the Mormon Authorities, who told me it was Satan who was making me question the doctrines of the church. I wish he had told me at the time of my interview that President McKay had already changed the word *doctrine* to *policy,* setting the stage for the "benevolent cessation of discrimination."[1]

I tried to talk to Dad about the new *policy,* explaining that I had received the same revelation twenty years before. Had I ignored it, wouldn't that have been a "sin against the Holy Spirit"—the *unforgivable sin?* I spoke with love, hoping for mutual respect, but he accused me of "arrogant attacks against the LDS Church."

On July 15, 1985, Dad wrote, "Apostates are the most bitter enemies in the world, and Bonnie is an apostate of the most vicious order. How we meet this new attack will take some careful thought. In the meantime, we have been abused so much for so long by Bonnie that the new attack doesn't hurt as it might have."

The same year a major scandal erupted when Mormon Authorities bribed a document dealer named Mark Hofmann and the incident led to murder. We happened to be staying with my parents when the story unfolded. I asked why the LDS Church would go to such lengths to obtain such a document; I wondered what they were trying to hide. Again, my logical questions were seen as attacks on the church.

In 1990, the very questions I'd asked my father five years before about the temple ceremony were resolved and the ordinances changed, thus validating the relevance of my questions. Dad was still working in the temple at that time.

In 1993, I was Rector at St. Stephen's Episcopal Church in Oregon. One day, Dad called to say that he and Mom wanted to visit us. They would drive to Oregon and arrive the following Saturday. I was amazed; they were eighty-six years old. When they arrived, I was still more surprised that they wanted to attend church with us on Sunday. The Gospel reading for the day was the story of Jesus visiting Mary and Martha in their home and teaching Mary.

I had rented a video of Barbra Streisand's *Yentil* to use as an example in my sermon, and they agreed to watch it with me. It is a story of a young Jewish woman who wants to be ordained a rabbi. Her father has surreptitiously taught her *Torah* and when he dies, she disguises herself as a man and goes to seminary. The similarities between that story and my relationship with my father could not be missed. Mom got so nervous she left and went to bed, but Dad and I saw the film through. In my sermon, I pointed out that the Jewish proscription against women in Jesus' day was even greater than in the film, and yet, Jesus was in Mary and Martha's home, teaching them. I quoted Galatians: "In Christ there is neither male nor female."

I thought our evening together was the most remarkable gift God could give me. But there was more to come. Mom and Dad sat on the forth pew to my left as I preached. We all hugged as the congregation offered each other their "peace," after which I celebrated the Eucharist, feeling the presence of God in every word and gesture. Congregants came forward to receive communion while Jack and I were preparing the bread and wine. When I looked up, Mom and Dad were among them, kneeling at the altar. Kneeling with their hands outstretched to receive the sacrament—from us.

I could scarcely see—blinded by tears—and the whole congregation was crying with me—in joy.

We never talked about what happened because there is no room for such a discussion in their church. But we didn't have to make words; making love was more than enough.

For my thoughts are not your thoughts,
nor your ways my ways, says the Lord.
For as the heavens are higher than the earth,
so are my ways higher than your ways,
and my thoughts than your thoughts.
For as rain and snow fall from the heavens
and return not again, but water the earth,
Bringing forth life and giving growth,
seed for sowing and bread for eating,
So is my word that goes forth from my mouth;
it will not return to me empty;
But it will accomplish that which I have purposed,
and prosper in that for which I sent it.
Glory to the Father, and to the Son, and to the Holy Spirit:
as it was in the beginning. Is now, and will be forever.[2]

---

1. Prince and Wright, *David O. McKay and the Rise of Modern Mormonism*, University of Utah Press, 2005, p.78
2. "The Second Song of Isaiah," from *The Book of Common Prayer*; *Isaiah* 55:8-11

Glossary of Mormon Terms
Used in This Book

1.   *Bishopric:* The three men in charge of a *ward*: a bishop and two counselors. There is no professional clergy in the Mormon Church; all righteous male members hold the priesthood and the leaders are chosen from among them—by revelation—for a specific number of years. They donate their time to the church.

2.   *Book of Mormon:* A book translated by Joseph Smith from golden plates, which purports to be the account of ancient inhabitants of the Americas. It is said to contain the fullness of the everlasting gospel.

3.   *Doctrine and Covenants:* A volume of scripture containing revelations given to Joseph Smith and his successors, including the Word of Wisdom.

4.   *Fireside meeting:* An informal meeting which often occurs on Sunday evening.

5.   *General Authorities:* The top echelon of leadership in the LDS Church. Members take vows in the temple to obey them without question.

6.   *Mutual Improvement Association:* Referred to as *Mutual* and *MIA*. The young people's organization (teenage) of the LDS Church.

7.   *Patriarchal Blessing:* A once-in-a-lifetime blessing given to Mormons usually after they've turned fifteen or sixteen, which gives them a purpose for their lives and reveals their eternal destiny.

8.	*Pearl of Great Price:* One of four books considered to be Scripture in the Mormon Church. It was translated and written by Joseph Smith and includes records of Abraham and Moses.

9.	*Primary*: The organization for elementary school children which meets once each week where they learn the primary teachings of the LDS Church.

10.	*Relief Society:* The women's organization in the Mormon Church.

11.	*Road show*: In the 1950's (and beyond), wards competed with dramatic skits, which they presented at their *stakes*. They were sponsored by the MIA.

12.	*Stake*: An organization of *wards* in a specific geographical location, similar to a diocese.

13.	*Temple Recommend:* A certificate that one is worthy of entering the temple and participating in the sacred rites.

13.	*Tithing:* Mormons are required to pay ten percent of their income to the LDS Church. Adherence is mandatory for entrance into the temple.

14.	*Visiting teachers:* Members of a ward who are assigned to visit specific households once each month to teach a lesson and determine needs in the home.

15.	*Ward*: A neighborhood Mormon community, similar to a parish.

16.	*Word of Wisdom:* A revealed health code that prohibits among other things, smoking and drinking coffee, tea and alcohol. It sets Mormons apart from other people. Adherence is necessary for baptism and obtaining a recommend to go to the temple.